Wakefield Press

Colouring the Rainbow

Dino Hodge is a co-author of the seminal essay 'Peopling the Empty Mirror: the prospects for lesbian and gay Aboriginal history' (1994), and a co-editor of a social studies text on Indigenous education experiences, *You Don't Get Degrees in Weetbix Boxes* (1994). His other publications include *Did You Meet Any Malagas?* (1993), an oral history book documenting intersections of racial and sexual identities in Darwin's gay community; *The Fall Upward* (1995), on spirituality in the lives of lesbian women and gay men; and *Don Dunstan, Intimacy and Liberty* (2014), a biography of South Australia's great reformist premier. He is associate editor of *You're Not Alone: 30 Years of AIDS Councils in the Northern Territory* (2016). Dino Hodge has a PhD in history from the University of Melbourne.

Colouring the Rainbow

Blak Queer and Trans Perspectives

*Life Stories and Essays
by First Nations People of Australia*

edited by
Dino Hodge

Wakefield
Press

Wakefield Press
16 Rose Street
Mile End
South Australia 5031
www.wakefieldpress.com.au

First published 2015
Reprinted 2015, 2017

Cover designed by Liz Nicholson, designBITE
Text designed and typeset by Wakefield Press

National Library of Australia Cataloguing-in-Publication entry

Title:	Colouring the rainbow: blak queer and trans perspectives / edited by Dino Hodge.
ISBN:	978 1 74305 393 5 (paperback).
Notes:	Includes bibliographical references and index.
Subjects:	Gays, Black – Australia – Anecdotes.
	Gays – Australia – Anecdotes.
	Aboriginal Australians – Anecdotes.
	Aboriginal Australians – Biography.
Other Creators / Contributors:	Hodge, Dino, 1957– , editor.
Dewey Number:	305.89915

CORIOLE
McLAREN VALE

Contents

Part Three

Acknowledgements

The Mirror

In 1994, a group of seven people (three women and four men) collaborated on the essay 'Peopling the Empty Mirror: The Prospects for Lesbian and Gay Aboriginal History'. I was one of the two non-Indigenous members of the group, which termed itself the 'Gays and Lesbians Aboriginal Alliance'.[1]

Two decades on, it is time to examine the mirror itself. The life stories and essays in this book collectively address the challenges posed by the 1994 group of allies. The book's contributors broadly consider indigeneity and colonialism with regard to gender and sexuality. As a whole, the book seeks dually to document a diversity of knowledges, experiences and contributions to Australian society of First Nations People from many walks of life, and to reflect upon epistemology and notions of recording and interpreting history.

My intention at the outset had been to work with community members and organisations as well as with academics in convening a national conference and then publishing the conference papers. As a preliminary step towards that goal, I convened a one-day Queer Histories Symposium under the auspices of the Australian Lesbian and Gay Archives (ALGA) together with the active support of the Northern

Territory Archives Service (NTAS) and the Northern Centre for Contemporary Art (NCCA). The symposium's theme was 'Sexuality across Race, Culture and Gender'. It was held in Darwin during May 2014 as an official component of the third Asia–Pacific OutGames, with a diversity of speakers from Australia, the Pacific and Asia. Subsequent consultations with community members and academics saw an invitation issued for me to proceed as sole editor of this book. A call for contributions was then distributed nationally and generated considerable interest. I am grateful to everyone who responded to that call with suggestions, comments and expressions of interest.

The contributors to this book discuss their lives, outlooks, beliefs and thoughts – but this is no ordinary knowledge. The telling of histories and the sharing of insights by First Nations People demands particular effort and courage. The reader has the chance to be taken into the confidence of the contributors, and to learn from their wisdom. We are indebted to the contributors for this opportunity.

A complexity always exists surrounding who is telling a story or documenting a topic, in what manner, and from which perspective. Some contributors have chosen to share oral histories or to write life stories. Others have prepared essays addressing specific topics or events. And some have written utilising an academic framework. My role as editor has been to gather contributions and to ensure these are presented in a format that is familiar and accessible. I have sought as much as possible to avoid influencing content, preferring to leave to contributors the decisions about topics to be documented and the information to be shared. Effort has been given to promoting clarity of expression and narrative cohesion, and the book's contributors have ensured that this task has been a straight-forward and pleasurable undertaking. Furthermore, I have sequenced the chapters and book sections with the intention of placing directly complementary or contrastive contributions together, and of presenting a development of content around the themes raised in the essay 'Peopling the Empty Mirror'. My thanks to the contributors for their trust in allowing me to adopt this role, and additionally to James Ward, Marcia Langton, Lyndon Ormond-Parker and David Aanundsen for their encouragement.

The book's structure develops the notion of 'peopling the empty mirror'. Troy-Anthony Baylis's introductory essay 'Looking In to the Mirror' defines the context for this book and outlines some key issues. The first section, 'Inner Reflections', makes visible some figures in the mirror through a series of life stories as told by two sistergirls, three gay men, one lesbian and one brotherboy. The second section, 'An Emergent Public Face', opens with essays revealing the impact of HIV/AIDS during the late twentieth century as an impetus for a growing public profile and discourse (with no intention of downplaying the importance of the social justice and liberation movements in the preceding decades that have continued into the present day).² This section includes two essays discussing elements of recent important debates instigated by inflammatory public utterances of a racist and/or homophobic nature. The final section, 'Looking Out of the Mirror', is comprised of essays by academics providing critical insight into various knowledge constructs and methodologies.

Oral history methodology has been used for six chapters. Rodney Junga Williams was interviewed by Kathy Triffitt in 2011. New interviews undertaken specifically for this book were completed with Naomi Hicks and Tempestt Sumner-Lovett (interviewed by Margie Fischer); with Brett Mooney (interviewed by David Hardy); and with Kai Clancy, Brie Ngala Curtis, and Crystal Johnson (interviewed by me). My thanks to Margie and David for undertaking interviews and then preparing them for publication; to Graham Carbery for transcribing one of the interviews that I recorded; to Caitlin Perry for supplying supplementary details to Crystal Johnson's interview; and, to Maurice O'Riordan and Gary Lee who, with Crystal's permission, proof-read her chapter.

The interview with Rodney Junga Williams was first published in the magazine *Talkabout* in 2012, shortly after Rodney's passing; I am indebted to Aunty Joan Lamont Willliams and Kathy Triffitt for permission to reprint the article.[3] The essay by Steven Lindsay Ross is an expanded version of an article first published in *Archer Magazine* in 2014, (see archermagazine.com.au for further details).[4]

Jim Wafer, lead author of the 1994 essay 'Peopling the Empty Mirror', supplied an extensive reference list for that essay, and it now forms the basis of the selected bibliography given in this book. I thank Jim for his initiative, commitment and spirit. Several HIV-related documents, reports and articles are included in the bibliography. Additionally, a history of the Anwernekenhe National HIV Alliance is available at http://ana. org.au/home/our-history. ALGA has given priority to collecting a range of diverse materials and to making these available for researchers. ALGA also has included a copy of the original 1994 essay on its website, located at http://alga.org.au/files/Peopling-the-Empty-Mirror.pdf.

Crystal Johnson's 2012 campaign poster, designed by Andy Ewing, has been incorporated into the book cover. My thanks to Crystal and Andy for permission to reproduce the poster.

Many people have supported this book through introductions to friends and colleagues, and by supplying information and resources together with suggestions, advice and encouragement. Nick Henderson, Michael Hurley, Daniel Marshall, Maurice O'Riordan and Graham Willett have been particularly generous. Thanks also to Dennis Altman, bryan Andy, Troy-Anthony

Baylis, Jim Arachne, Timothy Bishop, Jane Black, Dameyon Bonson, Bronwyn Carlson, Michael Costello-Czok, Vicki Crowley, Peter Crowley, Rosalina Curtis, Chris Dawson, Mark Deasey, Amanda Diprose, Kara Dodson, Lani Mau Dorante, Andrew Farrell, Neville Fazulla, Suzanne Fermanis, Catherine Fitzgerald, Robert French, Gina Gascoigne, Dean Gilbert, Kathryn Gilbey, Francis Good, Andrew Gorman-Murray, John Hobson, Bobbie Hodge, Wendy Holland, Chuck Kaminski, Rita Karaminas, Megg Kelham, Colin Kinchela, Melissa Lindeman, Graham Lovelock, Paul Marsh, Terry McClafferty, Miriam McDonald, Arone Meeks, Clive Moore, Caleb Nichols-Mansell, Starlady Nungari, Sandy O'Sullivan, Amy Peachey, Maria Pallotta-Chiarolli, Gary Proctor, Colin Ross, James Saunders, Gary Schliemann, Jenny Scott, Yorick Smaal, Gerard Sullivan, Phil Walcott, John Waugh, Sara Wills, Lana Woolf, Garry Wotherspoon and Jackie Wurm. Thank you ALGA, NCCA and NTAS. I am grateful for everyone's input and guidance. Thank you to my bush-walking friends for their thoughts and support. I apologise for not thanking every person by name; please know that my gratitude is nonetheless sincere.

On a more personal note, *Colouring the Rainbow: Blak Queer and Trans Perspectives* furthers a discussion surrounding some major themes canvassed in my oral history book *Did You Meet Any Malagas?* (1993).[5] Editing this new book similarly has been a privilege. The experiences and opinions of often-overlooked groups can reveal as much about dominant paradigms as they do about their own, thereby fostering the potential for stimulating discussions about Australia's histories and contemporary cultures. However, the impositions of critical self-reflection and frank thoughtfulness accrue not only to the act of preparing auto-ethnographical and academic essays, but also to the art of reading. As Lynn Gehl, an Algonquin Anishinaabe-kwe from the Ottawa River Valley, notes, 'a decolonised ally values their own relationship to the knowledge'.[6] In the Australian context, essays such as those by Damien Riggs, Barbara Baird, Gabi Rosenstreich and Sally Goldner provide us with fine examples of some aspects of what Gehl is asserting.[7,8,9] I hope that this book prompts more discussions and publications.

I am pleased to have the opportunity once again of working with Wakefield Press. Considerable thanks are due to Michael Bollen and all the hard-working staff of Wakefield Press for their professionalism, enthusiasm and dedication. Words alone are not enough!

Copyright of each chapter resides with the author(s). All author royalties from book sales are being donated to the Aboriginal and Torres Strait Islander HIV Youth Mob. ANTHYM was formed in response to the rising incidences of HIV among Indigenous communities. It is the first and only network of young Aboriginal and Torres Strait Islander people from across the country who have mobilised to raise awareness of HIV in their communities (see http://anthym.org for further details).

Dino Hodge
Editor

Contributors

Troy-Anthony Baylis, a descendant of the Jawoyn people from the Northern Territory and also of Irish heritage, is an artist, curator and writer. Currently, he is Curator and Manager, Programs at Tandanya National Aboriginal Cultural Institute in Adelaide. His own art practice has been subject of sixteen solo and numerous group exhibitions since 1993 in Australia, Germany, Spain and Canada. Troy-Anthony is completing a PhD at the University of South Australia through a major studio project and exegesis, *Deadly Mimicry: Indigeneity and Drag in Contemporary Artistic Representation.*

Violet Buckskin is a member of the Moolagoo Mob and a founder of Blak Lemons, a social and support group for Aboriginal lesbians in Adelaide. Her work with these groups includes after-hours support and mentoring for young Aboriginal gays and lesbians. She is the winner of the inaugural Grace Bawden Incentive Award for her work in Social Justice at the 2014 Gladys Elphick Awards, and she is recognised for her leadership for the Onkaparinga Women's Rugby Team. Currently, Violet is completing a Masters in Public Heath through Deakin University. She is a Kaurna, Ngarrindjeri, Narungga woman.

Maddee Clark is a genderqueer / genderfluid Bundjalung writer living in Kulin Nation, Boonwurrung country, learning and teaching. They can be contacted at maddee.clark@gmail.com.

Kai Clancy has dual Wakka Wakka and Wulli Wulli heritage on his father's side, and German and Irish ancestry on his mother's side. His totem is tawny frogmouth. He grew up in Queensland and was elected vice-captain in his final year of high school. Kai posts on-line educational videos about brotherboys and also tracking his own transition. Currently, Kai is completing a political science degree, and working with the Victorian AIDS Council as an Aboriginal and Torres Strait Islander Peer Education and Support Worker.

Brie Ngala Curtis grew up with her identical twin Rosalina in the central Australian community of Acknwerrnarrte, learning Arrente, Warlpiri, Luritja and Pintupi traditions and culture from her grandmother and other family members. She is an advocate for the human rights and health of sistergirls, brotherboys and all queer people, and presents at conferences around the country. Brie is a founding member of Sisters and Brothers NT, an advocacy and support agency launched during the Alice Pride Festival in 2014.

Margie Fischer is a freelance writer, performer, producer and community cultural development worker. She is a founding member of Feast, Adelaide's LGBTQ Festival with which she has been working as either Artistic Director, Project Coordinator or Board Member for nineteen years. Margie's most recent theatre work, *The Dead Ones –* an exploration memory, death and family through story-telling and photography – was performed in Adelaide, Sydney and Melbourne. She is the daughter of Holocaust survivors, which has given her a strong association with Aboriginal and Torres Strait Islander people with whom she has worked on many projects including *Queer Gifted and Blak* and *OutBlak Adventures*.

Laniyuk Garcon-Mills: born in Adelaide but with culture, family and childhood lying in Darwin, I live a transient life back and forth between cities. I am currently completing short courses and workshops on business management, and plan on starting a small business in the next year. Passionate about culture, environment and equality, I'm hoping to bring my beliefs into the physical form and create the change I believe is possible and necessary.

Ben Gertz is a descendant of the GuguBadhun and Ngadjon-Ji peoples of north Queensland, and of the Meriam people of the eastern Torres Straits. Born and raised in Townsville, Ben currently is based in Brisbane where he works as a policy adviser to the Queensland Government.

Samia Goudie is a Bundjalung Mununjali woman of mixed descent and was taken as child. Currently, she is the Senior Lecturer for the Aboriginal and Torres Strait Islander curriculum within the ANU medical school. Samia previously was an academic in Indigenous Health at the Universities of Queensland and Wollongong. In 2007, she completed a Fulbright Fellowship which allowed her to travel across USA sharing her research on wellness and resilience in Indigenous Communities. Samia identifies as a Queer activist who advocates for those who are the most disadvantaged in our communities.

Dr David Hardy is a freelance writer and choral singer living in Brisbane. His doctorate in creative writing at Batchelor Institute of Indigenous Tertiary Education in the Northern Territory explored the diversity of expressions of his Indigenous and queer identity. David's writing also draws on his career as an Australian diplomat in Poland, Indonesia, The Philippines, Samoa and Kiribati. His new book, *BOLD: Stories from older lesbian, gay, bisexual, transgender and intersex people*, published by The Rag and Bone Man Press is out in November 2015.

Naomi Hicks is a strong Aboriginal woman who leads her purpose in this world with love. Her passion for helping her Aboriginal family and community shines through her talents as a teacher, mother and artist. Naomi has worked with Elders to create The Journey therapy program which she used in her work in prisons and with at risk Aboriginal youth. She has developed workshops based on releasing trauma memory, and worked on a wide range of Aboriginal singing and healing projects nationally. Naomi's ancestors and children have always been her rock and guidance.

Dr Dino Hodge – Konstantino Hadjikakou – was introduced to notions of empire and colonisation by his Cypriot family, and to fluidity in identity and intimacy through his Greek cultural heritage. Born and raised in Adelaide, he lived in the Northern Territory from 1983 until relocating to Melbourne in 2000. He is an Honorary Senior Fellow with the Centre for Indigenous Studies at the University of Melbourne, and continues to visit the NT regularly for work.

Crystal Johnson, an Elder living in the Tiwi Islands, is a long-standing advocate for sistergirls and queer people. She has represented sistergirls in national committees and advisory bodies, participated in national health campaigns, and spoken at human rights conferences nationally and internationally. In 2012, Crystal was elected to the Tiwi Islands Regional Council, becoming the first transwoman in the Northern Territory to be elected to any tier of government. As Crystal Love, she often performs at Pride festivals and other events to great acclaim.

Dr Mark McMillan is a Wiradjuri man from Trangie, NSW. He is a Director of the National Congress of Australia's First Peoples, a board member of the Trangie Local Aboriginal Land Council and of Annecto, and a member and Node Leader of the National Indigenous Research and Knowledges Network. Mark became the first Indigenous Australian to join the University of Melbourne Law School when he was appointed a Senior Lecturer in 2011. He teaches Public Law and International Human Rights Law for Indigenous Peoples, and is currently working on projects relating to Indigenous nation building, Reconciliation, and Structural Justice.

Oscar Monaghan is a Murri man, currently living and studying on Gadigal country. His research interests include settler colonial and Indigenous studies and critical race theory. He has been published in several student publications, including *Dissent*, *Arna*, and *Honi Soit*. Other interests include making white people uncomfortable and working on his pirouettes. His online home is oscarandendear. tumblr.com.

Brett Mooney, a proud Torres Strait and South Sea Islander, was born and raised in North Queensland and the Torres Strait. He lives in Brisbane with David, his partner of twelve years, and has been employed for the past ten years with the 2 Spirits Program at the Queensland AIDS Council. Brett enjoys practising and sustaining his culture which keeps him outdoors a lot, and experiencing the world by walking in it for himself. He says the best remedy for being home sick is eating your own cultural food.

S. O'Donnell is the *nom de plume* of a man who found himself growing up in Wagga Wagga and Sydney during the 1970s.

Dr Sandy O'Sullivan is an Aboriginal woman (Wiradjuri) and a Senior Indigenous Researcher at Batchelor Institute of Indigenous Tertiary Education. She is an enduring Australian Learning and Teaching Fellow and is currently completing an Australian Research Council-funded fellowship examining First Peoples representations in museums around the world. Sandy's PhD in Fine Art and Performance focused on the intersections of sexuality, gender and Indigeneity. Her research work is often arts-based and focuses on identity and representation.

Steven Lindsay Ross is a Wamba Wamba man with cultural and familial connections to the Gunditjmara, Mutthi Mutthi and Wirajduri peoples. He has worked in many areas in government, including Indigenous water rights, arts coordination, local government, and policy and project management. Steven also is a published writer of policy articles, opinion pieces, essays and poetry. He is proudly gay and lives in Sydney.

R.J. Sailor is of 'many tribes'. His unique perspective on life, and his distinctive writing style were honed on the tough streets of Queensland where he was introduced to tertiary education through a jail outreach program. He travelled to every capital city on Australia's mainland before he travelled to Europe, North America and Asia. Sailor credits his long-term relationship to the rehabilitation he couldn't get from Government-funded agents and agencies.

Tempestt Sumner-Lovett is a twenty-four year old Indigenous woman from South Australia. She began performing in Australia and Canada at eight years of age with her parents, Betty Sumner and Monty Lovett, in their band Urban Dreaming. She is a singer/song writer and self-taught guitarist who has developed her own music as a solo artist over the past six years. Tempestt's inspiration and motivation for her love ballads come from her everyday experiences and the heartache that love brings.

Kathy Triffitt has contributed significantly to the ongoing development of HIV health promotion and prevention and to the health education needs of people with HIV in New South Wales and Australia over twelve years working at Positive Life, NSW (the voice of people with HIV since 1988), and in previous roles since 1988. She has also contributed directly to the development of policy frameworks in relation to HIV and to advocacy work in relation to the care and treatment of people with HIV.

Dr Jim Wafer has worked for many years with Aboriginal languages (first in Central Australia and more recently in the south-east), and is the co-author of a number of Northern Territory land claims. He has also published on various aspects of homosexuality, as it occurs both cross-culturally and in his home base of the Hunter Valley. His alter ego, Sister Enema Mundi of the Convent of Original Sins, moonlights as a conjoint senior lecturer in anthropology at the University of Newcastle.

Kym Wanganeen is a passionate and active member of the GLBT Aboriginal and Torres Strait Islander community. He is one of the conveners of the Moolagoo Mob (GLBT Aboriginal and Torres Strait Islander social/support group) for the past seven years. Since 2008, Kym has been actively involved in the FEAST Festival, showcasing his artwork and participating in shows such as *Queer*, *Gifted and Blak*, and *OutBlak Adventures*.

Alison Whittaker, a Gomeroi woman from north-west New South Wales, transitioned to metropolitan life to pursue legal, creative and public policy ambitions. She busies herself working in gendered violence, decolonising critical legal research, advocacy and activism. Alison lives and works alongside her partner, Lucy, in the inner west of Sydney, thinking over the finer points her of gardening failures, and the potential for a radical bogan epistemology.

Rodney Junga Williams (1962–2011), a proud Nurrunga-Kaurna man and a member of the Stolen Generation, came out publicly as an Aboriginal man with HIV in 1992. He participated in many national campaigns and spoke at international conferences. Rodney successfully managed HIV for twenty-seven years before passing in 2011 from cancer. His legacy is one of a fighter who stood up and spoke up about the importance of inclusivity within the response to HIV/AIDS for Aboriginal and Torres Strait Islander people.

Raymond Zada is an Adelaide-based emerging visual artist working primarily with photography, video and digital design. He's also an award-winning community radio broadcaster. In 2013, Raymond won the New Media category of the 30th Telstra National Aboriginal and Torres Strait Islander Art Award for his piece, *Sorry*, and in 2012 he won the Works on Paper category for *racebook*. Raymond, a Barkindji man with Afghan and Scottish heritage, grew up in Port Augusta and Marree, South Australia.

Introduction: Looking In to the Mirror

Troy-Anthony Baylis

The lived realities of colonisation have constructed a silencing force that mutes Queer-Aboriginality. It is as if history has constructed Aboriginality as being so pure and so savage, so purely savage, that if tainted by the complexity of sexuality and gender, mixed ethnographies, mixed geographies and mixed appearances, the whole look would be ruined. Aboriginal people would be regarded as not pure, not savage.

The sexual and gender diversity of Aboriginal peoples remains mostly absent in the recordings and interpretations of Australian histories, and these absences reinforce a hetero-centric reading of Aboriginal cultures.

There is urgency, if we are to be more inclusive of our diversities, to unsettle the ways that colonisation has constructed Aboriginality. Perhaps history, historians, and other members of the academy are ready for Aboriginality to celebrate its own diversities as subjects and objects produced by history and to allow for alter/native histories other than those imposed through colonisation.

One way of circumventing the effect of colonisation is to draw upon all imaginings of history, including colonial history, to create new mythologies, new artifice that transforms the past, present and future. As Roland Barthes puts it, 'myth consists in overturning culture into nature or, at least, the social, the cultural, the ideological, the historical into the "natural"'.[1]

1

Here lay opportunities to tip the ways in which Aboriginality is constructed on its head and instead to 'mythologise' with endless queer potential.

Querying queer history

From the 1960s to the 1980s, feminism achieved remarkable progress in advancing women's rights. Amongst the achievements was advocacy within the movement to broaden its scope and acknowledge its diversities – that feminism recognises the struggles of women living in low socio-economic conditions, women of colour, and women from different ethnicities all over the world who experience oppression and inequities because of their gender. Queer Studies must also continue to evaluate itself and acknowledge its cultural, ethnic, and linguistic diversities.

In a literature review of gay and lesbian public history in Australia published in 2004, Andrew Gorman-Murray writes that Australia might have a long past of same-sex desire, stretching back beyond European settlement, but the idea of a possible Queer-Aboriginal history is not pursued.[2] Generally, there is scant reference to Aboriginal sexualities in Australian histories. For example, in his book on the development of gay and lesbian culture in Queensland, Clive Moore recounts an incident in 1855 when two Aboriginal men seen having sex with a European man fled before police arrived.[3] Most published research regarding non-heterosexuality in Australia has excluded Aboriginal people though, in more recent times, this may be due to lack of information, concern over permission for use of knowledge, or other factors.[4] This absence promotes an assumption that Aboriginal people do not have the diverse sexualities that non-Aboriginal people have. Maddee Clark takes the opportunity of this collection to suggest in her essay 'Are We Queer? Reflections on "Peopling the Empty Mirror" Twenty Years On' that: 'Aboriginal sexual histories are often written by settlers with an anxious investment in believing that white settlement is justified, largely peaceful, and necessary.'

Rebecca Jennings supports the likelihood of same-sex desire amongst Aboriginal women prior to European settlement, although the early accounts of non-heterosexuality in Aboriginal communities written by 'white' anthropologists is problematic. Jennings critiques an observation by the Lutheran missionary Carl Strehlow, who interpreted sexual and cross-gendered activity between two Aranda women in Central Australia as 'unnatural'. She points out two key problems with Strehlow's account: writings by 'white' male observers have been invariably overlaid with European notions of same-sex activity as 'unnatural' and a 'vice'; and, there would have been limited opportunity for European men to record activities in women's spaces.[5] Whatever the circumstances in which accounts were witnessed, the writings support the possibility that Aboriginal peoples' sexual and gender practices may not be easily defined as heterosexual or fit within a binary system of gender.

Jennings cites further information regarding homosexual practices among Aboriginal women. The anthropologist Geza Roheim observed, when working in Central Australia in the late 1920s, a 'love magic song' in which women show their labia to each other. The oral artefact 'love magic song' – if indeed an unpublished song can be regarded as an artefact – extends to multiple possible readings that might subvert the assumption of heterosexuality in pre-colonial Aboriginal cultures. The act of women showing their labia to each may be interpreted as a homosexual custom and may also be considered a homo-social practice.[6] Another interpretation is that the observation itself may have resulted from the Aboriginal people deliberately providing misleading information to shock the Europeans and conceal knowledge.[7]

The Aboriginal custom of gendered spaces such as women's

camps and sacred spaces where women elders could live together away from the settlement to engage in women-centred activities, may have offered the space to build relationships of intimacy and such intimacy may have afforded erotic potential. This erotic potential disrupts static conventions of performing gender and opens up new categories for naming sexuality with the potential to remove labelling altogether, and to unsettle power associated with gender and sexual normativity. So, the potential of 'love magic song' opens up spaces for multiple perversities that disrupt gender, sexuality and the colonial framing of Aboriginal people.[8]

The fieldwork undertaken by Jon Willis considered same-sex attraction amongst Pitjantjatjara tribesmen. He concludes that 'although men may feel erotic attraction for each other, the gender and kinship systems of the Pitjantjatjara conspire to limit completely the possibilities for the physical, sexual expression of this attraction'.[9] The same could be said of a Judaeo-Christian tradition that has no place in its kinship, relationship or marriage structures for fulfilling same-sex desire.

Roheim, however, has suggested that young men during Pitjantjatjara men's rituals appeared to have been masturbating in the presence of one another.[10] This behaviour, however, might not necessarily be regarded as homosexual. Without knowing the sexual fantasies of the men involved, it is difficult to make any clear assertions about the presence or absence of same-sex attraction in these ceremonies.

It is possible when adolescent Aboriginal males went out on country for days at a time that conversations and actions were not restricted to hunting and analysing the land for fresh animal tracks. Their time spent together has erotic potential. They may have compared bodies or engaged in sexual behaviour with each other. I am not implying that these possible actions should be categorised within the binary of hetero- and homosexuality.

Rather I am suggesting that adolescents have sexuality, and their practices may be considered experimental, clearly more fluid than the binary.

The experiences of a number of same-sex attracted Aboriginal men in Darwin, Northern Territory, have been documented by Dino Hodge, whose findings and interviews published in 1993 provide evidence that there are non-heterosexual ways of being Aboriginal that have been practised since Australia was colonised.[11] The recorded stories in *Did You Meet Any Malagas?* also provide useful knowledge to dispel myths that 'queer' Aboriginal people do not exist, and demonstrate that the sexualities of Aboriginal people are diverse and complex and may have been so prior to colonisation. In an essay entitled 'Writing Queer Cultural Histories' published in 1995, the historian Robert Reynolds considers some of the issues raised by the book:

> Hodge does far more than reclaim a pure gay history of the Northern Territory. His questioning of gay white men reveals the way in which class and race intersect to create a commercial sub-culture dominated by relatively affluent white men ... It is in Hodge's interviews with Aboriginal and Asian gays, and two white men in close contact with Aboriginal communities, that the contextual and relational nature of homosexuality becomes clear. His interviews with Aboriginal gays indicate an understanding of sexuality that cannot be reduced to a Western model of sexual identity. This is not to construct Aboriginal sexuality as monolithic and static, or as an exotic other to the West, but rather to further contextualise dominant understandings of homosexuality and sexual identity. It may well be through such cross cultural analysis that Western concepts of sexuality will be most seriously challenged.[12]

Robert Aldrich, writing on colonialism and sexuality, has a relatively small mention of Aboriginal non-heterosexuality that is essentially drawn from an essay by the Gays and Lesbians Aboriginal Alliance:

> The history of homosexuality in Australia involves attitudes and behaviours of diverse cultures, both indigenous and migrant. Explorers and early visitors noticed, often to their horror, same-sex practices in Australia. Ethnologists and anthropologists now reject the argument that homosexual practices represent a 'white man's disease' unknown to Australian Aboriginals before European arrival. Evidence exists of 'boy-wives' kept by older men in continuing arrangements resembling marriage, as well as casual homosexual practices between adolescents and older men. Masturbation, interfemoral, subincisional and anal intercourse all appeared amongst Indigenous groups. Simulation of same-sex intercourse features in rituals, and oral literature contains references to homosexual acts. Traditional anthropologists proved taciturn or condemnatory in discussing 'sexual abnormality' or 'perversion' among indigenous people, and missionaries and public authorities in Australia, as elsewhere, attempted to eradicate 'immoral practices'. Many contemporary Aboriginal Australians remain reticent in discussing same-sex practices in traditional societies, and those who consider themselves gay still face double discrimination because of ethnicity and sexual orientation, encouraging reticence.[13]

The Gays and Lesbians Aboriginal Alliance, a collective of five Aboriginal and two non-Aboriginal Australians, proposed in 1994 a number of possible reasons for the reticence that are all tied to the impact of colonisation. They regard their only published text, *Peopling the Empty Mirror: The Prospects for Lesbian and Gay Aboriginal History* as experimental because of the insufficient writings in the field of postcolonial Aboriginal history.[14] I regard their text as vital. It is written from the standpoint of Aboriginal and non-Aboriginal people of various sexualities who use collaboration and critical narrative as enquiry. Their research may be foundational, or at the least extremely useful, towards a Queer-Aboriginal Studies discipline. Their insistence that silence around non-heterosexuality in Aboriginal communities is a direct result of colonisation offers not only opportunity to deconstruct the theory in which Aboriginal sexuality has been framed, but also reason to dismantle the act of colonisation and its effect.

Colouring the Rainbow: Blak Queer and Trans Perspectives provides us with reflective and critical life stories and academic essays that reveal and illuminate the worlds in which we live. The book's editor, Dino Hodge, has worked closely with the book contributors. I am grateful for his long-standing dedicated allegiance, and I congratulate all the book contributors on their achievements in creating and building our knowledge bases.

I call upon Australia's queer movement to work alongside and assist us to combat sexual and gender oppression, to make spaces for us to become more visible, and to value our knowledge by creating further opportunities for us to be heard from our own knowledge position.

Queering Aboriginality

The linking of Queer Studies and Native Studies can be problematic, as Chris Finley explains, because 'for the most part, neither discipline has shown much interest in critically engaging the other'.[15] Nonetheless, a number of scholars consider queer theory useful to be critical of how Native/Indigenous communities have been framed as hetero-normative, and they advocate creative expression, including visual arts, as one way in which queer-indigenous identities can create discourse and produce knowledge.[16]

Franz Fanon argues that 'decolonisation, which sets out to change the order of the world is, obviously, a program of complete disorder'.[17] According to Marie Battiste, decolonisation cannot be achieved 'without indigenous people renewing and reconstructing the principles underlying their own worldview, environment, languages, communication forms, and how these construct their humanity'.[18]

Qwo-Li Driskill, together with Finley, Gilley and Morgenson, argue that indigenous queer persons produce knowledge that opposes colonial representation, and that diversity amongst indigenous queer intellectuals has the potential to critically examine their own production within the power relations that were created by colonisation.[19] By queering Aboriginality, we not only set about challenging representations of Aboriginality brought about by colonisation, but question all representations of Aboriginality that are singular and fixed and constructed as heterosexual. Mark Rifkin asserts that 'heterosexuality is an equally inappropriate concept through which to consider traditional native family organisation, land tenure, eroticism and divisions of labour'.[20]

In this book, the contributors explicate 'Aboriginality' as 'Queer' and thereby open up potentials for transgression. They confront constructions of Aboriginality as untainted by sexual and gender diversity, and challenge assertions by Aboriginal people themselves who may regard 'queer' as not cultural or as somehow non-authentic.

The colonisation of Aboriginal/Indigenous knowledge in academic research

Although there is an emergence of Aboriginal people being represented within the western academy, the legacies of anthropological research have often resulted in depriving indigenous peoples of the opportunity to speak for themselves. A consequence is that when the researched 'other' has attempted to speak, they are up against an institution that has already constructed and colonised what it means to be Aboriginal. This is expressed by Linda Tuhiwai Smith, writing from the position of an indigenous scholar from colonised New Zealand:

> It appals us that the West can desire, extract and claim ownership of our ways of knowing, our imagery, the things we create and produce, and then simultaneously reject the people who created and developed those ideas and seek to deny them further opportunities to be creators of their own culture and own nations.[21]

Beth Blue Swadener and Kagendo Matua insist that colonisation is a way of representing, producing, inscribing, and consuming the 'other' through the silencing and denial of agency.[22] As a 'queer other' within the terrain of the 'Aboriginal other', my sexual and gender identity has also been colonised, and so it is important to offer a critique of the academy's own colonising practices, including those of Aboriginal scholars. It is essential to disrupt the colonising practices of the institution to bring into focus Queer-Aboriginality from its own knowledge position, and its particular experiences that colonisation has shaped.

Offshore, Queer Native Studies and Indigenous Queer Studies are both recent and emerging fields of research that unpack colonial hetero-patriarchy, and re-imagine non-heterosexual ways to be 'native/indigenous'. Queer Native Studies and Indigenous Queer Studies advocate that research in the field be situated from the subject's own knowledge position.[23] This is because, as Andrea Smith explains, the institution of the academy is implicated in the process of colonisation and because 'current scholarship reaffirms the assumption of settler colonialism'.[24] Linda Tuhiwai Smith supports this position:

Colonial universities saw themselves as being part of an international community and inheritors of a legacy of Western knowledge, they were also part of the historical processes of imperialism. Attempts to 'indigenise' colonial academic institutions and/or individual disciplines within them have been fraught with major struggles over what counts as knowledge, as language, as literature, as curriculum and the role of intellectuals, and over the critical function of the concept of academic freedom.[25]

The gap of knowledge within the academy regarding the gender and sexual diversity of Aboriginal peoples can be considered a product of the academy as a colonised space.

Although offshore research is non-Australian in its lens, it is useful because it has begun to unpack ways in which colonisation has constructed the gender and sexuality of indigenous peoples. In Australia, colonisation has had effect in a number of distinct ways that have arguably contributed to the silencing and denial of sexual and gender diversity within Aboriginal societies. There were policies that sought to dilute and then deny Aboriginal ways of knowing by removing children from their families; the removal, transferral, and confinement of Aboriginal people onto Christian missions; the non-recognition of non-nuclear family structures; and the establishment of a 'white' cultural default setting of hetero-patriarchy through British law, Christian morality and capitalism.

Queer Native Studies and Queer Indigenous Studies provide critical linkages between 'indigenous' and 'queer' identity; the subjects of the research have authored the knowledge though their experience, their stories, and through critique. Queer Native Studies advocates that research into queer indigenous people be situated within the academy and be pursued from the knowledge position of the queer indigenous 'subject' because 'current scholarship reaffirms the assumption of settler colonialism'.[26]

Speaking for the self

The notion of 'others' speaking for themselves is described by Norman Denzin and Yvonna Lincoln:

> A politics of liberation must always begin with the perspectives, desires and dreams of those individuals and groups that have been oppressed by the larger ideological, economic, and political forces of a society or historical moment.[27]

Stephen Kemmis and Robin McTaggart suggest that people who research from their own experience can contribute towards recovery from oppression and provide liberation from the restrictions of 'irrational, unproductive, unjust, and unsatisfying social structures' that have limited self-development and self-determination of oppressed peoples.[28]

Many of the contributors to *Colouring the Rainbow: Blak Queer and Trans Perspectives* employ auto-ethnography to represent their own experience within their essays. Auto-ethnography looks to extract meaning from experience rather than to depict experience exactly as it is lived. While it incorporates autobiography, it is not an uncritical historical account. Auto-ethnography puts the autobiography in context with the cultural and social, and a narrative structure leads to self-enquiry through the process. Further, auto-ethnography incorporates the notion of 'the personal is political' and decolonises by being centred on the care of the self and of others by feeling the voice within.[29]

The knowledge, experiences and interpretations of contributors to this book establish meanings that challenge a range of prevailing misconceptions.

Already queer: in native tongue

Native peoples of the United States have created a term for same-sex attracted Natives called 'Two-Spirit'.[30] Such

Two-Spirit people are regarded as having both male and female spirituality, thus defining non-heterosexuality as being 'in touch' with the feminine and the masculine. Maori, who are considered and consider themselves indigenous people from New Zealand/Aotearoa, have established cultural traditions of gender diversity and non-heterosexual ways of being Maori. These diversities are expressed in Maori language. The terms 'Takatapui' (same-sex attracted people) and 'Whakawahine' (transgendered people) *names* gender diversity and non-heterosexual relationships. Articulating these ways of being through Maori language is an action that has enabled Takatapui and Whakawahine to transmit culture from their own knowledge positions.[31] As a consequence, this knowledge can be employed to challenge British-colonialism and its introduced regulations for being and doing gender and sexuality.

Gender diversity in the Tiwi Islands of northern Australia was regarded as traditional and an acceptable part of Tiwi culture prior to colonisation.[32] 'Sistagirls' were traditionally called *yimpininni* and respected as nurturers within Tiwi culture, and this language is now being reclaimed. It is argued that once colonisation took effect, 'attitudes toward queer indigenous people began to resemble that of the western world and religious right, and gender became bound in binary opposition.[33] It is more recently through activism and the visibility of art practice that gender diverse Tiwi are once again recognised. 'Sistagirls' (or 'sistergirls' as identified by Brie Ngala Curtis in her essay 'Kungakunga: Staying Close to Family and Country' within this book) have contributed to dispelling myths around indigenous attitudes about gender as being either male or female.

In the essay 'Kungakunga: Staying Close to Family and Country' in this book, Brie Ngala Curtis explains how she changed her name using Arrente language to signify the 'feminine' and 'masculine', while also maintaining a frenetic connection to the language of her Luritja and Warlpiri cultural heritage:

> My skin name at birth was Jangala (for boy) but now everybody calls me Nangala (for girl). That's in Luritja and Warlpiri, but in Arrente we just have the same word and that identifies that person. Ngala is the skin name for both female and male in Arrente. I identify as Arrente and also the other ones – Luritja through my grandmother, Warlpiri through my grandfather, Warramunga and all the other tribes and languages I speak.

Being able to articulate queerness in indigenous languages is a powerful way of challenging the effects of colonisation that denied the existence of gender and sexual diversity in traditional culture. Perhaps with language you exist and may be viewed as a problem, but without language you are not recognised as existing at all.

Of Christianity

Christian missions in Australia functioned to carry out the welfare agendas and assimilation policies of the government – the intention of these policies being to eradicate Aboriginal culture. The social order of the missions was an attempt to 'civilise the natives', and it follows that this included conditioning particular ways to express gender and sexuality and to control 'sexual perversion'. It is not inconceivable that homophobia and transphobia are practices introduced by the Christian missionaries. Samia Goudie recounts, in this book, her memories from 1980s and '90s, and recalls Aboriginal pastors who preached homophobia and who claimed that homosexuality was not 'part of "traditional" culture' and that 'it was destroying culture [and] had no place'. Similarly, Steven Lindsay Ross reflects upon a recent instance of an Aboriginal sports star's homophobic commentary about gay Aboriginal people that stimulated a mainstream homophobic response, including from Aboriginal people. Presuming to know the Christian God's intentions about gay Aboriginal people and the outlooks of the ancestors is, unfortunately, a rather common response from our own communities.

For some Aboriginal people, however, remote Christian missions provided a haven and safety from the hell of life and death on the colonial frontier.[34] Crystal Johnson – a sistagirl who is an Elder, a mentor and an activist, and who is a truly remarkable survivor – insists that Christianity 'modernised' the Tiwi people by teaching the community values that have become entrenched in culture. Johnson has been able to reconcile and celebrate what appear to be conflicting belief systems.

The homophobic practices resulting from the colonial Christianisation of indigenous culture have also been identified by Native Queer Studies and Queer Indigenous Studies. Maori activist Elizabeth Kerekere writes that 'we are up against the mighty and continuing impact of Christianity on Maori culture' and that 'any acceptance that same-sex partners may have enjoyed in pre-colonial times is something for us to ponder and strive to achieve in this lifetime'.[35] Similarly, Rifkin discusses how colonisation brought Christian hetero-patriarchy to Indians (Native Americans) by imposing a nuclear family structure.[36] Finley suggests 'heterosexism and the structure of the nuclear family need to be thought of as a colonial system of violence.[37]

Articulating diversities and creating Queer-Aboriginal knowledge

I identify as a Queer-Aboriginal visual artist and the 'discursive objects' I produce are coded with Queer-Aboriginal knowledge. I want to situate my own work alongside the work of similarly identified artists to create conversations, explore intersections, and contribute further discourse. The work we create contributes to decolonising the ways in which our ethnicities, gender, sexuality, bodies, and desires have been constructed. What appears is the absence of an appearance of academic discourse to connect the instances.

There are countless Aboriginal and/or Torres Strait Islander artists, writers, scholars, poets, and other creators of knowledge, who identify as non-heterosexual and are non-binary in their gender identity. Some put themselves and their work in the public domain, and by doing so assert that gender and sexuality is explicitly connected to their cultural identity and cultural expression. Following the 'always was, always has been' position of Aboriginal ontology, it is also possible that many queer and trans Aboriginal people were not afforded the opportunity to publicly express their identity, or considered that they could or should.

Arguably, there are other spaces that incorporate work by queer and trans Aboriginal artists who have expressed identity through practice. A record of these occurrences could provide considerable knowledge towards a discipline of Queer-Aboriginal Studies, but without published analysis or promotional material it is difficult to know the extent of these possible histories. However, as Maddee Clark suggests, 'we don't need to be able to construct ourselves in written historical accounts in order to consider ourselves real and whole'.

Identifications

The Indian economist and philosopher Amartya Sen posits that we have multiple identities which can shift and change throughout our lives.[38] Although we define ourselves and other people define us, the language of insider/outsider identity labelling is not always in sync. It is exciting, perhaps anti-establishment, that as non-heterosexual and gender diverse indigenous peoples of Australia we do not share the same labels to define our identities of ethnicity, gender or sexuality. The sexual-and-gender-identity-acronym-soup (GLBTIQ) is not everyone's flavour of choice – sometimes we like to mix it up, and sometimes we feel it is not representational of ourselves.

Within my own writing I have employed the term 'Indigeneity' to refer to indigenous peoples globally whose land and culture may or may not have been colonised by other nations. I applied the term 'Aboriginal' to identify the pre-existing indigenous nations within Australia prior to European contact that included hundreds of distinct 'tribes' with unique languages and cultures. Where possible, I have used the names of Aboriginal and/or Torres Strait Islander nations. Although 'Aboriginal' is an introduced term, many indigenous peoples from Australia identify with it and the term is recognised within Australia's constitution to include indigenous nations from the Australian mainland as well as South Sea and Torres Strait Islander peoples.

'Blak' is credited to Ku Ku/Erub/Mer visual artist Destiny Deacon, having been developed as a strategy of reclaiming colonialist language to create means of self-determination and expression.[39] It has since become widespread in Aboriginal vernacular as a vehicle to express identity and subvert the racist notion that Aboriginal people are 'black', or rather are only identifiable as having 'black' skin.

'Queer' has been transformed from a language of oppression into an identity label, a theory, and a peoples' movement towards social, political, and identity liberation for sexual and gender diversity, but the term is not a good fit for all non-heterosexual and gender diverse people. 'Queer' is a problematic term because it was historically – and perhaps continues to be – associated with acts of violence towards people who appear to be non-heterosexual. This awareness stems from my adolescence in

Queensland, where non-heterosexual elders told me of horrific stories of being beaten and urinated on by police and called 'queer' because of how they expressed themselves through physical appearance.

I employ the term 'Queer-Aboriginal' both to name my identity and also as an academic field of scholarship that I am advocating. Just because Queer-Aboriginal identity is slippery and problematic to define, it is not an adequate reason to keep Queer-Aboriginal discussion silent.

It is the diversities of identity and our differences in worldview that has created the texture of *Colouring the Rainbow: Blak Queer and Trans Perspectives*. The editor has not attempted to streamline the language of identification to make it more consistent throughout – or thereby possibly more digestible for the readership. An understanding and appreciation of the slipperiness of our identifications is central towards learning about us. Language is also vital, I believe, towards developing a field of Queer-Aboriginal Studies.

Within the western academy, there have been limited explorations between the disciplines of Aboriginal Knowledge and Queer Studies. This lack of examination has resulted in an absence of recognition, discussion, and critical discourse about the complexities of gender and sexuality of indigenous queer and trans peoples in Australia. Lincoln and Denzin suggest that Critical Race and Queer Theory scholarship are at the forefront of questioning how history has 'silenced and/or misrepresented cultural difference'.[40] There is, however, very little intersection between these disciplines, and this is particularly so in the Australian academic landscape where there is no such field as Queer-Aboriginal Studies. I hope that *Colouring the Rainbow: Blak Queer and Trans Perspectives* will provide a valuable resource for this future discipline.

Part One

Inner Reflections – Life Stories

Napanangka:
The True Power of Being Proud

Crystal Johnson
(as told to Dino Hodge)

I was born in Tiwi Islands, in a little community not far from
Nguiu on Bathurst Island, in 1970. I grew up at Milikapiti on
Melville Island. My mum is from Tiwi, but my father is from
Yuendumu – he is a Warlpiri man. My father was older but my
mum was young. She was in and out from Bagot Community in
Darwin, where she met my father and fell in love. They moved
back to community at Lajamanu for a while, but then travelled
between these places.

My mum had three boys. I have four sisters and three
brothers – I make eight. My father had two wives, and then
other kids from different women. He was a Casanova – he
travelled around Yuendumu, Willowra, Lajamanu, Wave Hill.
It was just the way that he was.

After my dad broke up with my mum, I got adopted out. I
was about eight and my mother gave me to her first cousin in
Oenpelli, so she looked after me. Paula was a Christian who
worked for the Aboriginal Inland Mission church. We travelled
around preaching the word of God to other Indigenous people
in different communities. When I was thirteen, my mother took
me to Lajamanu because my father wanted me to be ready for

men's ceremony to be initiated to be a man. All of his siblings and sons were initiated men.

Mum – before she died – she was a big influence in Warlpiri society. She was a cook and made a lot giving out food. In return, her wealth wasn't the money, it was the respect that she got. That was more than money. If she was in trouble, all the in-laws would drive all the way from Lajamanu to come and bash whoever that man or woman was. Or if my mother wanted money, I would ring my brother-in-laws and straight away they would send her five hundred dollars. A lot of people don't see that in Warlpiri society. If you are good at something, you would be up on a pedestal and regarded. My mother when she died, she had a name, and she had a place to go to.

In Warlpiri society, you do sorry meetings when someone dies and cry for that person. The old ladies cut their hair right off and weave the hair, and they give that to the men to do their ceremony. They break a branch with eucalyptus gum leaves and they walk behind it to cover their tracks. We can't see it, but people who have witchdoctor powers can see the footprints. So when they do that, they cover the footprints so she can go to her home where she belongs.

My other brothers went through initiation in Lajamanu before me. First, they sing songs, and then they take you out bush. The mother's skin sisters bring gifts to the sons-in-law and for the men, like blankets, sheets, pillows, a radio, and food packs with corned beef and flour. You stay out bush for two months. You shoot kangaroos, and at night they have singing. When you come back, you can't go stay with your parents; you have to go stay at a camp for a month. They cover you with special materials made out of red ochre and oil, and they put red cockatoo feathers. They used to make woven belts, but these days they use material. And then they start singing. After that, then you be free. The men who look after us when we are out bush get promised to our sisters. So their children have to do the same for the next generation. There were thirty-eight boys who went into business with me.

My father knew at the time of my initiation that I was a sistergirl. They seen me with long hair, so feminine, still playing with the girls – I came out long before I was initiated. My father thought that putting me through men's business would change me, but it didn't. I said to my father: 'I'm the way I am.' It took them a long time to accept me. They knew who I was. My father is not stupid. He is a very well educated man, and he knew people like us.

And, you know, you see your brothers go through that pain. What happened was that my brother-in-laws couldn't protect my eldest brother during his initiation. They cut his hair. He got raped. That was payback for me. I don't know how he survived. He was crippled when he came out from the ceremony business. They told the police and the doctors that if they reported it, they would go around to my family's house and shoot them, and so my family members couldn't say anything. I got upset about it. I didn't want to talk to my father about it. I felt like he took my brother's life away. My brother left Lajamanu and he came to Darwin. He was traumatised. He was in the long grass, sleeping, being itinerant – and he used to say to me: 'You forgive me, you forgive me?' I said: 'I forgive you, but I won't forgive the men who did this to you.' My brother committed suicide. He overdosed himself. It was payback thing. And that's what happened.

My other brother got bashed in Katherine, and then he ended up getting sick and on dialysis; they said there was something wrong with his kidneys. It was payback. He was another person who drank a lot because a lot of bad things happened to him, too. There was this vicious cycle, you know, trying to run away from the pain but you can't. You get all these violent things happen to you – how can you forget about it?

My aunties used to bash my mum because I am a sistergirl. We never talked about it. Everything was all quiet. Hidden. I wanted to bring it out, but I couldn't. Nobody talked about sistergirls in Lajamanu and Warlpiri society. They used to kill them. Everybody had to be a man. My mother was bullied and my father's sisters used to spit at her. When she would see them and tried to talk to them, they walked straight past her. She started drinking and the family members used to fight with her and say: 'Your son is a poofter. He shouldn't be doing that, dressing up like a girl. You loser. Your son is going to die.' They said that to her every day in Lajamanu. They flogged my mum, but my mum used to fight back. She was always a fighter. She was the first Aboriginal woman to hold a black belt in karate and Taekwondo. She flogged all them big Warlpiri women. She would never have backed down for anyone. When I was young, she was all happy. You know, being an alcoholic, you gradually get sick. I did feel sorry for her.

My step-mother – God bless her – she told my mum: 'Well you might as well go now, Betty, because you have nothing. You have people picking on you.' And so she packed her things and left for Darwin, but the same thing used to happen there. When I had my nineteenth birthday, she said to me and my step-dad and a couple of other family members: 'Come to the park.' Once there, she said: 'Well, I want this for you. Here, your debt has been paid.' She just grabbed the knife from the birthday cake and she cut her throat in front of me. My uncle and I tried to stop the bleeding but the cut was just too deep. My step-father called the ambulance but she died instantly. I got a shock. You get the shock of your life.

My mother had a lot of respect but that didn't protect her from payback because a man is a king. A man has power. In a society like that, she didn't have no way. If I had a choice, I would protect my mum, but I didn't have a choice. I was forced into initiation. I didn't want to do it but I had to please my father. If I didn't, I would be disrespecting our forefathers. It's like, if I take you to men's business and you're my son, you have to uphold the law when I die and you have to keep the secrets with you. But if you don't and you break your promise, then I have to teach you a lesson in any which way.

I tried to help my brothers. You know, I would tell them: 'Go to counselling, Come with me. We'll take you to rehab.' I've been to rehab in Darwin and I've helped myself – but these things I couldn't do for my family. It's still in my mind, but I just have to deal with that in my life. You know, when you let that thing beat you, then you will suffer yourself and then you go down – you'll kill yourself. I said to my father: 'Why blame me when you knew that I was a sistergirl? I'm not going to come back. I don't respect you. I don't respect what you did to my family.' So when I seen him, I walked straight past. My father should have known not to take me and do those sort of things, initiations. But you know, I stopped and I thought: I was blaming him, but really I should blame the culture and the people.

I felt like: 'Why did it happen to me? Why did my family die for me?' A lot of people say: 'Why didn't you try and stop your mum.' I didn't know then about counselling or helping other people or where you can help yourself. My mum and my brothers are buried in Darwin. I go talk with them and I explain: 'If you only knew that there were ways of helping yourself.' And I can't put the blame on myself and on my sexuality. Now I would say to them: 'You can help yourself. You can overcome these things. I did. And you can.' But I was young then and more naive. If only my mum knew, and my brothers. I didn't go to school and learn things; I went to school later when I was in my twenties.

But it was a learning curve for me to take the next step, and to educate our people about gender, and about who you are and what you want to be. It's not the white man's thing. It is about freedom and I didn't have freedom. Freedom didn't come to me easily. So you know, my family had to suffer and to die because of freedom. If my mum was still alive, I would say: 'Mum, why did you do it? Mum, you should stop and think. You still could have a good life, regardless. Mum, you should see all the good things that I did. Mum, you should see, I've got a house back at Nguiu. Mum, you should see all my gay friends. Mum, you should see that I'm the first sistergirl lady politician in the Tiwi Islands Regional Council.'

I get respect from my community because I've been through a lot. I can walk in Warlpiri society saying that I am a sistergirl. They look at me as a woman. I still get criticism, but family members tell my other family members: 'She has a title and she has a name.' My name is Napanangka. I earned that skin title. I tell people: 'This is my title, this is who I am. I use that title for my mother. I earned my father's title, because this is who my ancestors were.' And if I still get criticism, I'll strip myself fully naked right in front of family and dance like a woman. Then I grab a stick or a bar and I crack my head or I cut my hand to show them the blood for proof.

I speak Tiwi, Warlpiri and Gunuwinggu. I speak a bit of Jawoyn from Katherine region, and I understand Yolngu Matha and Kriol. And I speak Marrithiyel – my grandmother's tongue, she is from Adelaide River near Litchfield National Park. When you have a language, the language comes with a country, with food, and with culture. You have to balance all that – if I speak a language, say Warlpiri, then I have to put myself in a Warlpiri perspective. I have to think, act, be smart, and be knowledgeable. When you speak a language, it is actually a title. So when I speak Marrithiyel or Maranunggu – they are two similar languages – they talk about country, and they talk about how we live today.

For me, when I speak Warlpiri, I speak hard Warlpiri. When you speak hard Warlpiri, you have to live the old ways. You have to be knowledgeable. When you talk to old people, you sit down and you have to put yourself in their shoes. When I talk to young ones, they answer in English. They understand, but they don't see the true outlook of life. This is the new generation: it's like half-English, half-Warlpiri. When you speak fluent Warlpiri, you are part of the culture; it's a different way.

I left Lajamanu to go to Darwin in late '89 and got a job as a Support and Recreation Officer at Bagot Community. From there, I moved back to Bathurst Island and I kept that job for nearly five years. I started thinking about a lot of things in my life. I've been through a lot of trauma. Yeah, and I thought I was gay. But the thing about me was I would dress like a man but I would tamp my hair out, I would still walk real funny, and I would always still have the little poxy, pinky finger raised when I held a drink. Oh my god! I was like: 'Oh, I feel shame. People might think that I'm gay.' But everybody did! People would say: 'Cyril, we know you are gay.' I met other sistergirls there during that time and I said: 'Well, this is the life I have to live.' Then in 1996, I packed up all my things and moved to Sydney with my cousin Praxi Tipungwuti. I went to Sydney to find out who I was.

Praxi found out information about support groups and one day she told me about a sistergirl centre in Petersham called the Gender Centre. She said: 'There is biggest mob sistergirls like you!' I was thinking, 'What the fuck? What's a sistergirls centre?' She showed me all these photos, and I said: 'They are all pretty ladies.' Praxi answered: 'They're not ladies. They're all men with cock!' And I was like: 'What! They are good looking. Look!' That mad bitch! She introduced me to the world of transgenders. I had a small portable record player I got from a second-hand shop and I used to buy records. One day she gave me a Patsy Cline record with this song about a crystal chandelier – and Praxi said: 'We're going to change your name. Fuck Cyril! That poofter name have to go, and you Crystal now. That's a spiritual awakening.' She was – for a black person – eccentric. And I was like: 'Are you going crazy, smoking lots of oopoonga?'[1] She replied: 'No, I'm not crazy, I can tell you. I can feel it now, I can see it now – you in a dress! We'll take you to a movie.' That's when we started going to cinemas. We went to the Gender Centre and she used to pull me along to meetings. And that's how I found my spiritual awakening.

I came back home and built my life as Crystal. I started volunteer work at the Northern Territory AIDS Council, meeting people there like Jed, Tarquin, Stanley and Greg. I became a member of the Top End transgender group 'Sista Girls', and I became the national Indigenous transgender representative. In 2000, I started writing for the magazine *GayNT*, first as Cyril and then as Crystal.[2] In my first article, I wrote:

When I go into the communities and see how my sisters and brothers live, I feel almost sick! Only in some communities though. If you go back, it mainly started with the missionaries. They would come from the Catholic Church and just push our culture aside. Back on Bathurst [Island] when my Grandmother was growing up, she didn't have any words to describe a gay man. They were just different. But since the missionaries came, they brought new prejudices and new judgments. They liked to tell my people what was bad and what was good. They tried to wipe out our culture and our beliefs. The white man's religion changed the way our people think. When I asked my people what they thought of gays, (I mean, I asked them in my own language), they just said that the gays were funny people.

Some Elders on Bathurst Island still can't accept us. They're still stuck in the teachings of the missionaries. My Grandmother is a very wise woman. She says that 'If you believe in one God, you should let him make the judgments and you should respect the land. The land and God are all part of the same thing. The people are all part of the land and so we shouldn't make judgments.'

I'm not going to make any judgments. On Bathurst Island, the Sista Girls get ridiculed lots. Mostly from the men. Even if you hang around the Sista Girls, you'll get ridiculed. There's not much support from our own people at home ... there's plenty of us though. At last count, I think there was about fifty-eight. Ranging from little ones about eleven years old to late forties. There's some lesbians on the other side of the island too. We all look out for each other but we've still got lots of our family that do support us. We've been around as an unofficial group for about fifty years, but we've now become a group that travels and visits other communities to have meetings about HIV, drugs, alcohol, transgender issues, and lots more.

For a long time, I felt like there was no real place for me, with my family pushing me away. But now, even my father has got a grudging acceptance of me. We just want family and ourselves accepted.[3]

We were talking about all these gender issues. It was just like clock-work. You know, when people show you articles and you talk about reforms – and they were talking about human rights. I was thinking: 'What are human rights and how come my people don't know about these sorts of things? Who is teaching them about human rights?' I had to learn about human rights, and I had to study it. Sistergirls were dropping like flies. Why were sistergirls getting bashed? Why were all these men bullying them? I was thinking: 'We got rights to say "No". We got rights about domestic violence. Is there a way of stopping these things?'

Around that time, the government gave money for pilot projects. Bathurst Island got grants to build a men's shelter and a women's shelter. The Catholic Church ran the men's shelter. I started encouraging the gay men to use the men's shelter and the sistergirls to use the women's shelter, but they got discriminated against. Gary Lee and Maurice O'Riordan helped me to write a letter to the funding body, asking them about having educational programs to educate the Tiwi people about transgender, gay, lesbian and bisexual – and to educate them about rights where sistergirls can be free to go to the women's shelter. So we sat down, and Strong Men's Group and Strong Women's Group started talking and educating them about gender rights and gender equity, and talking about how you can help people. It was hard at first, and then it became committees for Strong Men, Strong Women, and Youth Diversion. That's how everything all started – from using my ideas and putting it all together in this one letter.

I learned and I used that at the Club on Tiwi Islands. The sistergirls got sexually harassed when they went to the toilet and they were too scared to talk up. I said to the Club Manager that I wanted a unisex or some toilet where us sistergirls can be free. He didn't believe me and said to use the men's toilet. And I said to him: 'You are discriminating me. I am Crystal. I changed my birth name from Cyril to Crystal. This is who I am.' I got banned from the Club for six months. After six months I went back to use the women's toilet. I got banned for two years. And I said enough is enough. That's when I went to Darwin Community Legal Service and said: 'I want to win a toilet for sistergirls. I'm sick of being discriminated against in the men's toilet, and being humbugged by men.'

The Legal Service helped me to make a complaint to the Anti-Discrimination Commission, which I did in July 2003. That's when we started talking about the toilet. The Club said: 'You can have a toilet at the back. Sistergirls can use that toilet.' It was just a room, and I said: 'Is that a proper toilet? Is that toilet clean? I am not going to sign that paper unless they fix it with a flush toilet.' A lot of people threatened me. These were Elders from Tiwi Islands. They used my brother to come and flog me, so I turned around and I went straight to my home, loaded all the weapons in my car, and went straight down to the Club. I was tempted to use my gun but I didn't. I stopped and I thought: 'Now I'm being like them. I can be the other way around.' But my brother cracked me on the head. I was bleeding so I went to the clinic first and then I went to the police. Then I went straight to the Club – all dressed up – and said to my brother: 'You know what? A scar is only a scar. If you want a war scar, this is what I am going to give to you: every day of my life I am going to dress up – until the day I die. You are not going to change me. I've got the law to protect me.' I pressed charges on my brother and got a restraining order for two years. Then after two years, he said sorry for what he done. I said: 'There are laws. We don't live in the stone ages.'

In March 2006, the Club gave up. They wrote an apology letter and had to do training on gender diversity. And they paid me compensation – but money wasn't important. The important thing was that I got a room. It had a shower and a toilet. When we wanted to go to the Club, we would use that room to do ourselves up. We used to bring little perfumes. And, yeah, it was good. A lot of people look upon that as a big achievement for sistergirls. I'm that kind of person where, if I want to be successful in something, I go ahead and do it.

The Tiwi Islands shire council elections on Bathurst Island were being held in March 2012. Family members were talking that there's not a lot of things happening in our community, and who can we get to talk for our people and to stick up for our people. Well, they turned around and asked me. I said why me, and they replied: 'You talk up for Sistergirls. Can you talk up for us?' People were coming up to me and asking me. Praxi was saying: 'You got to do it, Crystal, people are suffering. You've got the voice. You talk up at meetings. You show them and guide them the right way in public meetings.' Everybody was encouraging me, and I said: 'Well, okay then, if this is the way to go.'

I thought that no-one would vote for me. I asked Andy Ewing to make some posters and lucky for me that I had friends to print them. I was going around house-to-house talking to a lot of people about if you vote for me in Wurrumiyanga ward, then I can help our community – to be the voice. It was wet season, but I just kept on doing it. When it came to voting time, I was tired from doing all the things that you do. I went home and had a sleep, and got up the next day. I nearly flipped out of my pants and I started crying because five hundred people voted for me! I got elected as a council member. And I think I was the first or the second trans lady to be elected in Australia. Yeah. I represent the Arafura side. We talk about all sorts of issues. We talk about the roads, the community, the budgets. I learnt a lot about competency and about codes of conduct, and about where we stand as council members and how we can voice our opinion and help our people.

You know, they start calling me Cyril in meetings and I got sick of it. My Uncle was saying, 'Oh, Cyril, he – .' I said: 'Through the Chair, this person is disrespecting me, and I don't want to be discriminated against in this shire boardroom. When I am here, I respect you mob as men. When I am on this table, my hat is Crystal and I am a female and I represent my people. My people voted me in here, not you mob. You are the same as me. People voted us here to fight for our people's rights and to make our community a better place. When I am out of the room, you can call me Crystal. You have to respect me. These are the laws. We, as a people, we make these laws to be governed. When I am here, you mob address me as Crystal.

Don't discriminate me. This is part of the Code of Conduct.' I got all the information together and I stapled it and gave it to everyone. I had big arguments with them and then they raised their voice on me. They got a shock, me saying that. Yeah.

Freedom is a word where people can be who they are and live in a place where they can feel good. Freedom is a word of many colours – more or less to set yourself free, to be who you want to be. Australia is big and vast, but it's free. I'm so glad that I'm an Australian. You hear about some people overseas who don't have freedom, but we do.

The Tiwi people were modernised through Christianity – the Catholics – and we've been educated. Tiwi people forgive. If I hit you, the next day I forgive you; I come and cry and I bring food to say I am sorry. Tiwi people are not angry people. They can be but they are placid people. They come and they say sorry. My brother Walter – God bless him, he passed away now – he was an Elder, but he learned so much from me. Before he died in 2013, he said to me: 'You made me open my eyes. I feel hurt because you are my little brother' – he always used little brother – 'and when people used to talk about you, it hit me in the heart. I used to cry and I used to argue with people. But I didn't mean to take it out on you, to hit you and flog you. I am sorry for what I did. But I learned so much from you. And I will call you Crystal. I respect you. You can be like me now. Look after my kids. You're the next caretaker for them. You fight for their rights. You fight for them, as I did for the Tiwi Islands. Your kids are my kids. You are the head father now.' It was a blessing – in other words, like, head aunty. He respected me like an Elder and he gave me the blessings. It was good. Walter died when he was seventy-eight. He was very a well-known Saint Mary's football player when he was younger. He turned round and he handed me his kids – and the honour of being an Elder. That's a title that I keep. Name have title, name have people, name has a country. I say to people: 'Yes, I am a sistergirl. Yes, I am an Elder. I earned that respect. I earned that title. I got that respect.'

Recently, the Alice Springs mob – Brie, Que, Shon, Carmen and others – asked me about sistergirls and trans people using the women's shelter, and I said: 'Oh, I'm sure they can, because over at Tiwi Islands they do.' It happened at Bathurst Island, and now it's happened in Alice Springs too. It was a big outcome. A lot of people say to me: 'You did a lot.' I say: 'No, I didn't do a lot. Everybody did it with me.' Yeah. I'm glad. I just want to inspire gay people and trans people and people of all walks of life. I had to go on that journey. And I'm still going on a lot of journeys, but that was the journey that I took when I was young. That's a journey that made me stronger, and I believe that I came a long way. But if it wasn't for them people – God bless them, they are with me – they turned that time into something and made me stronger. That is the true power of being proud of who you are and of being human.

Kungakunga:
Staying Close to Family and Country

Brie Ngala Curtis
(as told to Dino Hodge)

I was born in Alice Springs in 1984. Rosalina is my identical twin sister. She's trans as well, a sistergirl. My family originate from Alice Springs but from several different tribes. I grew up in my community, Acknwerrnarrte, learning tradition and culture around my grandmother and other family members. There would have been about seventy to eighty people, maybe even more. There was Arrente people there, Warlpiri and Luritja people as well, and Pintupi people. I grew up learning all these different languages. I speak Arrente – and Arrente has five dialects – then there's Luritja and Warlpiri, Warramunga and Alyewerre, and I can speak bits and pieces of some languages from Top End.

My skin name at birth was Jangala (for boy) but now everybody calls me Nangala (for girl). That's in Luritja and Warlpiri, but in Arrente we just have the same word and that identifies that person. Ngala is the skin name for both female and male in Arrente. I identify as Arrente and also the other ones – Luritja through my grandmother, Warlpiri through my grandfather, Warramunga and all the other tribes and languages I speak.

My grandmother is from the Western Desert. She was

Luritja Pintupi. Her name was Mona. She has passed away now. The first time she ever came in contact with a non-Indigenous person was when she was about maybe fourteen or fifteen years old. She walked all the way from the western desert into Alice Springs with her parents. Yeah, she was a very strong, traditional cultural woman.

I was around my grandmother a lot when I was a little boy. I was a really feminine little boy. I always used to play with the girls and dressing up and all that. My grandmother was the first person to catch me cross-dressing. She growled me only because of the fact that I was wearing her clothing. Oh, she swore, and I got upset and started crying. But she said to me to not worry about what people would say about what I'd wear as long as I'm happy. Yeah, we grew up really Christian as well. My grandmother was very Christian. Even though she was really traditional and cultural, she had a really strong Christian background and belief. And she imparted a lot of her wisdom and morals upon us and upon me personally.

I was about eight years old and at Barunga Festival, near Katherine. And I was this chubby little sistergirl – long hair – everybody thought that I was a little girl. Well, I was! I went up to Crystal Johnson – we used to call her CJ back then – who was teaching the young people. She was one of the youth workers and she was teaching young people softball. There were other sports like football and basketball but I said, 'No, I'm going to play softball with her' because she was so funny and vibrant. As she is today, she was back then. Anyway, when everybody went away and I was talking to Crystal, and I just looked up to her and I put my hands on my hips and gave her a real serious look, and said: 'CJ, are you man or woman?' And she looked at me and she said: 'I'm a boy!' Crystal is one of the first sistergirls I've ever met. At that time, being a little kid, that's when my curiosity started wondering about who I was.

It was around that time that I dressed up as a girl for Halloween. I think that's when people started becoming aware how I was really feminine as a little boy. I always used to get mis-gendered and mistaken as a girl. Later on in life, when I was in my teens, I knew I was different. Once I started reaching puberty, I knew within myself that I didn't want to change into a man – that I wanted to be a girl. I left high school because there was lot of bullying.

One day when I was a bit older, in my teens, I sat down with my grandmother and said to her about why she didn't mind me wearing girls' clothes. She said that there were always sistergirls in Aboriginal culture and there always were trans people long before European settlement in Australia. And people like her tribal group – being the last tribe to be discovered in Australia – I believe her for that because she didn't come into contact with a white person until she was a teenager. In Arrente they call us 'gwarregwarre'; Luritja mob, they say like 'kungakunga', same again, meaning like 'girl girl'; Warlpiri, they say 'karnta-pia'. The trans women at that time would join the women to do traditional women duties like cooking, collecting bush fruit, growing up the children, and making bush medicine. They'd go through women's ceremony and they'd be respected as women. They'd have relationships with men and be married because they'd be identified as straight women. Back in them days, men could have a lot of wives.

We started travelling with our parents when we were really young. We lived in Adelaide for about three years, when my parents were going to university and finishing off their degrees. Dad did Business Management and mum did Human Resources. We travelled a lot to the Top End in the Northern Territory, going on holidays with my mother's younger sisters. They have pretty much grown me and Rosalina up as well, and they're just like our mothers. And we've got other cousins, but we just call them brothers and sisters because we're in the same skin group even though they're my cousins. My mum is the oldest of about five other girls beneath her. They all have the same skin, Napangardi, and all their children are either Jangala or Nangala, or Ngala. So we are brothers and sisters; we don't call ourselves cousins. Yeah, we travelled around a bit. It was a good experience for me, anyway.

My feelings as a teenager were really intense. I've had family members saying, 'Oh you're reaching puberty now. You're almost ready to go through men's ceremony', and all that. But my father being a tribal law man himself, he sat down – because obviously he could see that I was different – and he said: 'No, it's your decision. You do it, whatever you want. If you want to go through it, you can go through it, but nobody's going to touch your body unless you say so.' Yeah, he's very strong and he gave us that option. I've never been through men's ceremony and I'm not intending to.

Rosalina came out when she was sixteen, so she came out a lot younger than me. For me, it was sort of evolving. I was always feminine when I was a teenager. Then I ended up going back to church, then cutting my hair short and trying to be straight and everything like that. I still believe in God, and I love God and I pray to Him. And just because I'm trans now, I believe that it doesn't make me any less, and I've not lost any of my values. God was always in Aboriginal culture, anyway. My ancestors believed in the spirit. The church that I did go to was an Aboriginal church so they didn't exclude Aboriginal culture at all – there's good and bad in every culture, so going to church is like enhancing the goodness of our culture: family is first, then there's food, and then there's dancing and ceremony. So going to church, we could still do all that. And I learned in church that eight of the Ten Commandments are still being lived in Central Australian Aboriginal culture today, so it is so easy for our traditional Indigenous people to adapt to Christianity. I wanted to go for the reassignment surgery straight away when I was about seventeen. But living in a small redneck town like Alice Springs at that time with no support and nobody around me, feeling isolated, I didn't have the courage to do it! I always thought about what people would think about me and the bullying – people would say bad names. People could see that I was sistergirl and then somebody would say 'No, that's a boy', and then people would make fun of it and say nasty words. It was really hard for me. And I guess for Rosalina, too.

I went into really dark, deep depression with attempts at suicide, feeling isolated, and having nobody to talk to. It seemed that there was no help at all then. I think that's when I started going to church, and I think going to church actually saved my life. Having God in my life actually gave me strength as well but I always knew that I am still a sistergirl. At that time, there were several cases of teenagers in Alice Springs who were committing suicide – friends of ours and cousins who we went to school and high school with. And it was just like a heaviness, a dark cloud going upon young people, and it went upon me at one point of my life. So I went back into hiding, like I had put myself away again.

Still, I realised there's still something about me that I'm not being true to myself, so that's when I first came out as a gay boy. For a few years I lived as a gay male, still identifying as a male, but I was still feminine. And so I was telling people I'm gay-slash-sistergirl – I'm half gay boy and half sistergirl. I've been in two relationships as a gay male. I think those both made me realise who I was as a sistergirl because at that time I was still feeling very anxious and depressed. But then I think it was my last break up that made me realise who I was as being trans and being sistergirl.

After my break up, I just left everything and moved up to

Darwin for a few months. I felt that I was going downhill a bit, like drinking way too much, hanging around the wrong people and getting in a bad crowd. Me and Rosalina got a place in Darwin and shared an apartment. Rosalina would invite Crystal and others over. There was one time that me and Crystal were sitting down, and I was playing Christian resources and videos on the TV – it was a real powerful and special moment where we were watching it and talking about good things. She called me by my male name, because I wasn't a sistergirl back then, and she spoke in Warlpiri and said, 'You know, God's going to use you to reach out for sistergirls.' I would have been about twenty or twenty one at that time, and I didn't understand what she meant. To me that was very prophetic. I had to go through my journey, evolving and finding myself. Today, I could see what she meant by that. Taking all of my knowledge and wisdom I've gained over the years from my experiences and people I've met, I understand that I've got a voice. And to see Crystal as a role model, standing up, speaking out aloud, advocating on sistergirl awareness and what's happening – this has given me that courage to get up and start speaking as well and to say, 'Enough is enough'.

I decided to move up to the Tiwi Islands to stay with Crystal around 2010. Crystal, in traditional way, she is our grandmother. Sistergirl way, she's more or less a big sister. When I moved there she gave me and the other sistergirls living up there very good encouragement. I realised: 'This is who I am, I'm a sistergirl.' Being around in a community where sistergirl culture is very accepted and loving, that gave me strength and courage to chuck away all my boy clothes and start living as a girl. Ever since then I've felt complete within myself and satisfied within myself. I don't think I could ever look back. And I know that my life is a new life now and it's only the beginning.

Crystal is the first Indigenous trans in the Northern

Territory to come out as sistergirl and to live a trans life in a modern way. She's travelled the world to talk at many conferences. She gives me advice how to be stronger and how to be a good role model. And she's really encouraged me to access hormones and assisted me in that. I think some of Crystal's major contributions and achievements are her voice. She's got a very powerful, prophetic voice – she's very articulate with her words – making, advocating and bringing awareness, and giving strength to sistergirls or trans or gay and lesbians living in remote communities. Yeah, she's the first transgender to enter a shire or political government in Australia. I think she's done a lot of sistergirls proud when she did that. I look up to her a lot. I get a lot of advice from her. She's full of wisdom and she's a humble woman.

Rosalina and I are identical twins. We are best friends but we are just like total opposites. She has been one of my biggest encouragement and strengths as well. People like Rosalina and Crystal and several other sistergirls actually gave me that courage to start my transformation from being a boy to a girl. But I believe that I had to go through my journey to become who I am today, and I've become a lot stronger. If I ever get the opportunity, I'll go through women's ceremony. Rosalina's been invited to dance with women a long time ago. The majority of my family have accepted me being sistergirl now. But it's so ironic because my father's side, they're so atheist, they don't believe in God or anything like that – oh well, the majority of them don't. But on my mother's side who are all Christian, they have totally accepted me and Rosalina as being sistergirls and trans, but our father's side have been a bit unsure. We've had more bad experiences on our father's side – even been called names and had bad attitude towards us from our father's side more than from our mother's side. But our parents are really happy and they're both very supportive of our transitioning.

I have been invited to go dance with the women for certain ceremonial or ritual activities. But the real sacred ones, I'm not ready for that yet.

Sistergirls do understand and do carry the culture, and they know about things. I think it's important that we do. A lot of the Tiwi Islands sistergirls know all the songs and the dances for men and women. In the central desert, a lot of sistergirls know a lot of the secrets of culture and dreaming. Like the way I was brought up, my grandmother imparted a lot of her knowledge within me. She taught me things that she didn't teach other people – I'm not too sure why. Maybe because I was different, but I feel special and privileged to have that within myself. She shared a lot of her knowledge equally to both me and Rosalina, and we share it to each other. My grandmother loved her bush medicine. Crystal's big sister, Napanangka, she had a lot to do with our upbringing as well and would teach us a lot of things. I think that we had the privilege of knowing, learning more, and absorbing more information out of them old people than what our siblings did. And today we are slowly imparting the knowledge to our other siblings – and to other people when the timing is right.

The biggest challenges for being a sistergirl in the Northern Territory is access to hormones, and that feeling of isolation, not only for myself but for sistergirls in general. Access to hormones is the reason why I moved to Sydney. A lot of Aboriginal Health Services aren't educated or aware of sistergirl or trans issues. Being sistergirl and trans can be really embarrassing because sometimes we feel ashamed about our body. You know, we don't want anybody to invade our privacy – well me personally I don't want that. When I go to a doctor, I'd rather see a female nurse or a female doctor. I always tell them that I want to be called and respected as female and as Brie. But it's much more easy in Tiwi Islands – the girls there just go to the women's side of the clinic. They're separate those clinics, there's the men's side and the women's side, so women will go to the women side, and sistergirls will go to women side, yeah.

I'd tried so hard to access hormones – there wasn't any doctors or anybody familiar with it in Darwin. I got lined up to see a psychiatrist, but I had to pay two thousand dollars to be assessed as transgender so I could start my medical transitioning. I said: 'No, blow that. Why should I pay when there's other ways of doing it.' That's just stupid! So I went back to Alice again and they said the same thing again: 'You have to travel. The nearest place is Darwin or Adelaide to see a psychologist and get an assessment to be diagnosed as trans to start medication.' A lot of sistergirls can't afford it because a lot of sistergirls living in remote communities are living in poverty and have no money and no support. So how on earth can you afford to pay thousands of dollars and the expenses of travel and accommodation and everything like that.

But yeah, I think that was my biggest challenge at that time being a sistergirl. There are a lot of other challenges, like going back home and making the community and other people aware about sistergirl issues – even about violence and discrimination against sistergirls. I know several sistergirls who have been assaulted. I have been assaulted a few years ago for being a sistergirl. I woke up in hospital, after being taken there in the ambulance, for being bashed for being a sistergirl and transgender. That was the pivotal moment in my life where I said: 'Well look at me: I was bashed for being a sistergirl.' That gave me a great strength within myself. I didn't want to feel sorry for myself so I turned that emotion around and said: 'I'm going to use this to empower myself. I'm not going to change for everybody. This is who I am, and I am only going to make my appearance and myself look better.' I didn't know who bashed me. They were black. I can honestly say that I don't get much discrimination or abuse from non-Indigenous people. The majority of it does come from Indigenous men. And that experience is pretty common with other sistergirls as well. Yeah, I think that probably the biggest challenges I'm facing at the moment are to fight against that discrimination and to fight against sistergirl violence.

I never used to speak publicly about sistergirl things before, but we lost a young sistergirl to suicide who was sixteen years old. That young sistergirl who was bullied and had no way out decided to take her own life, and she was a beautiful, gorgeous young girl. It's really heart breaking for us older sistergirls, and we said: 'No, we've had enough of this. There's no other organisation willing to support us and to help us, and that young sistergirl's death could have been prevented but she had no support at all. Let's make our own organisation.' So yeah, we made our organisation Sisters and Brothers NT, which is a support network advocating for sistergirl issues and for queer, trans, and gay and lesbian people in the Northern Territory. We were just going to leave it for sistergirls alone but I said to the other girls: 'No, we're not going to leave it just for sistergirls, we're going to open it up for everybody. What about the gay men and the lesbian girls and the brotherboys – Indigenous and non-Indigenous. We're living in the NT and there's no support for any of us.' So yeah, we decided to involve other mob and open it up. And a lot of other people – intersex, gay, lesbian – have joined.

We're developing an advocacy and referral service. Other organisations came on board like the NT AIDS and Hepatitis Council, and the Women's Shelter in Alice Springs. Now we've got allies around Australia as well, like trans organisations in Victoria. So yeah, there's these organisations and allies, but I think the greatest support at the moment is from the Women's Shelter and NTAHC. We've been coming together for a long time with NTAHC for the sistergirl retreats. We're a support network as well. It is very important that support happens, because if there's no support then there's going to be more high suicide rates in the Indigenous communities, especially amongst trans Indigenous people. We've been losing a lot of sistergirls over the years, and losing that other young sistergirl from Numbulwar community just last year. The majority of the Sisters and Brothers NT committee live in Alice, but we are all spread out through the NT. We've got some sistergirls from Daly River as well. We're trying to get other people involved as much as we can.

Crystal, Rosalina and Starlady put in proposals to the Women's Shelter to be inclusive with trans and queer people for safety access against violence, and that they cannot discriminate in providing services to sistergirls and queer people. Crystal first did that up in the Tiwi Islands a few years ago for sistergirls to access the women's shelter there. For this to happen in Alice Springs was a major breakthrough, and it was very good that it was reported in the newspaper. Since then, we've given an education seminar with the Alice Springs Hospital. And we've talked about human rights and our needs at the Mind Out conference, which is the LGBTI National Mental Health Awareness Conference[4] – Crystal, Starlady and myself were presenting at that one – and other conferences also, like the Australia and New Zealand Professional Association for Transgender Health conference.[5] We've got a powerpoint presentation that we use. Whoever of us mob who goes, we do the presentation all about sistergirls – and not only about sistergirls but the LGBTI people in the NT. We talk about suicide, depression, the lack of awareness, the lack of support, how we are going about educating and bringing awareness, and what our organisation is about. And Rosalina and a sistergirl from Ceduna, Simone, did an interview with Beyond Blue in Melbourne for a mental health awareness campaign.[6]

We officially launched Sisters and Brothers NT during the Alice Pride Festival in 2014.[7] We thought that would be a perfect time for our launch because a lot of people would be there from interstate and because the Pride Carnival has a lot of publicity. There was a formal event at Alice Springs Town Council, and Central Australian Elders Aunty Marie Ellis and Uncle Warren Williams spoke. They are both very renowned and well-respected Elders in the Arrente Nation and within the Alice Springs area. I think it was very important for them to come along and speak because they both accept diversity and they are aware of a lot of the issues that LGBTI people experience – and having a lot of family members who are diverse, they both are passionate about it. So I felt that they really needed to be there, and that people need to hear what they had to say and to show that support from Central Australia.

Uncle Warren gave a Welcome to Country at the launch, and Aunty Marie Ellis gave one at the Pride Carnival. I feel really happy that they wanted to do it. There was a panel discussion at the launch with Crystal, Que and me – we are all related to Uncle Warren in some ways: me and Crystal both call him Uncle, and Que calls him grandfather. He pointed out him being a law man, high up in the culture and in law, and mentioned that he gets a lot of negative comments spoken about why is he involved and supporting us. One of the main comments he said was about people moving away to come out as queer or trans. I feel that was kind of me and Crystal's situation, moving away from our communities to actually live our lives as being sistergirls. And there is a lot in those words when he said: 'They should come out in the front of us. They shouldn't move away.' What really made me emotional was when he said that if anybody messes with any of us mob, for us to go and get him. There was a lot of depth behind that, because it's hard to come out in the front of family and people that you've known all your life – and being

46

in a community where you've had bad experiences and a lot of judgement and criticism, especially when you know that that can happen again. So, I think that he pointed that out because he wants people to be more supportive and more accepting of it and not to be in that old mind frame, but to be more open about having a family member who is queer or trans or sistergirl or brotherboy. And for us to have that courage to come out in the front of them and don't travel so far away – to be who we are and to stay close to family and country.

Black, Gay in a Wonderland of Boogie

S. O'Donnell

Introduction

I was born in Sydney in the sixties but I consider myself a child of the seventies. My father was born in Caroline Street, Redfern, long before it became known as the Block. My mother was a home birth in Newtown.

Mum became the only female from her family to marry outside the norm when she married a non-white male, that is, an Aboriginal man. All my maternal cousins are ninth generation white Australians. My grandmother and grandfather were born in the Gundagai area; her family still is very well known in this town. My grandmother's old school mentality was that children should be seen and not heard, and so we were never allowed around her.

My father's Indigenous relatives were non-existent in my upbringing, and being Aboriginal was never really discussed. I was not even aware my father had any blood relations until 1982.

We lived first in Surry Hills and then Chippendale before moving out to Wagga Wagga in the Riverina district of New South Wales. The house at North Wagga was wooden and enormous, so it creaked and groaned. Watching the 1969 first moon landing in glorious black and white is a strong memory. Dad and mum separated in the following year, and then she and I moved into a public housing home. This is where all my schooling was done until I left Wagga at the end of 1980. A majority of the area's families were on social security benefits. I was never aware of any class distinction or even racial tensions; all the kids just knocked around together and had a great time. Our family being of Aboriginal descent was not a problem at all. The socially-entrenched discrimination only began when I started high school.

Sex

Our trips to Sydney during the primary school holidays were spent at my maternal aunt's her home in Maroubra. This place always had sand fleas that just jumped everywhere, and I never got used to them at all. Aunty Shirley's family were wax heads, that is, surfies. These cousins considered us so backward that they still thought we had our mail and milk delivered by horse. We were there most of the May and September school holidays and even sometimes over the long summer break.

By 1973, I was certainly aware that I fancied boys over girls. That year during the Christmas holidays one of my Maroubra cousins tried to sell me to some drug dealers. I was the exchangeable product for his marijuana habit. I was a bit perplexed what was going on but understood enough to feel sorry that it didn't happen. My cousin denies this event took place, even now, some forty years later. This one remarkable happening ignited my sexual awakening, and this sent me into absolute and complete overdrive. I then figured out that sex was a very powerful pursuit. I also knew that sex was not love.

The following school holidays this same cousin had sex with another male cousin while we were all sleeping in the same bedroom. When I got the courage to ask 'What's going on?', he replied 'Shut up and go back to sleep'. I hid under the cover and listened. I knew it was naughty but at the same time exciting. That other cousin would go on to have a sex change – something that was very much talked about in Wagga at the time. She currently lives in Brisbane and is very well indeed.

Boys were always meant to be rough and tumble, and girls were the objects of desire. I could see the other kids pairing off in primary school, and I tried to follow what was expected so that I could be normal. I got a girlfriend. I thought I was in love, and I went so far as the steal a music book by the Carpenters for her; she was very impressed! As with all young men, at the same time there was certainly sexual experimenting going with each other. It was all very hush hush and it was just mucking around to see who would take the bait for the next step, but being so young I had no real idea of what the next bit could be. I even fumbled sex with my girlfriend but she would have none of it – a good Catholic upbringing does that. I was sad and upset when she announced that her family were moving to Perth.

The holidays during May 1975 were spent at Bondi Beach with a Wagga friend who lived just around the corner. We were staying with his sister who was a live-in nanny for an army family; she first got the job in Wagga and then moved with them to Sydney when the husband was transferred to Watson Bay. I suspect she was a lesbian: she was like the house army sergeant most days, and once she even told us once that she 'had a piss standing up to see how blokes did it'. The flat was right across the road from Bondi Beach. This school holiday was absolute magic: all sun, sand and bronzed male bodies everywhere – well for me anyway. I figured out very quickly that the big smoke was the place to be. My friend was very straight-acting and our friendship was over when at the end of 1975 he announced 'I don't like your kind coming here'. I supposed he was annoyed I never made a pass at a him; he was not very pretty, anyway.

At the same time, my primary schooling was coming to an end and we were prepared for the next phase of our education in high school. The required sex education class was given and I remember thinking that this cannot be right: the penis goes into a vagina and this is called 'making love'. It was the fastest forty-five minutes of my schooling days and the teacher giving the talk was very red-faced while showing us the slide show.

Race

On the first day of the new high school year in 1976, mum was required at school to sign forms, like a cattle call with all of the new first form students and mothers. It was sad because I think mum felt she was losing me. This is the ritual of going from a child to a man! Society demanded that males should always be tough and rough, and this was enforced by the boring Wednesday afternoon ritual of sport. I had a go at cricket but, bloody hell, it was boring and I was useless; mainly I went to watch who was mates with who. I did like baseball and basketball, but as a general rule I was not a sportsman at all.

I had not made any real jump forward intellectually at all by beginning high school. It was hell for the new first formers. We were thrown to the lions, and the older students made our lives very miserable. Survival of the fittest and quickest was on the cards that first month. It took us about six weeks before the cliques of your new best friends were established. The usual attractive white girls all stayed together and they attracted the good looking young men. The need to be accepted was like a stench in the air. Those outside of accepted circles were open to humiliation by everyone. Also the 'rural kids' verses the 'townies' was a game played out daily. I had no idea milk came from cows.

The government of Liberal Prime Minister Malcolm Fraser instigated a scheme in 1976 where Aboriginal children in high schools received a fortnightly payment of $4.50 and also a yearly payment of $300 for clothes and sundries. Once it became common knowledge that the 'Abo' kids got paid, then the other 'white' kids really had the shits because they 'had' to go to school while we 'were paid' to come along.

The other kids who identified as Aboriginal were open to torture as most were from Ashmont, a most undesirable housing commission estate. I really had nothing to do with the these Aboriginal kids from Ashmont at all as I moved in a different circle. I tried my own version of assimilation when I bought exactly the same clothes as the white kids – brown suede boots, grey Levi trousers, and a white shirt and tie. The day I walked into school I was almost bashed as I had attempted to cross the line – no blacks into the whites-only club. But I was safe at high school because I led a group of five other boys. We stuck together and were inseparable. I was the top dog although mainly all I did was watch out for teachers while the others smoked in the basement locker room.

Uncovering the Gay World

I met Michael when his family moved to Wagga from Melbourne. Wagga was (and is still) a very conservative place. For a woman in 1976 to wear a caftan was outrageous but Michael's mother did. His family became my surrogate for most of the time. It was there I was able to watch older relatives, especially the grandmothers, come and be nurtured. Also, this family did not drink and that itself made them unique. They discussed subjects ignored at my own house, such as politics, world events, life events, Australia as a country, religion and the arts. This was also the year that my love of music came into being.

Physical Education became a looking contest for me. I was the first boy to grow pubic hair, and so my pubes became the weekly required observation point. This was no problem for me and I would drop my pants down at any given request, but only on Wednesday's in the Physical Education change room of course. Mind you, there was one male who was quite keen for an up close and very intimate inspection, and he said I should come to his house on the weekend. This 'weekender' became a sexual adventure where neither of us knew exactly what we were really doing. He made it quite clear I was not to speak to him at school for any reason. Anyway, I was already experimenting sexually with others, both male and female. There was the unspoken rule that we can do it BUT no mentioning of it to anyone or the adventures will be cut off or, worse still, exposed to all as a real live poofter in the school ranks. Looking back, you know you are doing something naughty and exciting at the same time, but you have no real name for it, as 'it' was never discussed.

These first two years of high school was when I met by chance some young university students. I would hang out with them at their rented house on campus. They smoked and drank, and so to me they were real adults. They were involved in the Riverina Trucking Company, the university theatre group. One girl told me she was a 'lesbian', and this did have to be explained to me. They also had three bean bags in the lounge room, which was very hip and happening for Wagga.

In late 1976, my mother received a letter from my father's then partner telling us he was sick. I used this as an excuse to go and see him at his home in St Peters, Sydney. I turned up one Saturday morning and boldly went to the address. I told the man who answered my knock on the door, 'I am looking for Timmy', and he replied, 'Yeah that's me. Who are you?'. When I explained 'I am your son', there was some general banter and I was allowed to stay for the weekend. Thus begun my monthly train hops to Sydney, sometimes alone and sometimes I brought along mates. This was all quite innocent but we had some fun.

Sydney was the playground of dreams. The return train

fares were so cheap in the seventies, and I explored the city with such gusto. I was not looking for sex at all, just the excitement of being there instead of the country. The return train left Sydney eight o'clock on Sunday night and arrived in Wagga at two in the morning. I would walk home to sleep, and then go to school for another week of boredom. I was never very good academically and found classes dull. Most of the teachers were just long-time, bored educational robots.

I took a neighbourhood boy, Kevin, on one of these trips. During the trip back to Wagga on the Sunday night in one of the dog boxes (the trains were the old wooden red rattlers), a man sat across from us. He was wearing a butterfly ring on his pinkie finger. Kevin asked him what that meant. He was very forward and said he was gay. I was dumbstruck as I had only heard the word poofter or fairy used in Wagga, and he was the first person to actually say out proud that he was GAY. He gave us his address, which was not so far away, and said we should come over any time. I had never met gay men who had secure jobs and a social life, and I felt that I had struck the mother lode. Now, going to this house was not a problem but the trouble started when it became apparent we were being regarded by the men as new sex things. One male visitor to the house made it quite clear he wanted to have sex with Kevin. I had to explain to him what this predator wanted; Kevin never came back to the house. I was there quite a lot watching and listening to this gay household interact. I did not have sex with any of them – just not my type.

This house eventually split and two of the men, Kenny and Roger, moved into a unit in inner Wagga. There were no gay bars, and their new place was like a gay coffee house. I started meeting lots of gay men from across the Riverina. No sex was ever asked of me or even given; just the atmosphere was enough for my own tranquillity. There was a semi-official gay group called the South West Association of Gays (SWAG), that sort of met at this house to discuss over coffee who had been where and doing what. Some of the men bragged about picking up 'straight trade' and having sex with men who did not consider themselves to be homosexual. Peter had one such affair with a RAAF man stationed at Forest Hill RAAF Base. After two years, he was killed in a car accident, leaving Peter devastated.

This group is where I met my first real 'Out Queen'. He was from Griffith and dyed his hair blonde (he thought he was Deborah Harry of Blondie). He was a screaming queen. Just being in his car made you a poofter and many of the others gays in Wagga considered him an embarrassment; I found this to be a double standard. His parents would give him money just to go away from Griffith for the weekend. He was training to be a theatre nurse but you knew it was a waste of time.

There was also in this circle a semi-political group of lesbian feminists: Grace, Mary, Jenny and Linda. They became a force of their own within the gay students at university, mind you, even with support not many wanted to come out as they were still afraid of what others thought. Jenny and Linda were having an open affair. All the other students in their living block knew and were quite accepting and it was not a problem to anyone. Mary took a fancy to Jenny and started having a secret affair with her, and all hell broke loose when Linda found out. Watching two big lesbians fist fighting is a sight to behold.

Coming out

The subject of my Aboriginality and homosexuality was never a problem within SWAG; it was just a non-issue. However, life at school started to get worse and I was threatened with violence and daily verbal abuse, sometimes even by the other Indigenous students. Kids learn very quickly to despise what they cannot understand. I may have been just too confident in my own skin to realise the ramifications.

A new art teacher started at the school in 1977. When I saw him in the art class I knew he was gay. It took quite a lot of courage to ask him when we were alone. His response was to give me his home address, saying 'Please come around whenever you feel like talking about it'. His house became an after school social gathering place; no sex was involved and he was purely a person who treated me like an adult. In a small town and being different, it was very interesting when sometimes you ran into other students at his place. Again, this was never discussed outside his place, and we were able to just hang out and be natural. The next code of silence was established.

I had a major crush on a male student in my school year. I used to get very annoyed that he had girlfriends, and was always glad when they broke up. He also went out with a girl who I was friends with, so sometimes we would all hang around together on the weekends. There was another student who oozed an aura about him. He had brothers who were mechanics and so, every now and then when I was at his home, we would ride on his bike and then help fixing cars.

In 1978 I did two things that outcast me even more. I was the first male to turn up to school with pierced ears, and I did away with the usual over the shoulder leather school bag and instead bought a five dollar 'Just Jeans' bag. I remember my step father trying to talk me out of using it at school; he didn't use the word 'poof' but I knew just on the tip of his tongue. My schooling was a mess and I was all over the place and coming out quicker than I or anyone else knew how to handle. In September, I advised the school principal to 'get fucked' and he expelled me on the spot. This was a saving grace for me, really, and now I was free to roam around Wagga Wagga and be myself.

My mother wanted me to go back to school immediately. A plan was hatched for me to stay at my Uncle Eric's place in Sydney and attend Randwick Boys High. I visited Sydney and stayed for a week but this enrolment never happened. As luck would have it, while I was in Sydney I bumped into the art teacher who had been very kind to me at school. We had dinner together and he wanted to take me to a nightclub called Signal in Darlinghurst. I was up for it but he got cold feet at the last moment.

The remainder of 1978 and all of 1979 I was just wandering aimlessly in Wagga, visiting people as I wanted to. My home life was a shambles, as my sister had 'outed' me to my mother, though for what reason is still a mystery. I became the local babysitter, so money was not a problem. SWAG decided to have a party about twelve kilometres north of town at Kyembra Smith Hall. The organising committee was set up to oversee Wagga's first ever gay party. We had no idea who would came along, as in those days there was no internet and all information was distributed by word of mouth. The hall was chosen for its isolation and this allowed for privacy. I was absorbing every bit of information I could from the gay group, straight people and anyone else I came into contact with. I knew Wagga was not to the place to live.

In most larger country town across the world there are always places men can go for anonymous sex activity, and Wagga did have such places. Some who went were gay, others were part-time gays, and some were men who had sex with men but did not identify as gay. All towns have this core gay element; you just have to look for it. Being discreet was always a requirement, as once you come out and people knew, you then became the subject of gossip or worse.

Danny, a man I have known for almost thirty-five years, once encountered one of Wagga's most well-known footballers. He was enticed into the van and driven somewhere for sex. Two weeks later he saw the same man and again got into the van. He had no idea there was a second man hiding in the back seat.

When he got in, he was held tightly and blindfolded. They took him a location where they both had very rough sex with him before bashing him with a baseball bat. He made it to hospital where he spent a week. He made no complaint to the police – remember this was a long time before homosexual men were tolerated. To this day, he has a fear of going out at night. I am sure there are thousands of stories of the same evil calibre that can be told about men who do not identify as 'Gay'. It's the good old country poof bashing that we all had to endure. I remember one night I was assaulted by a man on a motorcycle who stopped, got off the bike, and hit me over the head with his spare helmet.

Winning Boogie Wonderland

Sydney in the late seventies was still forming it own gay liberation movement. Together with four mates, we would frequently drive to Sydney for the weekend, going to Oxford Street venues such as the Tropicana and Flo's Palace. I was never asked for ID even though I was only fifteen. The first song I danced to at the Tropicana was Boogie Wonderland. Throughout 1979 I was a night person, visiting the families I knew, the university students and other places. The twenty dollars an hour earned by babysitting allowed me to start a life-long passion of buying music. As often as I could on Sundays, I watched Countdown on ABC television. This was required viewing for the latest pop music. Queen, Suzi Quatro, Skyhooks and Sherbet were my favourites.

For some reason I became convinced that my life would become worthless without schooling. Returning to my old high school was certainly out of the question, so I made an enquiry with Wagga Wagga High School. The principal was a bit reluctant but he accepted my argument that I needed an education for life and in February 1980 I enrolled. The problems started within three hours on the very first day. One of the kids there also had been at my old high school and he instantly shouted there's a poofter. I became the hottest news at school that day. I was able to access Abstudy monies that year, and I rented a house with three bedrooms. A friend moved in, as did an actor who was in a production with the Riverina Trucking Company. It was a great time for all of us, being sort of out and semi-independent together in an old rustic home with an open fireplace, Salvation Army op shop decor throughout, cheap dinners, cheap wine, and great company. This house for a while became a little gay ghetto and, because of it distance away from the high school, boys from school started to drop in to see how I was; this was in complete contrast to how they behaved at school. This, of course, was their way of asking for sex. But the best things never last.

I became the new whipping boy for the school's hatred, and not only was there a 'queer cunt' around but he was an 'Abo queer cunt', such was the language used. Within weeks I had had enough of constant abuse. My complaints to the teachers, counsellors and even the principal were met with 'Oh well, too bad'. I wrote to the editor of the local paper, the *Daily Advertiser*, stating I was a gay student at high school. I had not signed the letter but I did identify the school. The principal called me in and demanded that I leave because of this disgusting letter that had been published. I had not signed it, and so I called his bluff with the NSW *Anti Discrimination Act*. An Aboriginal male with attitude and some legal knowledge was not a wanted student. The principal was stopped in his tracks, but being at school became impossible. I was banned from Physical Education classes as the teacher thought I might be bashed. A female student sent her crazed bikie cousin to my home because she didn't like poofters. The bikie pulled a gun and, in that blink of an eye, I knew it was time to leave Wagga once and for all.

The letter to the editor had one saving grace, as a reporter was inspired to write an article about homosexuality. She contacted Camp Inc, a gay lib group in Sydney and spoke to one of the founders, Peter. Her article gave me the opportunity and courage to write to him. I confessed I was the author of the published letter. His response was that if I came to Sydney I could stay with him until I got sorted out. I was packing as soon as I got home that day. Peter was kind and friendly, listening and advising on what to do. I stayed for six weeks before finding lodgings.

Twenty years later, in 2000, I was able to help a student who was putting up with the same old homophobic situation at my first high school. I knew a young gay student, Mathew, through his mother. He was being bullied but his complaints to the principal were totally ignored, and even a visit to the school by his mother was no help. I was able to get him a pro-bono solicitor from Sydney. Mathew received a $5,000 payment but with an understanding that the school would not be made accountable. No official apology was ever made.

Later again, in 2009, my first high school held a year reunion. I spoke to the organiser, Kathy, and was encouraged to join a Facebook page. A few sent friend requests that I accepted. A profile called 'Tim Potter' popped up with a friend request. I accepted, thinking he must know me from somewhere. After only ten days hate mail started pouring in, mentioning events from school that only a select few would know. The lengths some homophobic and racist people will go to is unbelievable. I tried to figure out who it was but to no avail. The messages got worse and I almost did not go to the reunion. Kathy said 'If you don't show up, they will win', and so I got myself together went along. I may not have been great at sport, but along the way I've learnt how to win.

Pigeon-holing Trauma: Situating Demoralisation

R.J. Sailor

Introduction

Foremost I acknowledge clever Aboriginal and Torres Strait Islander people, past and present, who instrumented change – modifications were not an easy thing to do, nor is it now! Greater minds than mine agree that Indigenous is a more inclusive term to reference original Australian cultures, unless I'm defining difference. I am descended from First Nations inhabitants of Australia, and being a man who has sex with men (MSM) delivers me a double whammy. The intersections of Indigenous cultures, anatomy and sexual preference, together with human conditioning, pigeonholes me in demoralising crosshairs.

Microagression is an everyday weapon of the wealthy, industrial ruling class that dehumanises Gay Bi Lesbian Trans Intersex Queer (GBLTIQ) and Indigenous communities through disempowerment. The path from aggressor to target, like bullets to the head, obstructs equal community participation and affects individual psychological wellbeing. This auto-ethnography expresses my identity, with sexuality equal back-seat passenger driver on a lived rollercoaster ride as I recollect happenings in my life.

James Baldwin, a black American gay icon, described that rollercoaster after he marched on Washington DC with Martin Luther King Jr in 1963:

> That's part of the dilemma of being an American negro; that one is a little bit colored and a little bit white, and not only in physical terms but in the head and in the heart, and there are days – this is one of them – when you wonder what your role is in this country and what your future is in it. How, precisely, are you going to reconcile yourself to your situation here and how you are going to communicate to the vast, heedless, unthinking, cruel, white majority, that you are here? And to be here means that you can't be anywhere else.[1]

I now lay unprotected my bare, Bear body, textually mirroring my anguish not as an expert but as just a man. I hope to break through stereotypes which hang, it feels, like a noose around my neck, loose but ready to be tightened. Whiteness, at a certain time in one's life, essentially is something you detect but struggle to define as it seems normal. The modern globalist planner's privileged stranglehold seems undying.

Justice or just me

From the start, growing up under the Bjelke-Petersen regime in Queensland, I was told by the geneticists, racists and theorists that 'dirty half-castes' are good for nothing. This pigeonholing traumatised me, and situated demoralisation as a norm in mainstream spaces. The claim that Miggaloo[2] people are right all the time seemed like I could never be bright, unless I agreed with them. They have might on their side. As the first male child in my generation of immediate family with light skin, being called 'Whiteman' at home wasn't easy, however, acceptance in Indigenous spaces was rough and is still tough.

Genetics, scientific rationality and tyranny orders every detail of my existence based on my genealogy. Biometric viewpoints continue to create social determinants for me, positioning me subservient to all. My Grandfather, like many others, proved to be an extraordinary man: he bought land with his third of a standard wage that he was paid. My genealogy places me second generation from the Warrior, and sixth generation from a Prime Minister of England.

Scientific or social technologies and terminologies have become central pillars to race cults that divide and conquer the struggles encountered in one's lifetime. The transcendent propaganda machines are both non-Indigenous as well as traditionalist. When they find out I'm MSM, the strangulation tightens. I get scientifically, socially, and forcibly compartmentalised by most, and they deduce me as an abomination.

Aristotle's proverb that 'there is nothing more unequal than equal treatment of unequals', epitomises the intolerance and prejudices I continually confront. Prejudices from non-Indigenous and Indigenous people are omnipresent and abundant towards me. Being authenticated all my life by tea towel imagery of an archetypical boomerang-throwing Aboriginal man constitutes the voyeurs' racism and not my identity.

Please do not expect me to walk around shopping malls wearing a dhari³ either. My clan remains multilingual and recent contact cultural knowledge is well within my grasp, but I just love the urban lifestyle. Why can't I wear a blue collar shirt? I can't hunt or dance – I don't have to! The only grass skirt or lap-lap I will be wearing is a Versace or Prada at the Mardi Gras. The sad thing is that other urbanised people believe they are more authentic than me because they've reinvented themselves.

Assimilationists, both white and black, create erroneous cultural traits I refuse to follow! If other people believe that borrowing another society's traditional character authenticates them, that's all good. But don't tell me what I am or am not for the purpose of clandestine acceptance or removal. How do I disrespect my culture when there are many different Indigenous cultures in Australia; I own the fact that many are new to me and I'm willing to learn, when I choose to.

The modern thirst for authenticity makes it difficult for well-meaning Miggaloo people who I come across. I cringe when older Miggaloo people start calling me 'Uncle'. Respect is my core belief and was taught to me the hard way. I'm not the one who is creating the hysteria; I'm not the problem. Tell the traditionalist for the confusion, as they said this is protocol. Without generating lateral violence, I simply wish to unpack modern mythologies that keep GBLTIQ people unfriendly, because our community is newly-developing.

Being summed up in a blink is hard work, and that makes life so much more difficult for those of us removed from power. It continually arrests our development; perhaps some should be prevented from performing their ventriloquist acts. 'To be sure, behind this thought lurks an afterthought of force and dominion.'[4]

Geneticists have previously defined my identity as 'dirty half-caste'. This device controls others' gaze on me. Racists and traditionalists use similar belittling as a tool, unless I accept their model of what they think I should be. Theorists contextualise me by using their romanticised imagery. I feel like bashing, banging or slashing my head all at the same time when I am confronted with these facsimiles, but instead I either laugh or cry.

The 'poor bugger' apologists feel sorry for me because they think I'm a lesser person than them. I'm continually shown by authorities that white is uptight and out-of-sight of the fight, but it's their might that's always right, or I'm continually Blackfella whacked.

When dealing with Indigenous subjectivity within the

wider GBLTIQ community, the normalising power structures control my diversity to make it fit mainstream or mythological opinions. Alienation leaves me voiceless in countless discussions, pigeonholing objections to the backroom and leaving me with no spark for enlightenment.

Identity shift

I welcome acceptance into the GLBTIQ family, and acknowledge particularly the heroes of the first Sydney GBLTIQ protest march to Hyde Park in 1978. I understand Sydney's Mardi Gras began as an uprising against institutional brutality which caused a state of terror. The Mardi Gras has help create a safe place – from no space – for generations to come. This we *all* must never take for granted! Since GBLTIQ Brothers and Sisters have sometimes rallied alongside me, my identity gets compressed. In GBLTIQ principles, I'm racially discriminated against and shackled by stigma.

Exclusion by Indigenous peoples' xenophobia or heterosexism are alarming norms. These quasi-formulations of removal lead to many social determinants of health that eventually demoralise GBLTIQ community members. The consequent mental torture, physical blocking, and emotional challenges rail towards devastation.

Many Indigenous peoples use Sister Girl to identify women.[5] People are welcome to disagree, but this worldview is now an accepted conventional norm. Quizzing this innovative terminology is for those yet to come who may be questioning their gender or sexual identity. I got driven mad by the way my Uncle Tony – Tina Rose – was treated and the names she/he was called. My eyes redden and then fill with tears when I recall my non-violent pioneer.

There has been a shift over the decades where Sister Girl now also describes sexually-diverse men. Ideologically, others from my regional area determine that Sister Girls *must* take the passive role. Endorsement of emasculation occurs when meanings shift to suit the wider community's ethos. This simultaneously robs and serves one's Indigenous cultural nimbleness. My intent here is to attain clear-eyed acknowledgement.

I shyly accept that this terminology has become common practice but refuse to accept Sister Girl as symbolising me. In fact, I don't seek any lady-like representation of my cisgender being. Sister Girls are known to me as Trans or Intersex Indigenous people, and that's fine by me. I was told by them older mob which helped me with my sexual identity that they actually 'feel like a female trapped in a male body'.

What irks me is that other forms of GBLTIQ are made to fit the Sister Girl descriptor within the Indigenous lexicon of the Northern Queensland diaspora and beyond. The widespread use of this feminine reassigned title is new for me. Some Indigenous MSM I speak to at the poker machines often object to being titled Sister Girl.

While some fear being ridiculed for openly discussing such opposition, my hope is to contextualise for the layperson that many generalist notions about being MSM are reactionary for some, as the 'one size fits all' paradigm is for others. If it works for other Indigenous GBLTIQ to identify as Sister Girl, that's their prerogative; nevertheless, I negate identification as 'the other' you frock me as. Whenever I refuse to don the make-up of me from your mind, I'm banished to the wilderness. My familial constellation of Aboriginal and Torres Strait Island fusion is where I draw my thinking from.

Positioning my trauma

The first time I ran away from home was in 1982 on a hippy bus going to the Commonwealth Games protest. I turned thirteen as we drove into Bris-Vegas.[6] One reason I left was because I was being physically beaten by my eldest Brother and I truly thought he would kill me. My O'Umma[7] may have felt that she had no choice and granted me my plea. She wiped her weeping eyes and paid my thirty dollar passage, and I set off on what I thought was my freedom ride.

At fourteen, I was back from Brisneyland[8] and wrapping a stolen car around a lamp post down the road from my O'Umma's house. Tina Rose, who was still alive then, took one look at the cut in my head and said she 'could see my brain'. She had obviously seen blunt force head trauma before. Sadly, Tina Rose was murdered by her down-low boyfriend for her bottle of rum, robbing me of my 'Elder'.[9]

Tina Rose was lured out of her room, where others thought she was asleep, and was murdered someplace else. Tina Rose then was placed back in her room and tucked into her bed as if she had been there the whole time. The authorities had to move her murderer from the jail he got sent to, because Tina Rose's brother 'Tank' was there serving ten years and was willing to convert that into a life sentence. I often wonder what I would've done to him if I had got my hands on him. Being a far younger, fitter and stronger man, I would perhaps still be in jail. Her murderer eventually got out of prison and was considered a cultural 'Elder' down south where he was hiding in plain sight.

Older GBLTIQ people faced tougher prejudice and racism than me! As a real-life actor in this modern 'Indigenous MSM horror show', the glitches in the matrix of identity renaissance are ongoing. I have put it before that intra-cultural inclusion is acceptable! People of other cultures, languages, or ways of knowing seem to think that they fit into my cosmology by utilising other Indigenous customary familiarity as a means of acceptance. If I know the person or if they were taught by my mob – no matter if they're Blackfella or Miggaloo – then they're welcome at my place or space whatever their skin tone. Otherwise, take back that paradigm to where you got it. It doesn't work for me when I try to get my evidence-based interpolation accepted. Issues arise when I question the place of common ground or space between our ears. This occurs for me throughout black, white, queer or straight communities Australia-wide.

The genealogical research generated in this post-Native Title era has enlightened individuals to their ancestry. While I'm fortunate to have the surname I got, now many others know where their bloodlines originated. Before Native Title, most people I knew identified with the place where they were born or grew up. It never occurred to me how important identity and belonging is to the lost, hidden or stolen generations.[10] I took it for granted and never gave thought to my Grandparents being so far away from their homelands.

My Grandad, who passed away when I was ten years old, had a rudimentary Western education and could read and write. English was his fifth or sixth language, and so all my generation were taught the fundamentals of his native tongue. My scattered knowledge of Indigenous languages has assisted my healing process. The Indigenous knowledges that I've acquired have been hard-earned. And there are so many pan-Indigenous vernaculars and idiosyncrasies that I had never known until leaving home.

I read books objectively written from White Australian first contact, but these do nothing to validate me. Subjective urban history, written or otherwise, must allow for one's own post-colonial experiences. The ambiguity of the 'history wars' is still contentious in modern Australia. The eugenics my forebears survived still lives by my preservation, and is made factual by my existence.

How others perceive me is not my issue; that's their problem not mine! I learned early in life that sticks and stones ... I'm just happy to be older, alive, and free to choose how I live 'my life' as an MSM, loving the man who loves me. The hate and anger transferred to me literally destroyed any chance of normality in either GBLTIQ or Indigenous cultures. I now understand that the double entendre of my 'deadliness' has done this.

I feel Sister Girls have the right to be deadly too; they deserve nourishing love and care, and nobody should make them feel un-pretty. In the region I come from, most sexually-diverse men take on the Sister Girl persona and are discouraged from having sexual relationships with other Sister Girls. The active MSM in sexual encounters publicly deny their own sexual diversity or say that the submissive partner is Sister Girl but the active MSM is straight. Perhaps emasculation or denying my sexuality likewise played heavily on my younger self.

I was given no choice about coming out. I got dragged out, and was mentally, physically and emotionally crushed to within an inch of giving up. I was in a drug and alcohol rehabilitation centre before getting kicked out after supplying cannabis. Isolation unit visits seemed to have a revolving door process during the nine or so months I spent on remand. I spent some months as a fugitive, breaching my bail conditions by not reporting to a police station – this was no picnic either; I traversed three states while in a drunk and stoned state most of the time. Luckily, I had a return airfare in my name, however, I was in another capital city far from the airport my flight was returning from when my trial was brought forward a week or so. Again, I was living to run and running to live, not hiding but running scared again.

The case got thrown out, but I still porter the baggage. My opportunity to be the first in my family to get a university degree blossomed. The wasted time I spent on remand still black dogs me beyond the blue to this day, and now decades later is only semi-relieved.

Accepting heartbreak

The heartbreak of my Mother's death to a massive coronary sent my life spiralling. More poignantly, I lost my best friend! That was the only year I stayed out of prison for more than twelve months from the time that I went to Westbrook Boys' Home when I was fifteen until when I went to live in Melbourne aged thirty. If I remember correctly. All I really know is, I put my family through so much as a young rebel without a clue.

Opportunities peaked and troughed for me like a heart monitor, and continues to do so. My social and emotional wellbeing flows and ebbs as this rollercoaster of life tests my survival, while the waxing and waning of scholarship is my constant. The struggle with myself is a daily continuum, where either the good wolf or the bad wolf wins.

My long-term unorthodox, sero-discordant relationship provides stability. My better half is a Miggaloo who went through Aboriginal customary Law. My fairy's tale still jolts. It feels like I went to sleep on a park bench in North Queensland and 'nek minit' I awoke uptown, way down Mexico way, in South Yarra. How my worm has turned! It seems the cyclone I never thought would end, now eases. It never really stops, but the eye of the storm gets big enough to travel in, like Dorothy in the *Wizard of Oz*.

The first time this modern-day travel Murri needed a passport was when a Miggaloo friend asked me to go to Aotearoa New Zealand. My mate and his de-facto both have chemistry degrees, but morally could never concoct illegal substances for me. I could be rich; I may have paid my Higher Education Contribution Supplement debt, and my Stolenwealth trade-off supplement loan would not be eating away at me.

But the reality is that I may become just another statistic adding to the expanding figures of Black Deaths in Custody! My second cousin (Brother) was unarmed when he was shot dead in his bedroom by police. My first Cousin (Brother) died from a terminal illness in custody. My eldest Sibling (Brother) was found hanging in a watch house. Statistically I could inherently be next to die in custody. No outspoken Indigenous person like me is immune from dying in custody; being MSM adds to my susceptibility. The dramatic custodial deaths experienced by my family warrants my fear.

Academia has broken me free from my chains of ignorance and was instrumental for my jail house epiphany. Through my Malcolm X-style tertiary education beginnings, books proved my survival redeemable. Life after the early death of my Palawah[11] mentor needed work, he echoes in me periodically. It was he who started me on the entry level qualification whilst I was in gaol. I needed that bridging course for entry into university studies.

I was studying down south at the time of my mentor's passing, not long after returning from the Asia Pacific Forum's input to the United Nations Declaration of Human Rights for Indigenous Peoples. There we made our last stand, and fought a few landscape shifting battles together. I battle on for him, assisting to get his PhD awarded posthumously.

Unity or mutiny
The intellectual macrocosm of universities is the jewel in my tiara, and the pastoral care given towards my revival is undeniable. My phoenix-type serendipity is not mine alone; I can't express enough gratitude to those people who helped me, though at times it feels like I'm going somewhere but not getting anywhere. At least now I have light at the end of the tunnel. Previously it was just my burglar's torch shining the way.

I have a 'sandstone' university Bachelor Degree and a Diploma from a regional university, but I feel my employment is hindered because I'm too black for the whites, or too white for the blacks. I refuse to follow leadership appointed without my consent. I reckon the cows at Westbrook Boys' Home got better pastoral care than I've received in the mainstream workforce. I must admit, I'm not the easiest person to get along with, especially with those lacking cultural competency. Back in the day, intelligence wasn't a necessity for front-line activist speakers; alpha males ruled supreme, making me a product of that environment.

From my viewpoint, many Miggaloos either can't fathom what I describe or simply don't care enough about Indigenous people's lives. Many Indigenous people I know are far too concerned about feeding their families to object to or challenge what's going on within the Indigenous industry. Maybe they're just weary and broken. It's easier for everybody concerned to blame others, rather than seeing people as game changers. I too do this sometimes. I had no control in the defunct establishment, and seem to have no rights or role in these government-funded *nouveau riche* interventions.

Costume me however you choose, I refuse to be the Frankenstein whilst social laboratories are fine-tuning horrific futures for an unsustainable world. I don't have the answers, however, I know a lot more about my grassroots people and community than many so-called experts, because I have 'been there, done that', and am attempting to get on with it without hate!

Hatred has caused many woes in my life, and in this world. Hate is yet to solve a single problem. I was there when Indigenous peoples and Miggaloo supporters turned their backs on the Prime Minister at the reconciliation convention in Melbourne. I thought things would change dramatically. This was a giant mental leap for Indigenous Australians. It struck a match in me, lighting a post-colonial candle of accepting mateship with Miggaloos.

I compliment my full-time Bachelor degree for greater forward momentum in my healing journey. Previously, my readings for my Diploma were done under street lights while living in a park. That's when I wasn't in jail, of course, as I was when my cohort matriculated.

Nearly twenty years on since the reconciliation convention, I am finally accepting myself as third Generation Stolen. It was my Grandparents who were taken, not me. They had no choice in their destiny; I fled or fought. I'm so proud of what they achieved with the little they were given. My Grandad got a commendation from the King of England for saving multiple lives, but sadly lost his eldest son in the process.

These days, government funding makes us the wealthiest passengers in our own civil rights freedom rides. We're yet to receive much of the human rights we fight doggedly for. While my poverty could be eradicated with the pink dollar, this can only occur if there are responsible non-Indigenous GBLTIQ participants taking ownership of covert dissonance and sometimes overt racism. Understand that you Miggaloo people are the puppeteers pulling the strings of the Indigenous dominant discourse, and it is you who must educate other non-Indigenous GBLTIQ people.

Change, towards me, has been lethargic over the decades. GBLTIQ people are under-educated about Indigenous people as a whole, and this ruins many prospects for Indigenous GBLTIQ people. Glancing at my employment history, there seems to be a character archetype that is acceptable: one must remain loyal to constant yet disconnected negotiations from core business, and not fail too high – unlike the ventriloquists who continually speak for me and do what they think is best practice on my behalf.

Those pointing out Racism as the elephant in the room continually run into ringmasters who circumvent dissenting voices into a scream, then reappeal the same reworded stance at the negotiating table once that troublemaker is locked out or even locked away.

I continually get severed by traditionalists or heterosexists in Indigenous communities Australia-wide, and so I flee to larger cities seeking refugee status in the GBLTIQ community. There, GBLTIQ people holding archaic, Euro-centric notions refuse my hybridity and contest for equality, normally by using the local Indigenous population against me. Ultimately, I get shuffled back into the deck as a spade by card-carrying members of every population, GBLTIQ and Indigenous included. One uses the other to conveniently ostracise me.

Admittedly, I am one of the lucky ones, having been swept off my feet by a man who took me home to meet his parents. Still, my partner and I are constricted by blurred lines. My better half is forbidden to discuss his Tjukurpa to anybody other than his Anangu Brethen.[12] I'm excluded from many People Living with HIV (PLHIV) spaces, especially employment, because I do not have the blood-borne virus. The mainstream activists state that I 'must work with the Indigenous mob'. The aggressive black armband card is used on me by the gangs who get rich off the back of other people 'dying in the streets and jails', like many of my family, because experts either can't or won't admit they know little-to-nothing about Indigenous homelessness and helplessness. I had to endure this lifestyle as one of the most vulnerable population for much of my adult life.

It feels like nobody wants to know how my partner's aging, or how we have maintained my sero-negative status. It's big business keeping blackfellas sick because the greater the statistics, the more government funds they get. His viral load is undetectable, and CD-4 levels are high. We must be doing something right I think.

Poverty is still my norm, plus I'm still more at risk to die at a younger age than him. Perhaps some data collection I did about stigma and discrimination which underlined dissimilarity between Indigenous and mainstream diaspora of PLHIV is also another diffident conversation worth mentioning.[13] Government policies keep my partner and me apart, but prejudice denies my rights to equality.

Many Indigenous people I know are religious, and most are armchair commentators about politics. Mao Zedong commented on religion being the opiate of the masses, but gender politics is also an adopted spiritual ethos that I continually confront. My Grandparents were forced onto Christian missions. I was born into a political party: my clan groups were my government, complete with senate, parliament and cabinet. Drugs and alcohol had me fighting my own personal opium wars all of my adolescent and adult life. Despite being gelded as a colt by old regret, I've since grown up and begun living my own unrestricted life, loyal to my individual identity.

Foreign philosophy has delivered Post Traumatic Stress Disorder and created mass hysteria. The assimilation I underwent is comparable to the science fiction of Star Trek's Borg collective. Make no mistake, it is a tug-a-war between white and black assimilationists I speak to!

The Conflicts of Camouflage

Laniyuk Garcon-Mills

Born of a French mother and a Larrakia father, I was created
with the soft olive complexion my mother crossed her fingers for
during pregnancy. Not light enough to resemble my European
cousins or dark enough to be the target of consistent racism, I
have often been the recipient of compliments and intrigue.

> *Where are you from?*
> Guess, I say.
> *You're Italian? Greek? Spanish? South American? Egyptian?*
> *Mauritian?*
> Closer to home, I prompt – it's an island, a big island.

My appearance often falls into the category of 'exotic' and
unfamiliar, existing outside of the notion of what an Aboriginal
woman looks like, and very few people have suggested that
I might be of this land. A descendant of the oldest surviving
culture in the world.

Similarly, my gender presentation defies the stereotype of
what a gay woman should look like. Possessing the appearance
of white passing and conventionally feminine, I have navigated
myself around racism and homophobia by manipulating people's
perceptions of me. This included emphasising my whiteness,

changing my name, and lying about my ethnicity. Although these tactics aided in evading discrimination, my self-esteem and connection to family was greatly compromised, and these encouraged feelings of shame towards my culture and myself. It was the strength and self-confidence I gained from coming out that allowed me to view myself in an honest way and to reconnect with where I came from. My experience of entering and overcoming camouflage has been shaped, hindered and encouraged by a range of key people and events from the earliest moments of my life; understanding their roles has played a part in discovering and reclaiming who I am.

From what I recall and have been told, my early years were abundant with culture. I spoke language, went hunting and travelled throughout the Northern Territory and islands. I wore dresses painted with goannas and wild geese, went out bush for land claim meetings, and was showered with love from cousins, aunties, uncles, and cousins of cousins and aunties of aunties!

At four years old my life changed dramatically when my mother was nearly killed in a drink driving accident. Seated in the back without a seatbelt, she crashed through the windscreen on impact and landed on the car bonnet. Upon arrival, the first response team assumed she was dead. Two decades later and it's still too painful for me to discuss in detail the events of that night, or the consequences upon us as individuals and as a family. Although she recovered her physical and mental capabilities, my mother's emotional stability fluctuated. Separated before the accident, my parents' conflict was heightened and gradually my mother gained sole custody.

From the age of six, my stubborn and sometimes detrimentally independent mother raised my brother and me. Although her passion and persistence drove her through rehabilitation and made her capable of raising two children on her own, it sometimes meant she wasn't accepting of the help and support that was available. Unable to return to her profession after the car accident, she battled her way through bureaucratic mountains of paperwork and, head held high, refused things she felt she wasn't entitled to. No pity, no sympathy, no weakness, no vulnerability became the mantra of a woman who'd been through hell and back.

The same was to be applied to her children: no special treatment because we weren't a special case – she was going to make sure we had everything we needed to succeed. Even when that meant food on our plates instead of hers.

In her efforts to maintain minimal support, I started to notice that my mother was choosing not to acknowledge her children's Aboriginal heritage in paperwork for government and school services. I wonder in retrospect if she was avoiding special treatment? Perhaps she didn't feel entitled to claim when we weren't in frequent contact with family or culture? Perhaps she didn't want people to know we were Aboriginal in an attempt to distant us and herself from a relationship she no longer wanted to pursue? Witnessing time and time again the blatant denial of my culture to others developed in me the idea that it was advantageous to not tell people. I started to understand that there was something wrong with being Aboriginal and that people would look at me differently for it.

When the time came for me to fill in my own forms, I found myself stuck on that question more than any other. 'Do you identify as Aboriginal or Torres Strait Islander?' is a straightforward question with a sometimes complicated answer. Well yes, but I haven't seen my family in ten years. Does that count? Well yes, but you seem to think I'm only after handouts. Well yes, but I don't want you to look at me differently or scrutinise me because my skin is light. The misconception that Aboriginal people receive some outrageous amount of entitlement from ticking one box has created so much scorn and distaste from people around me. I've overheard racist sneers and jokes about this one question while queuing for government services, in doctors' waiting rooms, and even from my own European family. It seems to me that being Aboriginal is synonymous with 'disadvantaged' for the person behind the desk and 'moocher' for those in the line beside me – neither of which I want to identify with. The ability to be white passing encouraged me to choose which box to tick depending on how I felt I would be viewed for it. In my early teenage years, I would come to carbon copy my mother's technique of avoiding a second class status – only to create my own mantra of secrecy and shame. The box my mother avoided so that her children would be seen as equal came to be the routine tick of self-denial and camouflage that I would send out to the world every time I filled out a form.

Witnessing my mother's struggle, I felt an exaggerated sense of allegiance and a need to protect her. The turbulent nature of those years had a dramatic impact on my relationship with my parents, and this created a large distance between my father and me. In my juvenile loyalty and hurt over my single mother's pain, I came to resent my father. I developed a perception, regardless of how accurate, that he was a violent, alcoholic time-waster who offered my mother no support in her darkest hour. This resentment in turn led me down a narrow path of self-hatred as I made connections between the colour of my skin, the person I inherited it from, and the culture from which it came.

At ten years old, I started telling my curious peers my dad was Spanish to explain away my darker skin and hair. This would have been a confusing conversation for those who had known me to be Aboriginal, but for those who didn't know, it was a passable lie. It might be surprising that a child would go to such lengths to manipulate how people perceive them, but children possess the incredible intellect to adapt to what they learn as positive and negative behaviours. Even in my youthful innocence, I understood that exaggerating my whiteness would lead me to success and acceptance.

It was the mentality of conventional society and the institutions in which I existed that reiterated my growing feelings that being Aboriginal was inherently problematic and wrong. Estranged from my Aboriginal family, all I had to demonstrate what that culture encompassed was the alcohol and violence plaguing the Aboriginal people of Darwin, and the general conversations and behaviour of the adults around me.

Although my primary school in Darwin made great effort to teach children about Aboriginal and Torres Strait Islander cultures, it was not immune to racism and political opinions: some parents refused to let their children attend the school's annual NAIDOC week celebrations, and classroom banter often echoed household conversations over the unfairness of how much money Aboriginal people received from the government. These comments were not only ignored by witnessing adults, they were sometimes confirmed! One teacher in particular stands out for me and, to this day, I remember wanting to shrink into myself over her criticism of the dole and low-income earners. Despite being the most enthusiastic learner in that classroom with such willingness to participate, my raised-hand would be disregarded, and friends often gave questioning looks as to why I was blatantly ignored. Even though I asked the most questions and attempted to engage in dialogue, she still put no effort in learning how to pronounce my Kungarrakan name. Although she never overtly said she disliked me because of my low-income family and Aboriginal heritage, children are not so easily deceived. My understanding of Aboriginal people was developing outside of any interaction with my family. I strangely saw myself as separate to the Aboriginal community but still took comments and perceptions as personal attacks.

As a young child, I bundled these quiet thoughts and insecurities and wore them to my mother's family gatherings. My arm lying on the table next to my cousins', I couldn't help but peek at our differences in appearance and behaviour and want so badly to fit their mould. Every name at the dinner table was a celebration of French culture yet there were never any discussions on the meaning of my strange name or the culture it came from. I still think they don't know what Laniyuk means. Perhaps if my father had been of European background, then I could have distinguished him from his culture? His culture would be understood, celebrated and readily available in the wider community through food, clothing and the media. The violence I had witnessed would not be a symptom of race but of circumstance. The emotions I battled with would be personal, not cultural shame. However, in a European family in a racist community, I was all too ready to disown my Aboriginal heritage and claim for myself a more acceptable and celebrated identity. I approached my mother and told her I wanted to change my Kungarrakan name Laniyuk to Anne Rose. From that moment on, I was on a mission of self-denial.

I observed similar trends in my younger brother as we entered pubescence and attempted to find acceptance in our new hometown of Adelaide. Living in a predominantly white, upper-middle class suburb, we both engaged in white culture and attempted to adopt typically white patterns of behaviour in dress, music and pastimes. I avoided the sun in an attempt to fight the darker shades of my skin and, if questioned, I emphasised my French heritage. When asked about my father's ethnicity. I would shrug it off and just say 'Australian'.

My teenage years became a sanctuary for my self-denial. Thoughts or conversations about my father's family were out of bounds. Feelings of anxiety would come over me at the mention of his name and I would all but shut off at the mention of being

Aboriginal. It was not something I could accept, embrace or appreciate. My high school maths teacher confirmed these feelings when he told an Indian student that he could tell she wasn't Aboriginal because she wasn't sitting on the side of the road sniffing petrol. As an adult, I want to go back to that moment, jump out of my chair and 'how dare you' the hell out of him. As an insecure and self-loathing teenager, I just put my head down and calculated maths I might never use.

Leaving high school with a few awards and a mind full of optimism, I moved out of home and dived into the world, ready to be a part of something bigger. At university, I had hoped to find a group of interesting intellects that had been asking the same questions as I had. Instead, I found myself in another institution next to the same people I went to high school with.

What I wasn't expecting to discover was my sexuality. As with my thoughts on my ethnicity, I struggled to comprehend my sexuality in an honest, unfiltered way. Although different sexualities and genders were being discussed and celebrated by my liberal-minded generation, I couldn't digest the possibilities of my own sexual experiences. The union of impending adulthood and the euphoria of independence from family and institutional thinking led me to one of the most crucial and liberating self discoveries I have experienced.

The day I realised I was gay was a rediscovery of sight, of sound, of senses, and of understanding the world and my place in it. I had stepped out of my withdrawn, uncertain self and was standing on a mountain being catapulted towards self-understanding. I was buzzing with excitement! This was the first act in my adult life I could truly claim for myself as an expression of who I am. Unfortunately, it wasn't as well received as I predicted. The effect of the car accident on my mother's emotional processing meant that she couldn't digest my coming out rationally. Instead, I endured hours of screaming, violence and nonsensical accusations. For those few hours I felt the most unsafe I have ever felt in my life.

I was shaken and confused about why my sexuality would receive such a negative reaction, although ultimately I felt betrayed. The person I had shaped my life around and who I trusted to protect me, had tainted the most liberating and personal experience I had ever had. I couldn't bring myself to see or speak to her for two years. Suddenly I was filled with anxiety. There were days when I couldn't leave the house. I woke up crying at the idea of having to go to work, and went through a periodical cycle of depression. It would last just long enough for me to think that I should seek help, and then it would disappear just in time for me to rationalise that I was fine and had everything under control. When I realised that something wasn't right, I didn't know who to turn to. My doctor suggested anxiety medication that I didn't want to take, and at nineteen I didn't feel I had anyone to help or guide me. One facet of my life was shining so brightly as I celebrated and embraced my sexuality, while another left me feeling secretly isolated and lost without my family. I had lost the base of my support network as a condition to being open, out and honest with myself.

A good friend invited me to the Girls Lounge – a fortnightly queer drop-in at Second Storey, a youth health centre in Adelaide's city district. Winding our way through the heteronormative advertisement platform of Rundle Mall, past the preachers screaming that gays will burn in hell, dodging drunk leering men, and escaping spaces without a spare inch to represent us, we would find ourselves every second Friday at an inconspicuous, red brick building. Initially, I attended these gatherings to learn more about the queer community but very quickly realised how valuable they were for my self-development. I had discovered a safe place to ask questions, learn, connect with young queer people and share experiences. Everyone was at different stages of coming out, and those who were struggling could seek inspiration and strength from others. I didn't realise then but. in the face of my family's rejection and my building anxiety, Girls Lounge was the only place I felt one hundred percent safe. When I walked through those doors, there were other queer people with similar experiences. There were professional adults who didn't judge or reject any of my questions. Adults who were dedicated to making sure we felt safe, respected and educated. They facilitated and monitored discussions, made us aware of our rights and resources, and often just gave us a space to be ourselves creatively, intellectually and emotionally. We could cry when we needed, and speak honestly about what we were going through at our own pace. The ability to share progress and celebrate achievements for and with others was the most valuable aspect of Girls Lounge. It allowed those of us with limited support to understand the possibilities of our future through the experience of others in varied genders and sexualities. It was this simple act that allowed me to process my sexual experience and within weeks I noticed my anxiety was no longer debilitating; it eventually disappeared altogether.

Throughout my life I have often felt like there weren't many adults I could turn to in an honest way for support and guidance. I couldn't be myself because I was always hiding my identity and shameful of my experience. A key person in the development of my sexual identity and self confidence is a worker I met at Second Storey. Tiff was the first adult figure I felt safe around. She provided a calm welcoming space to lay out our thoughts and feelings, asking all the right questions to help us bring them back together. Tiff turned the Second Storey building into a safe haven for me and countless other queer youth. Her positive influence of rationale and understanding resonates throughout the Adelaide queer community, and it is because of her and other amazing workers in social programs that young people are overcoming the coming out process.

Unfortunately the Girls Lounge program and the male-identifying equivalent were cut in 2012 and, despite all of our efforts to lobby local politicians and community members, it was not reinstated. It was replaced with a watered down, age group-specific program, only to have the whole building shut down a couple of years later. The removal of these fortnightly gatherings truly shook me. I was reminded again that the queer experience and vulnerable queer youth are not valued as equally valid or adequately supported by our politicians (federal or state) or by our social system. Once more I felt betrayed – this time by those who stood on community platforms and used our needs as a way of promoting their status. Their lack of care instilled in me a distaste and distrust for the social system and the political farce. We were left with the main access to the queer world being gay bars and night clubs, and waiting itchingly for the Feast Festival to spring up and claim for two weeks each year the space that we so desperately wanted and needed to feel connected and widely accepted.

I was ready to find those answers about where I came from, and to get an adult perspective on my childhood and the events that led me to be the person I had become. I was ready to go home.

I picked up the phone and from across the continent I made phone call after phone call, email after email, until I had a number leading straight to my father. I called it, heart racing, breath shaking, and spoke to him for the first time in thirteen years. It wasn't the heart-warming conversation I'd been anticipating. It was a bit awkward and he was slightly shaken up and frustrated after years of waiting to hear from us. But what a floodgate! Aunties, Uncles, Cousins! You're not one of two kids but one of nine! You're an aunty! A niece, a grand-daughter, a daughter. Family.

Soon I was on a plane to Darwin, my home town, and was standing in front of the giant of a man that is my dad and the bundles of excitement and shyness that are my siblings. An estranged cousin coincidentally was making the same pilgrimage home to reconnect. and my aunties were whispering that they were coming home. The children were coming home.

Some faces and names were more recognisable for me than others, but everyone had a story to share of the last time they saw me or when we played together as children. One of the faces that always stayed in my mind was my Wetji (Nanna). Memories of her have prevailed throughout the years; speaking to her on the phone for the first time moved me more than I anticipated. After all, I hadn't seen these people in over a decade, and I wasn't sure how readily a relationship could develop just on the premise of blood. As I waited for her to arrive, I felt a small buzz of excitement to finally see her and get to know her in the present. As she stepped out of the car and as I came down casually to see her, I found I couldn't speak. I silently approached her as we put our arms around each other, and we stood and cried. All I could muster was a half-choked 'Hi Nanna' as we sobbed within a circle of surrounding family. The reverence that I have for my family's matriarch is deeply emotional and, to be honest, I can't quite pinpoint where it comes from. These people, places, stories and photos are so strangely emotional and familiar, and seeing features that I see in myself gives a sense of comfort that is unique to knowing where you come from. Dad took me to Laniyuk, the area on Kungarrakan land that I am named after, and he pointed to the crystal clear water and pandanas palms and said, 'This is your land. You're boss of this country.'

When people ask me where home is I tell them that Adelaide is where I live but Darwin is where I will be buried. When I hear those cicadas singing, or stand in the wet season rain, or watch the sky light up at night and look at the dark storm clouds brewing, I know that I'm home and I feel closer to the earth under my feet than just skin and dirt.

My brother accidentally outed me to my dad while watching one of our cousins perform drag. I think he struggles with it in the way that parents sometimes do, but he's never treated me or my girlfriend differently for it, and we've always been welcome separately and as a couple in his house and life. Once, when speaking to him about how an aunty would feel with me bringing my partner and coming out to her, he replied, 'We don't discriminate against anyone, daughter.' When I consider that my family has experienced racism from the most brutal forms of violence to the most bureaucratic forms of public housing and education, it blew me away to hear those words. How is it that people who have experienced others entering into their family home in the eighties to beat up the young black teenagers can hold no reservations in accepting difference? Yet the privileged have screamed at me on streets or belittled my culture. Politicians imprison our community, deny funding to rural housing, steal children and land, and disregard police brutality and murder – and yet my Aboriginal family attends rallies to support the fair treatment of asylum seekers.

The representation I have found and the acceptance I have received from my Aboriginal family has come to provide a similar base of strength that I was finding in my Queer community. The necessity I felt to compartmentalise and distinguish my identity to appease those around me is lessening as I develop a place in the Queer and Aboriginal communities, and gain strength from them to exist in a world where those identities are often not represented in their true forms.

I sometimes feel like I'm coming out twice to everyone I meet. Once that I'm gay, and a second time that I'm Aboriginal. Neither time I can predict how it will be taken. Being slightly tanned and a little feminine, I've inadvertently flown under the radar for most of my life. People are sometimes surprised to find out that I'm an Aboriginal lesbian, and at my most vulnerable moments this has meant that I've been able to manipulate people's interpretations of me. It's strange to first deal with shame that was given to me and, once I've battled through their bigotry, then have to deal with the shame of shame! I wish I had been in a position to embrace my culture and also be supported enough to confidently use language like 'my girlfriend' in the workplace with disregard for people's reactions. Being in a really strong and positive place in my life, it's hard to talk about feeling ashamed of these parts of myself that I love and having to explain why I changed my name. The act of forgiving myself is on the same pathway as forgiving those who instilled my self-hatred.

The greatest tool I ever had for exaggerating my femininity was my hair. The smallest act of wearing my long brown curls over my shoulders changed the way people interacted with me. I found they were more gentle, accommodating and more surprised towards my sexuality. Once I realised that I was fearful of losing my hair and the security it provided then I knew it had to go. I shaved it down to the scalp with a blade and rid myself of concern and barriers towards the viewing of my gender presentation. Having battled my way past the concern of perception, I have taken charge of my own development and am reclaiming my space in my life, with the most powerful act being the reclamation of my name. The cultural gravity of being named Laniyuk and the struggle it represents for me is so important in understanding who I am and where I come from. I feel ashamed to have ever felt shame towards it. It's a beautiful name from a beautiful place, and it took a difficult journey for me to understand that. The struggle I went through and the courage I've gained has given it another dimension of strength for me. In contrast to the ticking of boxes, I now affirm my culture every time I introduce myself as Laniyuk.

I witnessed an auntie's eyes light up when I introduced

myself and she told me that it was a name in her family too. She smiled at the aunty next to her and said the named lived on.

Although I am working towards change in my life, I still exist in world where those changes aren't necessarily embraced. I once played the guessing game with a young gay man and when I told him I was Aboriginal he said, 'That's okay. You can't really tell.' There's so much misunderstanding about two huge parts of my identity that it's hard to know where to start on this uphill battle. It's a disgrace how little understanding exists about the cultures that have thrived on this land for tens of thousands of years, and I feel this is a huge contributing factor for the misunderstanding and fear that is plaguing this country. I want to be part of the force that breaks that barrier. I am currently working towards my own business that culminates all my passions and helps me work towards a world I believe in: a space for everyone and everything that doesn't have that space on the 'Australian' platform. There's a lot I want to achieve through this business and it extends further than just four walls. I want to educate, re-evaluate, and create lasting change. I want a world where my siblings and cousins and the generations to come will never experience the sinking feelings I felt nor the horrendous stereotypes and negative associations I heard about Aboriginal people or members of the Queer community. I don't want them to feel the need to shrink themselves or camouflage into an identity that doesn't represent who they really are. I want my life to truly represent who I am and bring together my two dynamic identities. At this point, the geography of my family in Darwin and my queer community in Adelaide has meant that both aspects have developed separately in strength and confidence. Now I feel ready to bring them together and share who I am.

Atonement

Ben Gertz

Growing up in a place like north Queensland as an Aboriginal or Torres Strait Islander can present its fair share of challenges, and growing up as an openly gay person can be quite tough. Unsurprisingly, growing up in north Queensland as an openly gay Aboriginal and Torres Strait Islander is both challenging and tough! Despite the problems that both identity and sexuality can present in regional Australia, I still proudly call north Queensland home. Most aspects of my upbringing, whether physical or cultural, revolve around the region in such a way that I could easily be considered a unique product.

I am a descendent of the Gugu-Badhun people, who traditionally inhabited the bushlands of the upper Burdekin River catchment, as well as the Ngadjon-Ji people, who traditionally inhabited the rainforest around Malanda and the Atherton Tablelands. I am also a descendant of the Meriam people of Mer (Murray) Island, in the Eastern Torres Strait.

My father was born and raised in God's own country, Malanda, surrounded by the rainforest and dairy farms of the Atherton Tablelands. My mother, whilst born in Queanbeyan, spent most of her adolescent years in the spectacular landscape of Mount Isa, in north-west Queensland. It was in this arid landscape that my parents met and fell in love, and where, it could be said, my life began. My father soon transferred for work and my parents moved east to the coastal city of Townsville, where I was subsequently born and raised.

At a very young age, I developed a keen interest in the world and how it worked. My parents often remind me how from the age of three, I religiously watched the six o'clock evening news. Once I began to read, I would trawl through the pages of Townsville Bulletin whenever my parents brought home a copy. It is not every four-year-old who can tell you the difference between a Prime Minister and a Premier, as well as their names. Astute has been a word that people have described me as from a very young age, and I was often told that I was aware of what was happening in the world around me. Many of my thoughts and feelings were shaped by local and world events. Often, I would ask my parents a few tough questions on political issues and current events. I joined in at my Aunty Janine's union meetings, which frequently were held on the nights she had to look after me and my brother while our parents were at work or away. I guess from this information alone, you can understand why and how the next part of journey came to be shaped.

My coming of age story of self-discovery is one of great heartbreak to me. It is a story of an adolescence driven by personal fear – a fear of being victimised for my sexuality. I grew up in a Townsville where gay bashing was a sport. In the late '90s in particular, there was a period of time when it seemed like a day wouldn't go by without reports of violence relating to the victim's sexuality, or hearing of people being harassed because they were perceived as being gay. It all culminated in June 1999, when two letter bombs exploded in the Townsville offices of the Queensland AIDS Council. I was only nine when the AIDS Council's offices were bombed, but even I at that young age knew that the offices were targeted because it was a service frequented by the LGBTI community. It was apparent to me from a very young age that if you were Gay or Lesbian, Townsville was not the safest place to live.

The entire duration of my high school years were at Ignatius Park College, a Christian Brothers all-boys Catholic high school, known colloquially by many Townsvillians as Iggy Park or, worse, 'Poofters Paradise'. For me, as far as sexuality was concerned, it ironically felt as far from paradise as one could ever be. I knew from the age of twelve that I was attracted to and had feelings for other boys, so entering grade eight at Iggy Park made for a bit of an awkward and uncomfortable situation. Despite my seeming disdain, I feel immense pride for my time at Iggy Park. However, if I could experience my time there again, there are some things that I would do differently. Some experiences, whilst formative, I still wish to this day that I could take back. Regardless, it was my time at Ignatius Park College which helped shape me into the young man that I am today, and it was here where my journey of self-discovery started.

I honed my public speaking and debating skills at Iggy Park and, thanks to the continuing encouragement of my guidance counsellor, Ms Parsons, it was also where I solidified my interest in social justice and politics. Ignatius Park is a school which takes great pride in its sporting achievements, and no sport was off-limits to its students. It is the sort of place where it would be rare for someone to leave without at least having played a year of some sort of ball sports (and, if you're asking, rugby union was my sport of choice). It seemed like a day wouldn't go by without hearing of announcements of Rugby League trials, soccer training and, hell, even Ultimate Frisbee landed on the sporting roster during my last years there. Everyone had to participate in the annual swimming and athletics carnivals, and also run in the cross country.

Yes, as you could imagine, it was a school populated by fit

and masculine young men who played every sport imaginable ... surely every gay teenagers dream. Now, when you tell fellow homos that you went to an all-boys Catholic High School, it is often met with a response along the lines of: 'You must have had a lot of fun then!' While the 'fun' they are referring to never eventuated for me during those years, it ultimately was my high school years that made me appreciate the male form more. However, it was also this environment which fostered homophobic tendencies amongst students.

Many students would often use deride other students as 'poofs' and 'faggots' and, if you didn't fit in with the sporting crowd, chances are you would be derided as a 'homo'. As someone who was very much aware of his own sexuality when entering that environment, I guess that I took things very negatively. And so, to fly under the radar, I developed my own homophobic tendencies and at times I would lead the chorus.

If I saw another student with dyed hair, I would often call that student a 'faggot'. If I overheard a student discussing his musical interests, I would interrupt the conversation with something along the lines of: 'You sure do listen to some pretty gay music, homo.' One student in particular, despite being involved with the rugby league crowd, used to wear foundation make-up to school, and would give great attention to his image. Any conversation involving his name would be met with me describing him as 'a f*cking make-up wearing gay c*nt'. I later confessed and apologised to this student during affirmations a few weeks out from graduating. I walked up to him and said: 'I'm sorry for calling you a faggot behind your back.'

One event stands out still as being particularly memorable for me and it highlights my homophobic attitude was when I was in grade twelve. I was outside of classroom with two other friends, Nick and Andrew, waiting to begin our Tourism lesson for the afternoon. We had witnessed a few of the boys in our cohort who were active in the Rugby League scene, slapping each other on the arse in a jovial manner. Andrew, who even back then wasn't the slightest bit homophobic, spoke up and said: 'God, those meats are so gay for each other, they really do love slapping each other on the arse.' While his comments were of a sarcastic nature, I responded in the affirmative: 'Yeah, it's pretty f**king gay, they're such gay c**ts, slapping each other like that.' Andrew, sensing the seriousness of my comments, slapped me on the arse, saying: 'It's not gay, Ben, it's just a slap on the arse.' This riled me up to a point where I proceeded to deride Andrew as a 'faggot'. After being slapped on the arse by Andrew two or more three times, and after telling him multiple times 'to stop slapping my arse you faggot', he decided to pinch me on the nuts. I responded by grabbing him by the throat, pinning him against the wall of the classroom, and yelling: 'Don't ever do that again you f**king faggot.' Nick intervened, saying: 'Calm down Gertz. Just let him go.' It was pretty clear by the look on both their faces that they were quite surprised by my reaction. I caught up with Andrew a few years later on a trip to Brisbane, and over a drink he grimaced and said: 'Remember when you pinned me against the wall of the boardroom computer room?' Then he smirked and chuckled before continuing: 'They always says the most homophobic ones are the ones that are really gay, huh.'

When I entered the workforce after school, I got to work alongside many openly gay and lesbian colleagues. I could see how they were accepted not just in the workplace, but by the community at large. My time at Ignatius Park seemed like a world away, and it became very clear that the fears I had once held were in vain. It wasn't until I started my studies at James Cook University and my subsequent indoctrination in the world of student politics where I would discover the world of LGBT activism and advocacy. When, in my first year, I was elected as the Equity and Diversity Officer on the JCU Student Association Council, it was my job to organise LGBTI events and to advocate on behalf of LGBTI students for both the Townsville and Cairns campuses. It wasn't always such serious interaction amongst students however: it was around this time that I would occasionally find myself spending early mornings in college dorm rooms and share house bedrooms in the company of fellow students (many of whom weren't necessarily open about their sexuality either).

My experiences as the Equity and Diversity Officer eventually led me to become involved as a committee member of the Townsville Lesbian, Gay, Bisexual, Transgender and Intersex Anti-Violence Committee, the then local LGBTI advocacy body. This organisation was created in response to the increasing anti-gay violence that plagued Townsville in the late 1990s and early 2000s. Meeting and working alongside the committee members also helped to put me in my place. I had been living in fear of being a victim of homophobic violence, but many of the committee members themselves had been victims.

Working with this committee made me feel that I needed to do more work to fix the wrongs on my past. In 2011, I helped to organise the second Townsville Pride Festival. The following year, I was the public voice welcoming the introduction of Civil Unions in Queensland by the Bligh Government. I even kept my local member of the federal parliament, Ewen Jones, on his toes by giving him a bit of a grilling at a Marriage Equality forum in 2013. Additionally, I helped plan and run the Rainbow Fair Days organised by the Rainbow Youth Group, and I eventually joined the committee of the new LGBTI advocacy body, Stand Up With Pride. Despite the amount of work or good I do, I still feel as if I can never heal the wounds caused by past actions.

The most painful thing about my struggle with my sexuality was that I always knew deep down that my parents would still accept me for who I am. Still, I struggled to find an appropriate time to tell them. They were always there to support me when I needed it the most but I continued to harbour a fear about a very slight possibility they would disown me.

The fears that I had about my sexuality were in complete contrast to my identity as a young Aboriginal and Torres Strait Islander boy. I knew from the day I was born that I was Gugu-Badhun, Ngadjon-ji, and Meriam. Despite the often prevalent racism in Townsville and the challenges that it presented, I was and always have been comfortable in my own skin as a young Aboriginal and Torres Strait Islander man. This is because my family – and my parents in particular – taught me to feel strong and proud about my culture. However, unlike my culture, my sexuality was something relatively new in my life and I was never taught to be proud of my sexuality. While my parents are far from homophobic, homosexuality was not often a topic of conversation in our household. I felt, when confronted with coming out, that I couldn't accurately predict how they would feel. At the end of the day, I realised that my sexuality was something my parents could not provide me with guidance and advice on. I came to know that I just couldn't prepare for whatever experiences would come from it, and that eventually I had to jump in the deep end and learn to swim. Thankfully, though, help and guidance wasn't too far away.

My mob have never really spoken about homosexuality and its place in a Gugu-Badhun or Ngadjon-ji context, but I did grow up surrounded by countless Aunties, Uncles and Cousins who are loved and accepted by my entire family. After I came out to my parents, the first person I touched base with was Uncle Adam, my mother's younger brother. My Uncle Adam grew up in Mount Isa, but it wasn't until his university days in Brisbane in the early nineties that he became comfortable in coming out to my Grandparents. My grandparents, from what I have been told, barely batted an eyelid at this news. My Grandmother Pattie told me about how she could not disown her own son, especially given the discrimination she had experienced as a member of the stolen generation who grew up in the dormitory on Palm Island and as a young Torres Strait Islander woman. She explained: 'Gay people and Aboriginal and Torres Strait Islander people experience the same discrimination. People always try and hurt both of us because we are different.'

Nearly twenty years before I came out, my Uncle Adam had spent that time as an openly gay man, loved and accepted by nearly everyone on my mother's side of the family. After finishing university, he moved to Canberra and spent a number of years working for the Department of Foreign Affairs and Trade. He enjoyed a number of overseas diplomatic postings before he moved back to Mount Isa, where he began a long and successful career as a mining executive. Uncle Adam sat down with me over Christmas 2009 and told me a few unpleasant truths about growing up as a gay man in north Queensland. He also told me if I needed to talk that he was only a phone call or a Facebook message away. A few years later. after I told him of some recent relationship troubles and moments of self-doubt, he sent me this message:

> For my amazingly smart and brilliant nephew. A lot of people will tell you or try to make you feel you are not good enough. You are! More than! The mould will never fit so throw it away. Work incredibly hard, don't be distracted from your goals, remain youthful and adventurous, see the world, and only keep company of those who love you and want you to succeed. Lots of disappointments and burns ahead. Get used to it and learn from the setbacks. I am the biggest believer in setting your own course. You have an enormous future ahead, so knuckle down, get to it!!

Even before coming out, my Uncle has been a role model to me. After coming out, he also became a great source of support and someone who I could to talk with about things when I felt that my parents or others wouldn't understand. Uncle Adam's support and guidance made my coming out easier for me.

Townsville is not a large city. I regularly ran into friends and classmates during nights out on the town, and I was able to tell many of them about my 'recent' coming out. Many of my mates were quite happy to know that I was comfortable enough to tell them, and many have expressed their admiration in knowing that I am also comfortable in my own skin. However, sometimes I can't help but wonder, if I came out to my friends at school, whether the same joy and admiration would have been expressed. Perhaps without the time we have spent since, navigating the waters that existed outside of the boundaries of high school, the reaction from many of my friends would have been more negative than positive.

That said, I did have a few entertaining interactions when I came out to some of my best mates. Duane, a Wulguru-kaba man, said to me: 'It took you long enough brother!' All I could do was raise my eyebrows in confusion, responding with: 'How did you know?' He explained to me that I had an obvious lack of interest in women during high school (despite the fact that I would occasionally join other students in trading topless magazines and straight porn clips), and mentioned that I had some obvious mannerisms. I walked away from that conversation feeling as though I could have been the most flamboyant gay man in history. Another good mate, Josh, was completely shocked: 'I didn't expect you to say that mate! I couldn't tell!' My conversation with Josh, unlike that with Duane, made me feel that I was the most straight-acting gay man in the world. Even so, Josh was pretty quick to also remind me of some of my actions in high school. Afterwards, he said: 'You were pretty homophobic back in school, so you have to understand why I think this is quite a shock to me.'

While some people did express that they felt as though they didn't really know the bloke they had spent five years at school with, my coming out did not stop invitations to birthdays and backyard gatherings, or now more recently, to engagement parties and weddings. It was pretty clear that coming out to my friends did not change my social standing.

Many of my Townsville mates and fellow Iggy Park old boys now continue to meet after work on Fridays for drinks at our usual haunt, The Brewery. Over a couple of pints of freshly-brewed beer, we converse about troubles at work and about life in general. With the advent of dating apps such as Tinder, many of the boys often talk about their on-line experiences with some of the girls they have met, spoken with, dated, and even subsequently had, um, relations with. As these conversations would progress, I would usually sip my pint of beer and nod my head while intently listening – and feel, with my minimal experience with both tinder (and dating women in general I suppose), that I would have nothing to add to the conversation ... that is, until someone eventually turns around and says: 'Gertzy, have you had similar experiences with Grindr?' At the end of the day, I am still Gertzy to all my friends. To know that my friends still have my back and to know that I am included is all that matters to me.

A few years ago, I came across a quote by Lesbian poet and author, Radclyffe Hall: 'You are neither unnatural nor abominable, nor mad. You're as much a part of what people call nature as anyone else, only you are unexplained as yet – you've got your niche in creation.' Never in my life have words rang truer to me. When you spend part of your life fighting yourself over who you are, only to then spend another part of it trying to be accepted for who you are – you fail to realise and understand that you are the one who needs to accept yourself and be comfortable in your own skin. I have never shared my true feelings until this point, not with my family and not with my friends. Only through writing this do I feel it is appropriate to convey the pain and self-guilt I have felt for myself over a number of years.

While perhaps I am yet to fully accept myself, I have accepted the fact that I am very unique individual. It is one thing to be born as an Aboriginal or Torres Strait Islander, one of only 600,000 in the world, and it is one thing to be an openly gay man. To combine the two, you have a pretty unique combination.

For all my faults and all my fears, perhaps one day I will reconcile the wrongs of my past. I can never take back the self-loathing, or the self-hatred that plagued my journey of self-discovery. All I can do now is learn from those valuable lessons of my formative years, and move forward with my life knowing that my fears, for the most part, have been alleviated. In the meantime I will continue with my journey through life, knowing it may not be until in death that I will find what I have been truly seeking for so many years. Atonement.

My Totem is Tawny Frogmouth

Kai Clancy
(as told to Dino Hodge)

I have a dual Indigenous heritage on my Dad's side. One of my grandparents is Wakka Wakka and the other one is Wulli Wulli. The Wakka Wakka one comes from the Chapman and the Law side of the family, and the Wulli Wulli one comes from the Clancy side. They are neighbouring nations. Most people who have dual Aboriginal heritage usually have neighbouring nations, like Kulin and Wirajduri, or Wirajduri and Yorta Yorta. Wulli Wulli and Wakka Wakka isn't a common mix. Wakka Wakka is a big nation population-wise, and Wulli Wulli is substantially smaller. Wakka Wakka nation begins about five hours north-west of Brisbane, and going diagonally north-west about nine hours from Brisbane will take you all the way out to Wulli Wulli country. Because they are neighbouring mobs, they married into each other a fair bit.

My Dad's brothers and sisters were all born in Cracow, which is about four or five hours west of Bundaberg and Rockhampton. It's pretty rural. They don't have any beer on tap – that's how rural it is – so it's all fridge beer. Dad's Mum was born there, but he was born in Mt Isa because the mining jobs had moved to Mt Isa in the sixties. When Dad was growing up in Mt Isa, he would come between Mt Isa and Townsville to play football and do boxing, and that's where he met my Mum. They met around 1992 at a nightclub. Mum was working in the bar and Dad was a bouncer. And then I happened three years later, and my sister a year after me.

Mum is from Ipswich in Queensland. Her family are German and Irish heritage mix. They were the white settlers of Lowood, on Jagera country, all the way out towards the bottom of Wakka Wakka country – that was in the 1800s. They are the Manthey family, and they married into some of the Cooma mob, out in Cunnamulla, so there is Aboriginal Mantheys married into our German side as well. My Mum's Dad was born in Ipswich, and Mum was born in Ipswich. Mum's Dad was in the Air Force; Amberley RAAF Base is in Ipswich too. She ended up moving to Melbourne and living in Wantirna in the eastern suburbs. She went to America for high school as well. They were an RAAF family.

We were brought up in Townsville, which is off-country – far from country, actually. We had never been to country until we were maybe five but Dad always brought us up as proud Aboriginal kids. There was a big cultural intake and focus at primary school, so I got involved in all the Aboriginal groups there. We were mentored through primary school, and Dad had a big influence on us. I was ten when my Mum and Dad broke up and we sort of lost all that.

My Mum joined the RAAF when I was twelve, so we ended up doing the same thing – moving from Townsville to Sale in Victoria, and then eventually to Ispwich. I went to high school there. It was weird because we would meet Mum's family on the white side, and there would be family from Dad's side at my school as well, because lots of the Wakka Wakka people from Cherbourg moved to Ispwich and Inala. I hadn't met them but they knew my last name, and we just worked out the connections through that – so high school was with family on both sides.

By the time I was fifteen, I had gone through four high schools – one in Townsville, one in Sale, and two in Ipswich – and then a private school that had a really big focus on culture and lots of Aboriginal, Samoan and Vietnamese kids. I was asked to leave the Ipswich schools and ended up in this private school – but the story turns out to be good, because it really made me focus and get down into my work. I ended up having a leadership position at the school and getting a university scholarship at the end of high school.

So there was a gap there when I didn't see much of my Dad. He went into a pretty depressed state and he was really sad. It was a really rough time for all of us. These were the years when I wasn't having culture. Those years I was a wreck. And I was moving all over the country-side, from Townsville to Sale to Brisbane and Ispwich. I picked up again with Dad and all that cultural connection when I was in Ispwich, around fifteen.

At school we had a mentor who was really supportive. The songs and dance we learnt were from my people. Although he wasn't from my people, he was from Cooma mob, which is out west, he taught me songs and dances from my people that I hadn't learnt before – because it was different to how Dad was taught. And I met my cousins and family in Ispwich through the schools, and got more involved with them. I was involved with marriage equality rallies because I had lots of gay friends at that age, so I was hanging around with my gay peers. One time there was a rally for Aboriginal rights, and I thought: 'I'm going to that. I've been to the marriage equality ones a few times, so I'd better check out the Aboriginal ones.' I saw a few people who pointed me out from Townsville, saying, 'I know your Dad', or 'You can come sit here with me', and 'Your uncle is here in town right now' – they'd tell me all this, and then I just began getting more involved. I started going to the Brisbane tent embassy and doing more political activism stuff.

The tent embassy was is in Brisbane city, which was a fifty minute train ride into the city and then back again. If I felt like it, someone would come with me but often I'd go by myself. I was pretty independent. Mum was in the Air Force and would always be away, so people would come to look after us – like Grand-dad and Nanna from her side. We would do what we want and were roaming the streets at night. It was a housing commission area, not really the best place for young kids to run around but no-one else could look after us.

I was four when Mum first thought I might be trans. Actually, I thought I was intersex because I saw Tony Briffa being interviewed on *Sixty Minutes*, that was in 2000. At that stage, Tony was transitioning from Antoinette to Tony because a surgical intervention as a child for a medical condition that had left him confused. When I saw that, I said: 'Oh, this girl is turning into a boy. Is that what happened to me, you know, you cut my gonads off when I was a child, Mum? Did that happen to me?' And, she answered: 'No, sweetie. That person had a medical thing where they got both, and the doctors did that. And now they are just changing because that's how they feel, and the doctors didn't know' – or something like that. So I believed that only your biological body can determine whether you can transition from female to male, like, there has to be if a genuine medical reason or some sort of biological mishap physically for you to be transitioning. So I put it behind me. But I was still a tomboy and liked hanging out with boys and doing boy things.

I don't remember the whole conversation, though, about that *Sixty Minutes* program. My Mum reminded me about three months into my transition and refreshed it in my mind. She has carried it with her to the point where – now that I have transitioned – she feels like it is a *big* burden on her for not acting when I was younger. But there wasn't any awareness around

FTM (female to male) transgender back then. Trans women were visible; maybe Chaz Bono, Cher's son, was the only visible FTM – but I don't even know if he was public in 2000, it might have been post-2000.

Anyway, Mum didn't have resources or support, and didn't know how to act on it. Now she thinks that it's her fault, which it's not. She was googling and telling me things like: 'It was my fault. When I conceived you, I was stressing out because you were my first child. And when I stress too much, apparently it gives you too much testosterone in the fetus. You just came out like this, and this is why.' I explained to her: 'Mum, there is no scientific evidence to back that. No-one has done research on fetus and hormones. It's just an assumption.' I try to convince her that it is not her fault. I referred her on to Parents and Friends of Lesbians and Gays support service, which she likes. She hasn't met with them, but she talks with them. I tell her that it's not her fault, but it's her mind and I can't control what she thinks. I feel really sorry for Mum sometimes. It's taken a burden on her.

Dad's really fine with it. His biggest worry is my actual physical health. He has always had a sense of me being different, transgender maybe. As his first child, I wouldn't do Barbie things, and we would go kick a footy out the back. And then down the track, around 2008, he ended up having a biological son. I was thirteen then. Dad wasn't living with us and we didn't see him in that period. It was traumatising at first when my brother was born because I thought: 'There I go. Dad's happy. His pride and joy. His son is right there. I'm a no-hope child. Dad's got a son now, and he's happy.' I sort of lost it. It's just how it was. But now I've transitioned and he's cool with it and very supportive. I was always close to my Dad but now I feel like I'm closer. And he's happy that he's got two sons. He's cheering.

There was lots going on when Dad got re-married and had

another child. I was moving to Sale, leaving all my childhood friends behind. I got depressed when I got to puberty. My mates were changing, and I was changing in a different way. I remember thinking: 'I'm different from these guys, and I'm not one of those girls, then what the hell am I?' For as long as I can remember, being separated from my mates by gender during ceremony and Corroboree would upset me because I was being taken away and put into a group where I didn't belong. Still, I did it because that's what my Elders told me to do. It got heavier about fifteen onwards, watching the boys dance as young men, because I obviously wasn't going through what they were going through. Whereas, as kids, it's like there's really no difference here. And seeing my peers as young men and wanting to be like them instead of standing back – because that is what happens during Corroboree when the boys go into the dance, the girls stand in the back of the line. And that is quite literally how I felt: standing back from the guys. I was kept back at that stage. I was pretty sociable still, and I wasn't kept back academically. I was kept back with those physical facets of my life. I wasn't being me.

I went to a private Catholic high school for the last years, and I was elected as a female school captain, like, vice captain of the school. Before I transitioned I looked naturally very feminine with long blonde hair, and I was really petite. I had to wear a school dress and transitioning would have been so messy. I didn't want to go through that. Leaving all the people behind from my school had a big benefit for me – no discredit to them, it's just maybe Year Sevens and Eights weren't ready for a transition. I just wouldn't want to be a distraction to everyone at school or to myself, and I thought that it may not be best option for my mental health. But I had to weigh up the options as well. I was only months away from leaving high school, and that isn't long enough to weigh up your options. This is a big, irreversible, life-changing decision, and I had to weigh it up. It took me about a year to weigh up. I was starting to identify as transgender about six months away from leaving high school, but I didn't really come out until a year later. It was in that last year of high school that I came across FTM transgender. I was following lots of blogs – and this is happening with lots of people my age on the social network site Tumblr – you have your own blog, it's sort of like Myspace but more wordpress type of Myspace. Like, you just write your thoughts and feelings and you put in photos, so it comes out like a wordpress layout but it's very neat and the aesthetic is nice. That's where I found a lot of queer blogs and, through following these blogs, I ended up following androgynous blogs – which is like androgynous lesbians and androgynous women. And then on one of these androgynous blogs, there was 'I am a trans guy', and so I looked at it. That post had hyper-links with the pre-transition blogs, and then later posts, like one month on 'juice' or T (testosterone), two months on T, and so on. It is an amazing timeline of someone's transition. I was inspired by their strength. It started to make sense, and I realised that I needed to do it for my own welfare. That's when I came out as transgender. I didn't really have any trans peers around me. That is the unique thing about me. Lots of people usually have a friend who has done it. But I was seeing these people and watching their change happening on-line.

I've been making YouTube videos since I began my hormone replacement therapy. I love being able to show how much I've changed. It's good for myself and it's good for other people too, I guess. I use it to document my progress and see all the differences in myself over time. For other people, it's a really good resource for motivation and also a referral tool for people who might be going through the same thing. Lots of transgender guys do those videos – the transition is so physical and you can see the differences in hormone treatment over time. I had two motivations for posting YouTube. I didn't want people to make up excuses for me. I was going to tell them straight up why I transitioned and how I felt. My first video, 'The Life of Kai', was my life story in a ten minute video. I posted that first video for awareness and empathy, and for education – to get people to know why I am doing this without people going, 'Oh, this is the sex change person', or 'They are doing it for attention'. And it was documentation of my process for my self-reinforcement. If I can keep recording myself, then I can see the visual and the audio changes throughout my transition. There are differences each month – the voices, face fat, facial hair – and they're all big changes.

I didn't talk beforehand with my parents or family because I don't really talk to my parents about those sorts of things in my life. They've been in and out of my life since I was thirteen and they are never really physically there. I don't text them and say, 'Look, I'm making videos', unless it's using Mum's DSLR camera. I use my Mum's camera sometimes; she's got a good camera.

My transition started in February 2014 with my hormones. I say that is my coming out because it is. I posted a photo of my drugs so everyone would know and call me Kai. I posted the first video that night, too. I didn't know there was any other Aboriginal transgender people apart from sistergirls, and about a month later I found the group Brotherboys and Sistergirls. I was like: 'Okay. So this group has got brotherboys on their name, so will they have any brotherboys?' The first post I put was pretty obnoxious: 'Is there any other brotherboys here that are really into their culture?' And then Dean posted, 'Yeah, me. I am Wirajduri culture man, considered Elder.' He transitioned nearly a decade ago when he was forty-two years old. Jay, a brotherboy in Melbourne, posted too. I was really happy with that. I felt like there were other people like me around, which I was totally unaware of. You just didn't know because there was no resources at all coming up in google or Facebook. Jay was the first brotherboy I met in person, and then I ended up meeting heaps more. There are about five in Brisbane. They've all started to come out of the woodwork now – because I put videos up on Facebook and began talking about being a brotherboy. And Dean and I recorded a video together that we posted on YouTube. We discussed aspects of the brotherboy experience, and Dean explained about his initiation into manhood a couple of years back.[1] There are people coming out as transgender who are Aboriginal, and there are people coming out as Aboriginal who are transgender! They didn't really identify in the past with being Aboriginal, because they thought that they lost it. Which is something that I considered as well – would I lose my culture for this transition? What are the consequences? I thought I could be losing my culture, but I asked my Elders and they were fine with it. It was a risk that I was willing to take – or else I would have been years in depression, or something.

There was no mental preparation for asking the Elders. I just had to get it over and done with. I love being young and who I am. It is a good feeling. I wouldn't want to be trapped and young. Participating in men's business is a grey area. The door hasn't opened yet. That's later down the track. I think a lot has got to do with internal organs, like your ovaries and that sort of thing. Carriers of life are considered women, for women's business. Once those are gone, and then the carrier of life from there is what the appendage is down there. Even though I don't have that, I think they are willing to have an exception. I just know that I can't play didgeridoo, and I can't participate in ceremony as I haven't had the go-ahead yet. Many young men haven't if they've got a history of drugs or bad things; they won't get accepted into men's business either. It's as simple as that. And like lots of my cousins, we don't live on country, and when we go to participate in culture, it's very rare we get to do that. I'm negotiating with Elders to learn some men's songs, but I'm content with where I'm sitting now. It doesn't bother me as much as it did being separated with the women. That was more traumatising.

I also made a video with Mum's camera about fund-raising for top surgery that I posted on social media. I asked my friends and my Mum to talk about my surgery and how much it'd mean to me, and then I talked about it too. I put an emotive sound track in the background and plucked the strings of those emotions to make people empathise with me about what I'm going through. I organised it to be around the day of my birthday so if anyone wanted to give me birthday presents, it could be a donation to the surgery fund-raiser. It was a really successful campaign. I was a bit worried at first but a lot of people helped out. My Mum helped out, too, so that bumped it up a bit.

Medicare for top surgery gives a rebate for a mastectomy on each side. I think breast cancer patients are fully rebated, but if it's cosmetic – in their eyes – it's a tiny portion. If you're a male on your Medicare card, it will cover hormones because males who are testosterone deficient are allowed to have access to the hormones at the PBS (Pharmaceutical Benefits Scheme) schedule price. Whereas, if you've got female on your Medicare card, then you're paying for those hormones at an extra price – about thirty dollars more a month.

You can get your passport changed, I think, to your preferred gender, if you get a letter. For birth certificate to be changed, you've got to have surgery – but that's only the removal of your reproductive system. You sacrifice your reproductive system so you can be identified as the gender you want. That could mean just removal of the testicles; you can still have your penis.

Or just removal of your ovaries – but you don't have to have a penis – and that considers you to be male. So you need to be infertile. Some trans women still want to have their body and that part of their body. It's barbaric to take it away.

Dad was worried about me not being in a relationship, and not being loved in the future. He didn't mind me liking girls; he was happy that I had girlfriends – that just meant that his daughter wouldn't get pregnant. But when I first transitioned, Dad was worried that I wasn't going to get a girlfriend. Now I have a nice girlfriend. She is really supportive and she is from north Queensland too. But, yeah, Dad's happy. That was an underlying fear for my family: will he find a partner, and I guess I have!

I've connected with a nation-wide Facebook trans support group created by a lady in Lismore, northern New South Wales. The transgender community knows discrimination when they see it, and it's very rare for them to discriminate against other people but sometimes there is racism. Recently I called out someone for her racism against Arabic people and Islam. She was posting about 'freedom of speech' – 'we have a right to be against Islam and Sharia law' and 'traditional Australian values – reclaiming Australia'. That's racist. And it's *really* offensive to Aboriginal people. Like, what are you trying to reclaim? Is this really your place to reclaim? And impose? That's where I see a hypocrisy about a fear of Islam taking over – the British colony with Christianity took over the Aboriginal population here. Some people say, 'I feel like a minority in my own country'. Well, hello, I'm an Aboriginal person and I'm a minority in my own country. I'm more afraid of a British colonialist telling me who I am and what I should be doing.

I called the woman who made that post a racist and deleted her off Facebook. She wrote this massive tirade about me and said I'm a racist. One of her trans women friends – she is white as well – she was like, 'Oh, he's not even Aboriginal'. And my Mum replied when she read that: 'He's Aboriginal. I know his Dad. I'm his mother. What are you on about?' And then there was: 'Your baby looks white, not Aboriginal. Why is he claiming that?' My Dad is Aboriginal, and my sisters and brothers and cousins are dark. What about recessive genes? And this is in the trans community! You'd think they'd know discrimination when they see it.

For an older trans woman to police someone's identity is just like someone telling them: 'Well, you're not a woman, because we know your past', or 'We know that you used to live your life as a man. You're not a woman.' Who's to say that I'm not Aboriginal? It's just ridiculous. What does Aboriginal look like? What does a woman look like? They've been through that, and I know well and truly they've been through that. I'd rather not be called white than not be called a man. I think that's been my whole life-long battle with being Aboriginal. It's not even the Aboriginal community that does it, because they know that I am an Aboriginal. They know my Dad. They know. They are the accepting ones. It's just the people outside the Aboriginal community who have this sudden power to judge others, and I see that in the trans community. It's a reflection of the broader population, too.

I'm studying a political science degree, majoring in international relations and public policy. I became interested because of the things that I was doing activism-wise during high school. I was pretty involved with the Labor Party, back in Queensland. I was volunteering with the Minister for the Arts and Environment at her electorate office when I was sixteen. That was an interesting experience because I was so young and someone high up took me under their wing. I went to Bond University, on the Gold Coast, for my first year. They do trimesters there, and I finished three semesters in one year.

The environment and the nature of Bond University is not for an Aboriginal person let alone for a transgender person. It's a really pretentious university, and the students are very straight. There are no kids there who are out of line, alternative – they are privileged kids who go to this university because their parents can afford it. It was that formative time for me and I left Bond so I could transition – and I was on a full scholarship. I enrolled in Griffith university, which is on the Gold Coast as well, and I was happier. I've got six subjects left – a semester and a half. I'm doing two subjects now. I'll probably just do another two and then another two, and finish half-way through the next year because I'm working.

The Victorian AIDS Council had advertised a position for an Aboriginal and Torres Strait Islander Peer Education and Support Worker. A couple of my friends were telling me to apply for it. I was giving a speech for the Wheeler Centre in the Victorian State Library and some VAC staff came along, and so we talked. I applied and I was pretty happy that I got the job. I moved a few weeks after I finished university for that semester. Now I'm studying on-line via correspondence. The job is working with Aboriginal people around reducing the HIV infection rate and with people living with HIV, so there's a lot of support groups and sex education. I don't see a career in politics – you see Aboriginal politicians who get elected and then everything comes undone because of racism. Aboriginal people in politics are demonised and every move they make is watched and criticised. I wouldn't want to put myself in that position. But I'm not involved with the Labor Party anymore; in saying that, I'm not involved in any political party. Policy is an interest of mine and I'd like to do more policy work later down the track.

Part Two

An Emergent Public Face

A Story to Tell: Rodney Junga Williams, 18 February 1962–24 November 2011

Rodney Junga Williams

This essay is based on an interview with Kathy Triffitt that was published first in *Talkabout* magazine, March-April 2012, together with a forward by James Ward and Neville Fazulla. It is reprinted here with the permission of Aunty Joan Lamont Williams and Kathy Triffitt.

> It is with great sadness that we have lost, but not forever, one of our true fighters for Aboriginal and Torres Strait Islander people's rights in the health and HIV arenas. Sadly, on 24 November, 2011, we lost Rodney Junga Williams, a proud Nurrunga-Kaurna man, after his relatively short battle with cancer. Relatively short, as he managed his HIV successfully throughout the last twenty-seven years. He has left a legacy that will be long upheld, one of a fighter who in the beginning and to the end stood up and spoke up about the importance of inclusivity within the response to HIV/AIDS for Aboriginal and Torres Strait Islander people.
>
> His pride was out of this world, for his family, his friends, his culture and the communities of both Aboriginal peoples and those affected by HIV. His laugh was infectious, his generosity was welcoming, his activism was sincere, sensitive and difficult. He was an instigator, an innovator, some say troublemaker and others say peacemaker – we don't care, we loved him for who

he was. His activism and those of others in the community paved a way for all of us to maintain vigilance regarding HIV in our communities. His activism and commitment is well described in his final interview with Kathy Triffitt (in August 2011). It's what drives us to do what we do. We understood the difficulties, we stood proud with him even in the darkest of hours, and although he has left this place we know he will always be looking down upon us.

We say thank you Rodney Junga Williams, son, brother, father, uncle, cousin and friend to many. Thank you for being who you were, for doing what you did. Thank you for your passion and your trailblazing. Your last interview so well encapsulates your longstanding commitment to humanity. We will see you again, wait for us! Miss you, our brother! Nukunya.

James Ward and Neville Fazulla

Coming Out in *Talkabout*, August 1992

I was looking at a photo from my very first interview in *Talkabout* (August, 1992), when I came out publicly as an Aboriginal man with HIV. Coming out was in some ways the culmination of a long process of coming to terms with being positive and gay.

I've had such a public life living with HIV, travelling all over the world speaking about my experiences. I've been interviewed many times and my face has appeared in a variety of magazines and campaigns. Twenty years later I'm not dying from an AIDS-related condition, but cancer.

I gave my first interview to *Talkabout* so I wanted to give my last one to the magazine and to Positive Life NSW, which I have a lot of respect for.

Growing up in South Australia

I'm one of the stolen generation. My family come from South Australia originally – the Yorke Peninsula, where the Aboriginal people call themselves Nungas. My tribes are Narrunga and the

Kaurna. They were moved into the district of Gawler, which was on the fringes of Adelaide. To work in Adelaide, we had to wear a dog tag, as we called it.

We lived in my grandmother's house with my mother's sisters and brothers. The Department of Community Welfare visited one day when my mother wasn't home. Representatives found the living conditions inappropriate for a five-month-old baby and removed me from the house that day. I was put into foster care and was eventually adopted into a non-Aboriginal family. I grew up in a suburban part of Adelaide.

I had a very different experience as a member of the stolen generation. My birth mother was allowed access to visit me, whereas that was not the case for others. Once they were taken by welfare, they were taken. My adopted parents were Anglican Methodist and wanted me to have contact with my family. This didn't happen weekly or monthly – maybe a couple of times a year. At the time, I didn't know who these people were. I just knew them as friends of my parents. It wasn't until I was ten years old that I was told I was Aboriginal and the people visiting me were my mother, brothers and sisters. That was a defining moment in my life.

At the age of fifteen, I left and lived with friends on the coast. I gradually found my way to Sydney around the time the first cases of AIDS were reported. People didn't know very much about it, especially in Adelaide. I became involved in organising the first Aboriginal solidarity group to visit Nicaragua in 1988. I was the first out Aboriginal gay to work there, but I was still in the closet about HIV/AIDS. It was a touchy subject in the Aboriginal community.

SILENCE = DEATH

I was diagnosed in 1985. It was definitely a key moment being told, as a young person in your early twenties, that you've got

AIDS. It changed everything. I was given my diagnosis and a death sentence and told to enjoy what time I had (approximately two years). It changed my behaviours and attitudes to life in general. I went from someone who had hopes, dreams and visions to nothing. It was about five years after my diagnosis I realised that maybe I'm not going to die. As more information became available, there was a slight hope that we could have a life.

A lot of the gay men I socialised with at the time were the first generation of AIDS activists in Australia putting a voice and face to this pandemic. I needed to be a part of that. One of the greatest slogans to come out of the movement was SILENCE = DEATH. This is as true today as it was then. If you keep your mouth shut and don't say anything, that's the worst thing you can do. I found myself going to lots of meetings and getting access to information that was more factual and optimistic than anything the media published. I became more and more aware of the media lies and distortions.

The information we generated was about removing fear, empowering people and giving them hope. The media became the subject of our criticism. We challenged the hysteria and misconceptions generated, for instance, by the notion that some people were 'innocent' victims of AIDS, while gay men weren't. We also challenged the depictions of passive 'AIDS victims' or, on the other hand, infectious 'AIDS carriers'.

Highlights and milestones

One of the highlights is my involvement in the development of NPLWAC (National People Living With AIDS Coalition) in 1990. This became the National Association of People Living with HIV/AIDS (NAPWA) in the early '90s. It was the first national voice for people living with HIV. To see that happen was definitely a very proud moment. We were moving through the fear and becoming stronger. There was so much stigma and fear around HIV. Along with a strong political direction came positivity and hope. HIV-positive people were now working in local and national government. All of a sudden there was access to this whole enterprise of organisations and people. That was a pretty incredible thing to not only witness but to be a part of. It was time for people to stand with us and not allow us to be marginalised by AIDS.

Campaigns like the Grim Reaper (1987) by the National Advisory Committee on AIDS (NACAIDS) motivated us to get into health promotion and to produce our own responses. We focused on living with HIV, dispelled the myths and challenged the fears. We built a public profile allowing people living with HIV/AIDS a human face, as opposed to what we were seeing in the media. We were living with HIV/AIDS, not dying. Aboriginal social and support groups started to grow nationally. What I witnessed was a community that grew and evolved and actually made me so proud to be a part of. Responses to HIV/AIDS were driven by ordinary people, friends and families.

Fit for a Queen

As HIV-positive gay men, we wanted to reclaim our sexuality. For me, that was tied into the injecting drug users (IDU) movement. We all worked together. Back then, there wasn't such a separation in ideology and organisational structure. Once it was identified that HIV was passed on through needles, we organised the first gay needle exchange at Mardi Gras. We wore a t-shirt with the slogan *FIT FOR A QUEEN*. We had a caravan set up where people came in to get safe injecting equipment.

We were a group of gay men who used drugs and had sex parties. We also set up the first ever poz-only space with a needle exchange in one room. We had people on-site to show guys how to inject safely if they needed a hand. There was lots of poz on poz sex. It was the first time guys could be free to be themselves and not have to worry about the fear of disclosure and of negotiating sex around HIV status. Poz people could get together and feel safe and free in that environment. It was very empowering. We were quite radical back then. It was an underground movement, which became a distinct part of gay culture.

It's all about choice: being able to make decisions and choices not only about sex but also how we live as people with HIV.

'Knowledge will help us to survive'
We needed to make information accessible to our communities. I was the only Aboriginal person, at that time, and a lot of people came and spoke to me. I worked across many boundaries and borders – HIV, gay, and IDU communities, including my own black community. When I returned to Adelaide from Sydney, I worked with Nungays, the first Aboriginal gay and lesbian support group in South Australia, which trained people who worked with young Aborigines. We brought mothers and fathers, aunties and uncles together. In 1994, we coordinated and ran the first Anwernekenhe national HIV/AIDS and sexual health conference for gay men and sistergirls at Hamilton Downs, Alice Springs. Being one of the founding members was definitely a highlight. It still operates now, but under a different agenda.

I've been blessed with many highlights in my life. In 1992, I helped set up NUHIT (Clean Needle Program) at the AIDS Council of South Australia (ACSA), and was elected the first Aboriginal president of People Living with HIV/AIDS South Australia in 1999. I also coordinated Black N Out, the first Aboriginal Arts Festival which was part of FEAST (community arts festival for the lesbian and gay community in Adelaide) before returning to Sydney to work in Aboriginal health.

Being the first Aboriginal gay man to speak at an international conference on AIDS was pretty amazing as well.

As the Aboriginal spokesman for the National Association of People Living with HIV/AIDS (NAPWA), I convened, supported and led their Aboriginal and Torres Strait Islander response in policy, advocacy, education and prevention, and gathered grass roots community support. As Co-convenor of PATSIN (Positive Aboriginal and Torres Strait Islander Network), I also helped in getting *Two Songs for Healing* recorded. This was our first fundraising project of awareness, dedicated to all those who lived, loved and lost loved ones to HIV/AIDS. The songs are an acknowledgement of our collective past, a celebration of our survival, our learning and our deep connections to all that is past, all who we have lost, and all who remain.

Although HIV/AIDS was relatively new to Aboriginal people, its social symptoms – grief, discrimination and stigma – were not. Aboriginal communities were going through their own multiple deaths, with families losing dozens of people from every healthcare issue, drugs and suicide. It was as if a big cloud descended across us all. I believed that knowledge would help us survive. With this in mind, I wrote *Aborigine Must Be Free: Let's Control HIV*, which was published in 1992. This was the first HIV/AIDS information and educational booklet of its kind in South Australia, both culturally appropriate and sensitive. It was soon distributed nationally and eventually had three editions published. The process of putting it together came from Aboriginal people both infected and affected, young and old, straight and gay.

'HIV doesn't discriminate ... people do'

With members of my family, I was involved in the ANCA (Australian National Council on AIDS) national campaign, *HIV doesn't discriminate ... people do* (1992/93). It was the first campaign produced by positive people in the world. We were all people living with HIV, not actors. By presenting our stories and a public face of living with HIV, we challenged people to rethink their attitudes. We stood up for our rights.

I've said it many times before: gay men are some of the most resilient people you will meet. The way we responded to this pandemic and continue to respond to the many issues that confront us as LGBTI people is something we shouldn't take for granted. It's not easy putting yourself out there on a daily basis.

I was at the forefront of a movement that was changing people's ideologies and lives on a daily basis. I think the response to HIV has changed the way people live their lives. It has changed the way people have sex and talk about it. It has changed the way people think about drug use. I don't think that anybody thought that it would change the world as much as it has.

Changing face of HIV

HIV has a different face now. In many ways we've gone back to 'normality'; many are getting on with their lives and their day-to-day routines, like working. In 1996, with the advent of new treatments, people's lives started to change. There was a shift from dying to preparing to live, with no discussion on how to do this. Some people still haven't been able to get their head around that. Because they lived for a long time thinking they were going to die, it's been hard to change/adapt. Because I was active in the community and working, I was able to make that transition a lot easier and maintain it.

In Australia, HIV isn't a death sentence any more. There are programs now where people can be retrained to go back to work. That should have happened around fifteen years ago. The best thing anyone can do is to keep living. Be active, whether it's working, volunteering or just being part of life or the world.

If people lock themselves away in their homes and in the past, they will become depressed. Depression is an issue for people living long-term with HIV and we don't talk about it. It's really important they get information and speak to their doctor because that will change their life. Depression can be treated. I don't know why in the community we've overcome this horrible spectre of AIDS and yet there are still taboo issues like drug use and mental health.

Gift of friendship and love
I've had some of the most amazing experiences over the past eighteen months. I've experienced so much beauty in this world. Unfortunately it wouldn't have happened if I didn't have cancer. The good has been good, and the bad has been pretty bad.

The next two to three months is about being with the people I love, my close friends and family. I also have my blood family in South Australia. I've been very blessed that I've had some amazing friends who have stood by me. The radiologist at St Vincent's, the nurse down at IBAC (Immunology B Ambulatory Care), the staff of Sacred Heart Hospice, and my HIV doctor of ten years have provided the most amazing support and guidance throughout this journey. I want to acknowledge their gift of friendship and love.

I was very sick from chemotherapy. My goal was to go over to California and London to see two of my oldest friends and to say goodbye. Through the healthcare profession, as well as my friends, I was able to do that trip. Now it's about letting my life be as organic and natural as possible, and enjoying the time left with the people I care about.

I want to be remembered as someone who didn't shut up, someone who stood up and faced the fear. It's always been about people that have no voice, access and equity – ensuring that the Aboriginal voice is heard. I feel very proud to have been a part of the HIV/AIDS movement and to have been friends with the first generation of activists.

My HIV has been and continues to be manageable. I have 500 T-cells, undetectable viral load, and yet I have cancer and two months to live. Who would have thought that I would not die from an AIDS-related condition; that touches my funny bone. The irony is too much. (*laughs*)

My Story, Your Story, Our Story: Recollections of Being Aboriginal and Queer in the 1980s and '90s

Samia Goudie

Names of people who have passed appear in this essay.

I dedicate this essay to Aunty Mary Davis, one of the Illawarra's leaders and Elders, now sadly passed.[1] Aunty Mary was a leader of the Illawarra Aboriginal Advancement League in New South Wales.[2] She was a health worker in the days when Aboriginal people were seen in tents located at Coomaditchie Reserve,[3] and before the Redfern Aboriginal Medical Service[4] had started the community controlled health movement.

I am extremely fortunate that Aunty Mary was one of my mentors and inspirations, along with Elders Aunty Iris McLeod, Aunty Faye Allen and Aunty Joyce O'Donovan. I also wish to acknowledge the Aboriginal community in the Illawarra, and the ancestors and Elders past and present, specifically the Wodi-Wodi and Wadi-Wadi[5] and other groups from the Dharawal people of that area and the Yuin Nation that spreads along the coast from La Perouse in Sydney and south into Victoria. I thank the people who live there now and who continue to care for Country, particularly those who I worked and lived with and who, to this day, remain strong friends.

Lastly, yet importantly, I acknowledge my friends, peers,

colleagues, and people in the communities where I have worked and lived as a Queer proud Aboriginal, First Nations Bundjalung[6] Mununjali[7] woman. I especially thank those who let me into their lives and who I travelled with into their passing. I wish this had not been so; however, it was and is also a big part of this story.

I offer a narrative rendering of my personal experiences in San Francisco during the early 1980s, my return to Australia, and events into the '90s. Specifically, I recall the work done to address prejudice, homophobia, and the need for service development particularly targeting the Gay, Lesbian, Transgender and Queer communities as well as the first Nations Peoples of the Aboriginal and Torres Strait Islander communities.

The Castro, San Francisco

Peter (not his real name) was to have his leg removed. Although only twenty-four years old, he was frail and a strange cancer was eating his body. No-one could explain why. 'Play your flute for me', he asked in a soft weak voice. I shyly played while a monk gave him his last rites, and then he was gone.

The year was 1982 and I was living in San Francisco.[8] I worked in a high-end lingerie shop located on Castro Street, an area well-known for its high population of Gay men and sex bath houses. I was twenty-two and remember the fear that had started to emanate around the streets. The environment I called home became quiet and afraid. Peter was the partner of a friend, and they had put out a request for help with his care. Peter was bed-ridden and extremely ill. As a result of my involvement with Peter, I was sought after in hospice work for the next two years, eventually becoming active in the training of others as more and younger people, both male and female, succumbed to the dreadful disease that was emerging as HIV/AIDS.[9]

The link between the disease and being Gay was being

emphasised by the press. Homophobic attacks rose significantly. This was evidenced through my personal experiences and those of friends. The Castro became very quiet, very still, and very haunted as young people struggled to make sense of this new world. We began to hold meetings to talk about how people felt, including a weekend retreat where about a hundred people came, all GLTBQ.[10] Many spoke of how they had struck off diary addresses for nearly all their friends as they had passed. People wailed in grief for fear and for each other.

The week following the retreat, one of the young men came to the shop where I was working. He remembered me from the weekend gathering and we struck up a conversation as he tried on various gorgeous fine silk kimonos. Finally he settled on a brilliant pink and purple kimono that was subtle but lavish. He paraded up and down the store, preening like a peacock. 'Isn't it glorious', he said. 'Yes, it really suits you', I replied. 'You look and must feel fantastic in it.' He smiled and then dropped his eyes, and when he looked up small tears were forming. I wondered out loud what was wrong, and why was he so sad. 'This is for my funeral, lovey', he explained. 'I don't want people to forget me, and I want to look good.' When I went to his funeral a month later, everyone was dressed in drag and their finest clothes as requested. Bright music was playing as we passed his open coffin, where he lay wearing that kimono. I have never forgotten him.

Australia

I returned to Australia in 1984, and then over the next decade travelled back and forth to New Mexico and San Francisco, before finally settling in Australia. I started working with homeless youth in Gympie and at Cherbourg,[11] running a young women's health project. After this I moved in the 1990s to the Illawarra, south of Sydney, where I started working for TAFE

(Technical and Further Education) and later for the Illawarra Area Health as an 'Aboriginal community development and sexual health educator'.

I had no university degrees although I had completed diplomas in natural medicine, massage, and community development. However, I did have enough experience and passion due to undertaking hospice training in USA and through my extensive work with troubled and homeless youth. In 1997, I enrolled at the University of Western Sydney, where I completed both a graduate certificate and a masters degree in Applied Science and Social Ecology whilst continuing to work full time in my position with Aboriginal Health in the Illawarra, Shoalhaven and Eurobodalla.

The truth, I observed back then, was that a lot of people 'blamed the Gays' for bringing this 'disease' of HIV/AIDS. This only seemed to heighten the homophobia that already existed in the wider community and especially within the Aboriginal local community, where people also tended to 'blame the Gays'. At one point, I joked with one of my lecturers that my sub-thesis for the Master's degree should be called 'The year I became Black and Gay'.

Meanwhile the rates of HIV were increasing, and some of the first cases were showing up in the Aboriginal community.[12] While some were Gay, it became apparent that the main at-risk group in the Aboriginal community was heterosexually-identified people. Among the reasons that we identified for this were that people were reluctant to disclose their sexuality, and that people would become intoxicated during Sorry Business (mourning activities following a death in a community) and have unprotected sex with people other than their partners. Also, some people were doing ritual cutting with infected blood on knives. Additionally, others were injecting drugs and sharing unsterilised needles, especially in prison populations, where the

Aboriginal population was four times greater than the non-Indigenous population. These factors increased the risk of cross-infections. People generally were reluctant to talk about 'safe sex' or be tested for HIV. Thus, a major task in my work was educating people about the truth of these issues.

Testimony – Joy Wurudjuri Williams and 'Cultural Grief and Loss'

The theme I chose for my Master's degree sub-thesis was what I called 'cultural grief and loss'. I made a video called 'Testimony', that was based mostly on interviews with Joy Williams, who has since passed.[13]

Joy was a Wiradjuri[14] woman whom I knew well in Wollongong, and who at the time was taking the Australian Government to court for damages she suffered due to her forced removal as a child under the *Aboriginal Protectorate Act*. She had grown up as girl 'number 9'. Joy was incredibly talented and yet also very much damaged due to the abuse she had suffered at the hands of the state welfare system. Ironically, she lost the case due to her testimony being considered 'unreliable' because of her mental illness.

The topic of 'cultural grief and loss' came from Joy who was in the TAFE class that I was teaching about grief and loss. I set an assignment for this class in which the students needed to pick a topic; Joy asked if she could choose 'cultural grief and loss', and I agreed to this. It was during the same time that research was starting for the Royal Commission into Aboriginal Deaths in Custody[15] and the Stolen Generations Inquiry,[16] as well as the making of early films such as 'Stolen Generations' by Darlene Johnson.[17] The terms 'transgenerational',[18] 'historical trauma',[19] and 'stolen generations' were still not widely-known. Peter Read's work was published around that time, and he is credited with the coining the term 'stolen generations'.[20]

This issue was something I could well relate to in many ways, as I had only recently met my own birth mother. The general Australian population knew little then about the brutal truth and history that was impacting Aboriginal people's lives as a result of the invasion and subsequent colonisation of people's lands. Many Australians simply could not relate to the pain that many of us suffered.

Joy and I would have long conversations and often discussed being Lesbians or Gay; we both preferred the term Queer as we felt less labelled and locked into some fixed identity. Queer was still a new name in the 'Community' at that time. The taboo was huge if you identified as Lesbian, Gay or Queer. We perceived it as being less difficult for men than for women. Being an Aboriginal woman with no children and no man resulted in being silently treated as abnormal, and I often felt judged and on the edge of things in the community due to this.

Aboriginal Pastors even preached that being Gay or Lesbian was not part of 'traditional' culture, that it had no place today, and that it was 'destroying our culture' (note the singular use of culture rather than cultures). I often thought about the irony of these statements, and of the wrath and bitterness expressed by these Aboriginal pastors. After all, Christianity surely was never a part of the so-called 'traditional cultures'. However, the strong mission enculturation experienced by many in the Community resulted in a tendency to express the same views. Many of us felt silenced and very alone, and even frightened to speak the truth. I and many others felt sadly ostracised, and some whom I knew took their lives simply because they no longer could take the ostracism.

I had been spat on and called names in public. I remember distinctly in a work meeting when two workers walked out in shock because I had pointed out that I am a Lesbian. This was during a process of contributing to the development of the first Aboriginal sexual health strategy. I can still hear one of them yelling as he stormed out about how I had 'deceived' everyone and that he 'did not need to know' and 'thought it was absolutely disgusting'. He further refused to work with me. Everyone at that meeting sat stunned speechless for a full minute before they adjourned so they could 'take in and process this news'. This was the climate at the time working in this area. It was tough and personally painful to go through.

Despite or maybe in spite of these reactions and attitudes, I was spurred on to take further action, to do my job well and to help educate and break down the prejudices in the community in which I lived and worked.

What we did

In those days I spent a lot of time at Coomaditchie 'reserve' near Port Kembla and what is colloquially known as Hill 60 (Port Kembla, Wollongong Illawarra).[21] This is a site where many Illawarra Aboriginal people had been moved to, either from Hill 60 or after leaving the Bomaderry children's home in Nowra and other missions up and down the east coast.[22] These people were all moved to what was then officially known as the Mission or colloquially, even to this day, as simply the Mish (or Coomaditchie).

The Mish was a focal point for many in the local community and we used the old tennis shed for gatherings and meetings and long cups of tea and yarns. A section of the community living there decided, together with me, to try to tackle the issues of prejudice and fear. We began to write funding applications to run a peer education project that the community named 'Scrubby Jacks'. We secured a small grant from the NSW User and AIDS Association, and another small amount from Illawarra Area Health. We also received food and art supplies from various sources. I did a lot of begging and borrowing in those years.

The process of 'Scrubby Jacks' consisted of meeting one afternoon a week over twenty-four weeks with guest presenters introducing their service and what they did; alternatively, we would visit services and see them for ourselves. A core community of roughly sixteen of us attended all sessions and, as a community, we decided upon the themes that we wanted to learn about and share. The sessions lasted between four-to-six hours. We also included the young Aboriginal boys from Juvenile Justice and youth under care with the Department of Community Services.

Scrubby Jacks purposely was run as an open event, which meant people started to come by just for a cuppa and a yarn or to paint, or just to sit and watch and listen. The local children often came directly off the school bus, and they ran around hugging everyone and sometimes painted with us. At the end of the twenty-four weeks, we had to decide how the information we had all learnt could best be disseminated to the wider community. Coomaditchie has a strong culture of painting, and so this was the preferred method. Thus, over a further ten weeks we individually and together painted murals and large artworks on wood addressing different themes, each of which had a small story accompanying it.

The main focus was breaking down prejudices and also educating people about risk behaviours in a culturally-appropriate manner for the community. This resulted in approximately twenty-four large pieces of art and some smaller pieces. We used photo negatives to make posters, tee-shirts and service flyers as additional new resources.

The people who attended the entire whole program were then paid to go out and run a workshop with peers using the materials and tee-shirts as materials. Other services were encouraged to use the art works in their workplaces to indicate a focus on Aboriginal and or Torres Strait Islander people's health.

We decided that we needed a launch to start this element of the peer education process. Consequently, I approached the Wollongong City Gallery to see if we could hold an exhibit and installation with dancers and Elders, and catering for the event with bush tucker. At first the curator was not so interested; in her mind the works were not interesting 'as they were not traditional enough'. What constituted being 'Aboriginal' in the art world was still quite narrow and was certainly controversial. Somehow over time and a lot of tea, she came around to seeing the work differently, and thus we held an exhibition opening with great success. More than a thousand people signed the visitor's book over the month the work was exhibited. This had a profound impact on the local community as articles started to show up in local news and on television, while reviews of the exhibition were positive.

It was at this time that we decided to hold a concert education day at Coomaditchie to coincide with the exhibition and World AIDS Day, which we would call 'No Prejudice – Caring for Country', and for which we made special tee-shirts with artwork designed by the local artists. Attendance was free, and Aboriginal, Islander, and non-Indigenous peoples were all welcomed. This would give people the chance to bring as many agencies and service providers together in one spot to show films and have stalls. I was determined that the concert would have quality acts and up-and-coming talents of the day.

This had never been done before at Coomaditchie. At first, there was some resistance from my fellow non-Aboriginal workers as they felt for some reason that it would exclude non-Indigenous people. Again, this reflects the levels of discrimination and prejudices of those times. However, we were determined to face both the racism and homophobia head-on and so proceeded to organise it. The event in 1997 was so successful that we decided to make it even bigger the following year. In 1998, we included a forum on homophobia for local schools, more films, and a tree planting in memory of those who had passed.

All of the performers at these events donated their time, as did our small team at Illawarra Area Health (including Sylvia Campbell, Iriaka Ross and Lorraine, Narelle, Coral and Daryl Brown), who all worked tirelessly with me sourcing funds and equipment, and promoting the events via fax and radio announcements. This was before Facebook and Google, so the Aboriginal Koori, Goori, Murri 'grapevine' was the best method to communicate, together with flyers, news articles and radio interviews.

The Indigenous and non-Indigenous performers included the likes of now-famous bands such as the Blue House, Tiddas, Vince Jones, Bette Little, Emma Donovan and Leah Purcell, as well as local dancers and didgeridoo players. 'Queen' MC of the day was Vanessa Wagner alongside with Pauline Pantsdown – both of them in drag. The community loved them. As both were popular and well-known MCs and comedians, Triple J, a national radio station based in Sydney, picked up the event. On the day it broadcast live from the site throughout the whole event. People streamed in from as far north as Sydney and from the south coast of NSW. We had a special Elders resting tent with food and people to care for our Elders, as well as a rest area for performers with refreshments. Many performers were impressed with how well they were looked after and also commented on the quality of sound engineering and stage management. Recently, I spoke with Pauline Pantsdown and she shared how she remembered the event as being very welcoming, warm and moving. She said the next day she was in Sydney at a major event with thousands and had been abused and had beer bottles flung at her. Pauline still remembers the special feeling of the day as one of the highlights of her career.

At a conservative estimate, some 600 people came and went

during the first event in 1997, making it a huge success. Being Gay, Lesbian, Transgender, Sista Girl or Queer was out of the closet in this community, and many Aboriginal and non-Aboriginal people commented on how amazing it was to meet and do such events at Coomaditchie. People were brought together in all sorts of new ways.

Over 1500 people signed the guest book on the day of the 1998 event. As it ended, I remember standing back and taking in the much larger crowd, which was still sitting in the fading light as Ruby Hunter's hauntingly rich voice echoed across the landscape and while people in silence planted bush tucker and 'Native' Indigenous trees for those who had passed.

All of these activities and events were truly self-determined and driven by the local community members, with us as the Aboriginal workers helping to facilitate the projects. All this work was done out of an old tennis shed – the only community space at the Coomaditchie 'reserve'. It is still used today. Lorraine Brown and the whole Brown family deserve special mention as the drivers of these projects. We were awarded a 'Consumers Best Practice Award' from Illawarra Area Health. More to the point, through these early efforts, much changed in this community, and this was palpable in interactions and in future projects. Lorraine, reported the Koori Mail, explained that 'we hope that the increased awareness will lead to reduced health problems in Aboriginal communities'.[23]

Conclusion

This story is my story, your story, our story – and a part of history now. I am not ashamed to say I am Aboriginal and Queer, though to this day I often deal with the prejudices that still exist. I try and walk proudly in my identity despite a level of homophobia that persists in all our communities, just as racism also exists. As with racism, these issues are difficult to change, and they often exist as an unseen burden that many of us carry. Prejudiced beliefs, homophobia and racism all do have an impact on the health of our peoples.[24] These have had an impact on my health and well-being and continue to do so. There is still much work to be done.

However, looking back I feel that in those last years of the '90s we did make a difference in the Illawarra and beyond, and that the artists from Coomaditchie and my co-workers contributed a lot to challenging and changing attitudes. Of course, this led to further projects that were initiated and often self-determined within the wider community, and ultimately also led to further education and employment for the workers who helped to organise the events.

Many, like myself, undertook degrees at university, some at a doctoral level, and they often were the first in their families to do so. Many of these people continue to work at the coal face of education and community health and well-being. There are ongoing challenges that need to be faced in relation to prejudices in communities of all forms, as well as what is now being called 'lateral violence' and that has a huge impact within many communities across the country. This is important, the history is important, and these stories are important.

We should never forget the struggles of those who came before us, and always be grateful for the ancestral spirits, Elders and wise people who have fought long and hard for what we all have today. I hope this personal glimpse back to these early years becomes known. The people in the Illawarra have made a huge effort and should be recognised for this.

I remain grateful and privileged to have gained my grounding in working within community from passionate, strong and courageous people. I will never forget these times and the continuing impact upon me in all that I do and how I live. I thank them all.

That Rope Pulls Along Many People

Brett Mooney
(as told to David Hardy)

I've ended up working in a service that I needed when I was growing up. This is my story, which ricochets between my personal and my work as a promotions officer in the 2 Spirits program at the Queensland AIDS Council.[1]

I'm Brett Mooney, a Torres Strait Islander with South Sea Islander descent. My mother's people are from the East of the Torres Strait and our language is Meriam. My dad's people are from Vanuatu. My grandmother was stolen when she was seven and brought to Queensland to build the sugar cane industry. Off the boat, they were put to work cutting down trees and ploughing and creating cane paddocks. When you think about Queensland's history of slavery, we were political tools.

I come from two families, my adopted family and my biological family. Both mothers worked in the health sector, and both contributed to the community. They had their share of achievements, and like everyone else, their disappointments. They've used disappointment as a driving force to move forward and achieve. I hope I have that trait ... I think I have.

When I left the Torres Strait I came down to Mackay. I was living with my sister and brother-in-law, and contract-planting cane in the Burdekin. I was the baby of the gang at just twenty-six, but most were forty- or fifty-year-old men. I'd ask myself, 'Is this what my life is meant to be? Is this my purpose, to serve but not to live something you create for yourself?' It ate away at me.

My cousin helped me to make changes. He's played a big role in my life and I can't mention my own success without saying his name – Dr Shannon Springer. He was a local doctor in Mackay, well known throughout North Queensland and now living on the Gold Coast. Shannon's an inspirational fulla, who respectfully understands the culture of many people in order to provide them with effective service. Shannon grew up in Mackay, so he understood the people from the get-go and was able to communicate effectively with the Aboriginal and Torres Strait Islander and South Sea Islander community. It's not that difficult but it's something you need to wake up within yourself. I think Shannon used that tactic on me.

So here was I in Mackay thinking, 'You can stay here and live from pay to pay and be drinking from week to week.' I don't have any issues with that but I wanted more. My cousin had to study in Brisbane and invited me down. I was planning to move to Sydney but they said, 'Stop here because it's closer to get home if anything goes wrong with family.' In Brisbane he supported me through a series of certificate courses, and then a Community Service diploma.

A turning point was being asked to speak at the graduation ceremony at South Bank TAFE. Twelve months earlier, I was hand-cutting cane because the wind had blown it down and the harvester couldn't pick it up; now, I was in Brisbane with a diploma. Mum and my Aunt had flown down and they were crying. My cousin's saying, 'Shut up mum. He hasn't even got it yet and you're crying.' When I got up to speak, I didn't need to prepare anything. I just told my own story, about the three months leading up to my move to Brisbane, and Shannon who said you can either do something or else swim in that same school of fish as everybody else, where nothing changes. And about giving back, because my mums gave back to their community. When I finished, the Dean came over to me and gave me his cap, and then them mob big cry. Some students waste their time, but when you pick fruit, move down, dedicate yourself to learning and come to the other side, that was when everything else followed. I was more than muscle. I was brain too and I had something to contribute.

In 2003, I began my prac at Open Doors as well as a prac and then part-time work at 2 Spirits that was known then as the Queensland Aboriginal and Torres Strait Islander HIV and AIDS program.[2] When the part-time contract finished I moved to the Gold Coast as a male health worker at the Kalwun Health Service until the 2 Spirits position became full time. They didn't have any Torres Strait Islanders and I think they were looking for a little bit of youth, so I got the position and moved back to Brisbane.

My bridge over the raging river

Growing up and being gay was really difficult because of my culture. Men are seen as the valuable ones and I was the only boy in my biological family. I was surrounded by uncles and wanting to do what men do: hunting, spearing turtles, spearing dugong, making family. As a teenager I was in trouble, fighting every weekend. When I look back, it was all a cover. Whenever there were moments I felt gay, it freaked me out to where I had to commit acts of violence to confirm me being straight. People knew not to muck around with me. I must have put them mothers through hell. They worried silently because I'm the first gay kid in the family. As much as traditional mothers love their children, an organic love, I think they are confronted very deeply about how to love a gay child. It's new to them.

141

As my mums worked in the health sector, they knew gay health professionals and so had their own self-learning. I don't think they had issues with me being gay but I can't speak for them because I never had that conversation. I think they silently dealt with it so that by the time I did come out they were cool. They reminded me, 'I don't care what you do, I can still smack you in the mouth if you play up, because I'm your mum.'

I was twenty-seven when I came out and even then not fully until I was in my thirties. When you're twenty-seven, you know nothing but when you're thirty, that's when you start realising your mistakes and don't want to repeat them. Early on, when I was in a relationship with a very understanding French woman, a lot of the older Torres Strait Island gay peers would say, 'When you're ready, we're there for you.' At that time I wrote it off as 'What the fuck are you talking about', but knowing that others knew and were totally okay with it helped me to become me. I came out to a few at first until I knew it was safe to come out to all my family. I wanted them to understand that I'm Brett. That's what I am. I'm not gay. I'm Brett. I still love your kids, I'll look after your kids, I'll defend them to the last teeth in my mouth, I'll cook, I'll clean. I'm still that person, but what I do with my personal life is different. I love someone who happens to be the same sex. That's the way I roll.

When I first came out, I had that much anxiety. I was with my cousins at this nightclub, these five boys playing pool and I walked up upset, crying and said, 'I've got something to tell yez.' They thought someone had done something to me and they were ready to bust him but it wasn't anyone – it was me – and I said, 'I'm gay', and they turned around and said, 'Fuck up, go and get another drink. We don't care.'

Funny, but revealing who you really are in those few words puts you on the cliff edge. You either fall off or step back from the edge, with relief. Some people fall. Some kick their kids out of home and disown them. It's the trauma of finding out whether they love me or hate me or will be the butt of their jokes. My cousins, the girls first, set my foundation, each with a role like pavers on a footpath. There was no way them bricks were falling out because they got slack. That's the moment I knew that I have people who love me, the same people I grew up with, share meals with, nurse their kids, hunt with, cry with when we lose someone close, laugh when we're all happy. They were my stepping-stones, my bridge over the raging river.

Now I teach them and others that being gay isn't about what you stick your dick into. There's a whole other life to it and I want them to understand that. When I come home, it's to fill my cup with culture and family. I'm not there to wave the Mardi Gras flag in front of them old people, expecting their knowledge to suddenly change. Who you are isn't about every colour in the rainbow. I want them to see me on the inside. They come from a different time and if you want them to understand who you are, take small steps and walk with them. And that's the way they'll understand. You're teaching them more for the next generation that will be more accepting, who'll say, 'I have gay kids and that's alright.'

A lot of traditional gay people go through the same stuff of pursuing the LGBT side of life and the cultural side. They take from these two cultures to make a life for themselves. That's what I've done here in Brisbane, and when I'm homesick or grieving I cook my food like coconut curry chicken, grating the coconut first, smashing the ginger and garlic. I can hear the advice by my mothers – when to add, how much to add. It's like I'm at home.

Mr Big Eye and the English Fulla
Prior to moving permanently to Brisbane, Shannon asked me down as part of his wedding party. As they knew me as a

run-around who loved the nightlife and the music and dancing, I was on house lockdown. This was my first time in a proper gay scene, so I asked my cousin if I could go out. I went to The Beat nightclub and the sex just hit me. In my culture, my people would say you're a Big Eye, just looking and never satisfied. So Mr Big Eye went for a look and I saw everything, from the most flamboyant people to the most, well – their version of straight acting. I was getting stared at, and there's this little English fulla who tapped me on the shoulder. He asked what I was doing and I asked him the time and he said quarter to four in the morning and I said, 'Is it the time you city people start looking for someone to take home', and he looked interested but I added, 'Brother, I'm not like that, I'm not from here and I just want to talk', and he looked like someone who has just been slapped.

This fulla was David. We started dating and we've been together for thirteen years. The relationship offers me security and greater understanding of western gay culture. What we've created is like a bank account: the more you put in, the more you get out. For Island people, if you look after your garden, the better your fruit will be. I am now on my way to owning my first home, and I've travelled to England eight times.

When we were there one time, David asked me why I said to people I am Australian, as he only knew me as a Murray Islander. 'You don't speak like most Australians, don't live like them, don't eat their food, and don't celebrate the things they do', he commented. It made me think about how I identify as a traditional person and as a gay person, and about the balance required to make me who I am. I find in my work with young same-sex attracted kids that they struggle to find this balance. One of my personal hates is the L G B T I LMNOP WYZ. It's a crock of shit. The kids are trying to be the 'G' and do what the 'G' people do, or trying to be the 'T' cause this is what the 'T' people do. It's not working for them. The problem is they're chasing a letter, and I tell them the best they can do is the best I can do. I can only be Brett. I can't be gay Brett, just Brett. Why do you want to label yourself further than the name your mother gave you. You don't define who you are by saying, 'Hi, I'm gay Tim.' That's nothing. How many different sugars are there? At the end of the day, it's still sugar, still sweet.

That rope pulls along many people

Everything I have done since I left home as a gay man is a piece of string. Every experience is string woven into rope and that rope pulls along many people from down the back when they grab on to it. That rope's only meant to guide them through and then they jump off and experience themselves and make their own rope. When I do my work with community, and when I lead them, I don't lead from the front, but from behind. It's easier to see a straggler and help them go forward. When you lead from the front and don't look behind, people fall back. From behind, I can pick them up, put my arm around them, they put their arm around me and we walk forward to the same place.

In the 2 Spirits program we're responsible for creating awareness and providing information around HIV and STIs and trying to prevent people from becoming infectious. Our success is the whole of community approach, making sure everything we do is culturally appropriate and that we create sustainable outcomes. We don't build dependency. Communities are given their own responsibility, as they are the only people who can fix the issues within their community.

When I work in urban, regional or remote communities, I tell my story. They can relate to it. Sometimes we laugh at ugliness and this can help unpack issues in their life that they haven't been able to because they've looked at it from a certain perspective, not the bigger picture. Like, for example, intergenerational trauma and how alcoholics around the street could be there because of child removal back in the day, thus feeding that cycle of depression and sorrow. When you keep breaking people like that, despair leads to drink, fighting, violence, don't care, no respect, no one respect me. We talk about that.

We work with communities, and the first thing we do is to go to the people who own that community – they're the old people. I draw on my own experience with Elders. I bring them up to speed, listen to them, and slowly educate them and create awareness amongst them about today's issues. We ask them about their community, and we talk about Elders in other communities and the resources we have developed with them that have had a positive impact on their kids. We help make them aware of behaviour and mental health issues that come with LGBT people and that their community, wherever it is, is not shielded from the ugliness of life. Even when we support a target group, we will take a broad approach first by teaching the community to look after those people, and by reminding them that they are and always have been part of their community.

Even though I don't live on Murray Island, I always say I'm a Murray Islander. That's mine. So I always make sure, before I do anything, that I'm involving the whole community. I put everyone on the one level and only then do I look specifically at the target group. If they are at risk from us identifying them, we might have to remove them and have a consultation outside, like bringing them to Brisbane if we have the funding.

For target groups or individuals, we sometimes start with activities like art or makeup, which helps lower the anxiety of communicating the issues. We also use fishing, healing lakes, and other men's and women's places that are known to local people. We draw on all that gives people identity, and use those traditional practices and protocols. When our people designed them, they weren't created for one day or one month but a whole lifecycle. And not just for straights.

The five in our team have different backgrounds. What we create is about what has been lived and experienced by every gay member in our communities. This, along with cultural appropriateness, means that there is no way we can't communicate with mob. Sometimes we have gone into a community and they've had sorry business so we can't do what we planned. Our 2 Spirits way is to ask if we could offer any support. 'Do you want me to cook something for you?' And you mourn with them. You help the community to heal – because you're going to go back. And when we do return, they remember and are thankful that an outside program understands sorry business. For the outside person, they might say it's a waste of time but that's them using western thinking on a culturally appropriate protocol that we adhere to. It's the way we do our work.

HIV and ignorance
When we look at HIV, Western service providers will go into a traditional community and say why it isn't working. It's because we are not Western people. You don't need a PhD to work that out. From a community person who has lived with these issues to a service provider who is supporting the issues, I have learnt how to communicate what needs to be said. I don't want to keep going back and telling them that you need to do this or you need to do that; and I don't want communities thinking that because they are so remote and removed that the world's issues won't affect them. HIV doesn't give a stuff about the world's issues and it does not care how remote you are. HIV and ignorance are left and right hand and one can't work without the other.

Ignorance comes from a western point of view, of treating people like we are all the same when we're not. For more than a century, never once have they used an Indigenous approach to health. When there's a black issue with health to be dealt with, we get pushed to one side. A lot of programs today are attached to blackfulla misery where you have mainstream services accessing blackfulla money to implement a fly-in, fly-out program. They're not worried about trying to make people stand up for themselves. The key is to involve them. When you get used to someone coming in and doing things for you, you don't give a stuff what mess you make. That approach is entrenched in some of our communities.

What we do is equip them sufficiently to be able to become a community that deals with sexual health issues, HIV and sexuality issues. And that includes providing them with other service providers. We have a large contingency of mainstream service providers that rely on 2 Spirits. But even that's not enough. An even greater holistic approach would be to address basic needs, like water, the roof over your head, access to food. When there's a black misery approach to policy and funding, one sector gets all the funding and these others get left behind.

Regional and remote communities are mostly without the services and resources that we have in the bigger centres. I have lived in a remote community with only a post office, an island shop and a health clinic. When engaging with workers in these communities, we need to be mindful of what health issues there are already, and that we create a structure that doesn't have a negative impact on their existing daily service delivery.

I have never done anything by myself

I have now been with the Queensland AIDS Council for ten years. I was fortunate to work at the start with the three most inspirational people in my career – Tony Coburn, Brendan Leishman and Wilo Muwadda. They hammered home how important it is for our work to be black and culturally appropriate. I'm thankful to those who have influenced me and helped me grow as a professional, to have earned their trust that when I open my mouth and speak that my words are heard and that they are honest and true. I grew up without having that type of information or the support that I now help provide. Being same-sex attracted, I certainly had cultural support from my peers but not the type of education and awareness that I know is important for all same-sex attracted people.

Tony, Brendan and Wilo were the ones who said, 'You have all this skill, now let's turn it into a trade.' It's important to say that I have never done anything by myself; it's only been with the help of others. Working with my people makes me want to go to work. Watching them learn and seeing them achieve makes me want to go to work, as well as helping the professionalism of newcomers. Passing on professional knowledge is like passing on traditional knowledge.

It's important that the community stays linked together, especially for guys who aren't from Brisbane, but from further north. By staying linked, I don't mean drinking every Friday but where we eat our own food, talk the way we talk, and practise our culture. We have two social support groups, gar'ban'djee'lum in Brisbane and, in Cairns, Yupla Mipla Ahfla.[3] They operate as extended family groups, so what same-sex attracted people don't have with their own families at that point of time, they have within the group. You have a mum, a sista girl who will mother you like a mother, and strong Aunts like myself who will help if there's trouble. There's cultural responsibility that goes with all that – and I mean black gay culture.

We'd rather eat the goose

We have a number of culturally appropriate programs in the 2 Spirits office that would create good, sustainable outcomes if only we had the funding. We're not about plucking the golden goose to line the nest with glory feathers. We'd rather eat the goose.

Condoman is our longest-surviving sexual health resource

in Queensland.[4] That's because our people own it and are very proud of it. At the time of the multi-million dollar Grim Reaper campaign, the first Condoman campaign in 1987 received just $4,000. When Condoman and Lubelicious were revamped in 2009, they gave us another $4,000. These new designs incorporate the Torres Strait Islander colours so that it now represents both Indigenous communities. We were inundated with requests for posters and educational comics, not only from across Queensland but nationally and internationally. This was yet another effective black campaign that has been put together and run by black people but poorly funded.

When I used to meet up with government people, all I wanted to do was chew 'em up and spit 'em out – but they only heard the bite and not the message, so I've had to modify my approach even if the annoyance is still there. We are still a portfolio being passed around, like 'it's your turn to deal', but we're not a deck of cards. We're tired of having some fulla who's had nothing to do with blackfullas in his life pick up the portfolio and want to implement improvements in our health. It's gotta stop. Black misery equals 101 hands that aren't culturally appropriate, and that leads to failed outcomes or outcomes painted up to be good but are really, to us, nothing.

Whether it's health or our legal status or equity, everything is tied to colonisation and the ignorance of the colonisers. We will never move forward until we unpack this. As traditional people, we understand that. When we bury our dead, we don't go to work on the same day that we put them in a hole to bury them and then go back to work. There's a system that we have which has been with us since the dawn of time, and these systems work for us. As Aboriginal and Torres Strait Islander people, we also can't be ignorant to politics as it's the way the country is run. We have to educate and inform policy.

Murray Island showed what we can do

By the time I finish working, I'm not going to be able to say, 'We are in charge', but I will be able to say that I took part in cutting the road towards that day. From my first job cane cutting, I helped in July 2014 to coordinate one of the biggest-ever global Indigenous HIV conferences.[5] This was when I, as a Murray Islander, showed the world what we can do professionally. Being part of 2 Spirits and with my colleagues, we proudly showed people our work. We spoke to people from Mexico, New Zealand, Guatemala, Chile, Jamaica, and many African nations, and to Canadian Indians and First Nations People from America. I have never felt more fulfilled, including when I was performing for them at the opening ceremony – and I never dance culturally down here.

This was a moment for my mums and my family, a moment for my nan who got stolen, and for my struggle in getting to where I am now. I was proud to let this international mob know that I'm part of a traditional response to HIV that has more outcomes than western service providers supporting the same people. I was letting them know that this is how we rock and roll. They understood our work. As Indigenous people of the world, they understood that all we want is for our people and culture to survive without prejudice.

OutBlak Adventures

Violet Buckskin, Naomi Hicks,
Tempestt Sumner-Lovett, Kym Wanganeen,
Raymond Zada

OutBlak Adventures was a performance project exploring personal, funny and moving stories of coming out and what's it like to be different in and out of family. The show was created by eight performers and artists from South Australia's Aboriginal and Torres Strait Islander gay, lesbian community, together with family members. They are Chris Bromley, Violet Buckskin, Naomi Hicks, Liz Hurrell, Tempestt Sumner-Lovett, Kym Wanganeen, Raymond Zada, Claudine Buckskin, Violet's mother, and Naomi's children and nieces. The nations of the performers include Gunditjmara. Kaurna, Latji Latji, Narungga, Ngarrindjeri and Wirangu.

The show was mounted in 2010 as part of Feast, Adelaide's Queer Cultural Festival, and featured song, storytelling, dance, drag, theatre, visual art and multi-media. As well as the Feast performances, it toured country South Australia, to Murray Bridge, Barmera, Whyalla and Port Augusta. *OutBlak Adventures* was a national first.

This chapter has been contributed by five of the eight performers, in collaboration with Margie Fischer, the project mentor.

Kym Wanganeen

OutBlak Adventures gave me the freedom to speak from the heart. I felt liberated speaking to a room full of friends, family and strangers. It took a lot of courage for us eight performers to travel around regional South Australia talking openly as Aboriginal people about our sexuality and sharing our joys and struggles. For some of those who know us, it was the first time they had heard some of our most inner thoughts and experiences that only being Aboriginal Gay and Lesbian could bring. What stands out the most for me during the *OutBlak Adventures* tour is how we were like one big family, bonding in a way that will stay with us for the rest of our lives. I felt a real connection between each of us performers, a refreshing realness and understanding.

For the opening in Murray Bridge, I rang my Aunty Mum (God Bless) and asked her permission to speak about the suicide of a very close and immediate family member. I was passed onto the eldest brother, and explained that nothing identifying would be said. I explained also that it was important to mention the suicide in the show, as there may be someone watching that could be contemplating suicide or someone in the audience who may know of someone that is feeling that way. As I spoke to him, I was crying down the phone in the dressing room. He said to me that if it will help anyone not to go down the same path, then it was okay to speak about it.

My Aunty's choir was opening our show with a Welcome to Country performance. Seeing her sitting in the front row and seeing me open the show was nerve-racking to say the least. I had to not look at her in the front row because I knew if I did I would of broke down crying on stage, and I had to focus on an empty seat near the back row every time I looked toward the audience. This is some of what I recounted:

There were times I have lost important people that helped shape my world ... losing family/friends/mentors ... One of those sad times was in Alice Springs, a very close brother/friend who helped me gain the courage to accept my sexuality and be proud of who I am. I remember him visiting me, bringing me a bunch of flowers and a carton of VB beer as a house warming present. It was only a day or two later that he was found hanging in his backyard. Every time I looked at those flowers in the vase, it would leave me in tears.

Then there was my cousin/brother who, like me, also was dealing with his sexuality. We were like each other's shadows: where one was the other wasn't far behind. While I was in Alice Springs, he was admitted to hospital in Adelaide. Shortly after he hung himself in the closet of his hospital room.

To lose these two significant people in my life made me feel completely alone, and helpless. Their deaths left me devastated with a sense of helplessness, that I couldn't be there when they were feeling sad, the same way they were there for me.

Every time I jumped on that tour bus, I was overwhelmed in knowing that this is it: I'm leaving myself open and vulnerable on stage for the world to see, but also that strong sense of pride knowing that we are doing something unique and inspirational for all who come along to the show. We ended our tour in Adelaide to a full house at the 2010 Feast Festival.

What we achieved throughout that tour was not only gaining a 2011 Ruby Award, but also an empowerment in knowing that we pushed our boundaries for an outcome. *OutBlak Adventures* was a journey of self-empowerment and personal growth, and it was about empowering others as well. It was a trailblazing journey into regional South Australia, too. We came together to share the innermost of ourselves, for all those that come from a place of homophobia and racism. We took our stories to the socially-isolated, we spoke the unspoken to our families and friends, and we connected personally to the audience, stirring up emotions either directly or indirectly.

Naomi Hicks

I was the Coordinator of *Queer Gifted and Blak*, which was what the show was called before it became *OutBlak Adventures*. Being asked to be the Coordinator was an honour and an opportunity to face my own challenges and fears. The Aboriginal and non-Aboriginal lesbian community in Adelaide is small: you know everyone, you've been with them or might have, or know who they are. The project was challenging as physical fear comes up about being an Aboriginal woman and a lesbian and everyone knows about you. Being the Coordinator and a participant was a professional job I could do with safety and be myself. We needed to be comfortable as a team. I trusted from the beginning that we were the right ones for the project. As an artist, the project gave me the opportunity to express my individuality and I was able to express what being an Aboriginal lesbian was to me. The goal for me and our family was to make a DVD music clip.

The clip has my sister, Amy, and my children, nieces and nephews in it: Whitney, Felicity, Tyrone and Shanika. I asked the kids if they would like to help me create a new song about their Mum being a lesbian and they said yes. Jesse was twenty, Whitney was eleven, and Flick was eight. I took off for the night and when I came back they'd already started. I was gobsmacked when I listened to their stuff. I was shocked and cried at how willing they were to accept me: they had no shame. I said: 'You sat at home all night and did this?' They did – and they kept going. They were totally keen.

The song is 'My Mum's a Lesbian and It's Okay'. They were in the energy, so I made time and built the song further. Jesse and I composed everything, and then we went back and forth with them again. We had Apple Macs and photos, and all the kids and I sat down with the lyrics of the song and we talked and wrote things down. The key things we wrote down are what I love about you and what is precious. For the show, we filmed us singing the song and added the photo images.

My Mum's a Lesbian and It's Okay

My Mum's a Lesbian and it's fine by me
My sisters gay and it's okay
Doesn't make her any different today
Hey hey her name is Nay
Doesn't matter if my Mum's gay

I have many amazing loving, caring children
My daughter's names are Jess, Whit and Flick
I love them so much I cuddle them to bits
At times I feel I'm not a good enough Mum
Blow that negative thought I am awesome

Mum teaches me to speak up when I'm upset with her
We are growing up with lots of love and feeling free
We are able to believe in all we want to be
Dream the biggest dreams and fulfil them you see
Dream, believe, achieve, we will receive

We must listen and care for each other
Because I don't have all the answers and I'm learning
It is our love, forgiveness, understanding
Compassion is my yearning, Hey I'm fine being gay
Freedom in my life every day

What I love about Mum, is she is the coolest
Round and round the roundabout it's just the fullest
Fun, fun, fun in the world
She's the best Mum in the world
What I love about sis is she loves me for
Who I am and I'm proud that she's gay
And it's okay, it's okay
What I love about Mum is she's so smart
And she has a great loving heart

I came out when Whitney was four – that was in 2002. I went to Feast's 'Picnic In The Park'; I felt equal at Feast. I taught the kids to accept everybody, I allowed them to grow up accepting and respecting diversity. They are older now and they still accept everyone and anyone. Whitney is sixteen now and has her own values and she is still accepting. I taught them to be free to be whoever they want to be, safely and freely. Right from when they were very little I taught them about drag queens and they loved the Dog Show at the Feast Picnic.

I had been part of a Feast song writing project before, working with Heather Frahn. The *OutBlak Adventures* project was about Aboriginal lesbian and gay people coming out to family and community and being safer. It was about Aboriginal lesbians and gays uniting together to face, to share and to honour each individual journey of coming out, and using personal experiences to support anyone else in the community who needs to feel safe and have someone to talk to.

It was so good to see the project grow beyond an idea. It allowed the participating artists who accepted the challenge to create one hundred percent what they wanted to create. The structure of the project and the show was flexible. The artists grew from creating an idea, to seeing, hearing and feeling the preparation and final presentation ... see the seed planted nurture and grow in to an amazing flower. Professionally, it helped me to learn more coordinating skills through helping each artist draw on their own story creatively. It all boils down to an amazing team.

This project brought us together. The group was so diverse, and it was a real education on types of being gay. There was family kinship between the performers. There was also a genealogical connection. Chris Bromley, one of the artists involved, was my second cousin and I didn't know. I was talking to another cousin who laughed at me and said: 'He is your cousin!'

I loved taking the show on tour as it continued to widen community personally and professionally for both Aboriginal and Non Aboriginal people. The project got me looking at my personal position in my community. At times it was tough, but I trusted the challenges and I learnt lessons of how to grow as a person.

Violet Buckskin

I had the opportunity to tell my story and so I did. If someone had told me in 2009 that I would be writing my own play and be performing on stage I would have said: 'Get fucked! I can't do that shit!!' But it happened.

It started when Naomi Hicks sent me an email chatting about this new project that she and a woman named Margie were trying to pull together for gay and lesbian Nungas to perform at the Feast Festival in 2010. Okay, I accepted to attend the meeting but said can't promise I will do it.

At our first meeting in Hindley Street, they were discussing concepts and ideas of what the show could be about. At the second meeting I heard the others speak about what they are going to do and I thought: 'Hang on, I could do my coming out story', and wondered how could I do it. I had a strong idea but didn't know how was I going to put it together. From then on, we met a few times as we put together our own pieces of performance. As I wrote my script I knew I couldn't play three people in order to tell my story, so I thought that it was a good idea that my mother could play the two parts that is herself and her sister who is now deceased. My mother accepted and said she would be honoured to be a part of my story and that she wouldn't mind being on stage in front of people to tell it.

We had to practice in our own home so my mother and I, after getting the script down pat, asked my three sisters and their children to be our Nunga audience. As we all know, blackfulla's biggest critics are their own families, ha! My mother and I were so nervous that day but we got through the play. We got a big cheer from all the kids and my sisters gave positive feedback. From then on, my Mother and I never looked back as we knew we were on our adventure, and so we performed in the *Queer Gifted and Black* in 2009.

Phew! The fucking show is over and it's time to celebrate. I ticked off one on the bucket list. The result for me was to see my father finally accept me by seeing life through my eyes and storytelling. This strengthened the bond between us, and he apologised for past events. He is now one of the biggest supporters when it comes to the Aboriginal LGBTI community.

In 2010, Margie called everyone asking: 'Hi guys, if we get funding to repeat the show, will you be willing to do it again?' For us performers in the group it was very interesting but scary at the same time because we wanted to tour everyone's stories to South Australian communities to show our own mob that we're not ashamed of who we are. When it came around, I made sure my play was up to date and a bit more tweeked to perfection and then, with the help of my mother, we went on our *OutBlak Adventures*.

Tempestt Sumner-Lovett

Coming into *Queer Gifted and Blak* – which became *OutBlak Adventures* – was a major change for me because I didn't have a gay and lesbian support group; it was hard to relate to people before the project. Naomi Hicks, the coordinator, invited me to join. I knew her through family, and I knew she was a lesbian.

At the time, I was nineteen and I'd only been out for two years. I had been to the Pride March when I was eighteen, and I went the Feast Festival opening night party. It was awesome. I didn't know there was an Aboriginal gay and lesbian group. I saw Naomi at the Pride March as she was part of First Australians in the March. Naomi introduced me to Feast.

I was out to my family. I have always had gay men in my life: they were always fun and my Mum loved them. My Aunty, my Mum's sister, is gay. I didn't want to go through being gay because I was nervous about my Dad. I was sixteen or seventeen then. I lost friends at high school as the news went around that I was gay, and they stopped talking to me. Then everyone went to separate schools. My new friend said she didn't care if I was gay but then she got distant. At my new school, I met a girl who was a complete lesbian with long hair, then she cut her hair short and she came out. Dad made jokes and said that I'd better not be a lesbian. He was probably joking but I took it that he was serious. So when I came out to my siblings I told them not to tell because I didn't want me Dad to find out. The following week my Dad wanted to catch up; when I met up with him, he put his arm around my shoulder and said:

I want to talk to you about something. Now I know you don't like boys and that's okay. If you ever need to talk you can come over. Now, stop your drinking!

I think my step-Mum found out and told him. That was the year that I went to Pride March and met Naomi.

OutBlak Adventures tour rehearsals were exciting. Before the shows when we were all getting ready, there was so much positive energy and nerves flying around. We all just bounced of each other. It was a really good thing to experience. We were each other's support. Performing in the country was new, and I was scared and excited. I talked to people after the show and I remember people giving me a pat on the back for coming out so young. Lots of people congratulated me. I loved hearing other people's coming out stories. It was good to see all of us had the same battles.

'Feelings' was the first song I wrote. It's about a girl who is a friend and you want more. She is straight and being more than friends could be more complicated and risky.

Your eyes give me feelings
That I can't explain
And your smile is like sunshine taking out the rain
And I don't want to see you as more than just a friend
But I can't help these feelings I'm feeling for you

CHORUS
I've got these feelings inside and I don't know what to do
I've got these feelings inside
I feel for you. I feel for you. I feel for you.
Do you feel it too? Do you feel it too?

I think I want to tell you how I really feel
And I can assure you that these feelings are real
But I don't want to see you as more than just a friend
But I can't help these feelings I'm feeling for you

This song is about my first relationship – a relationship that you know is a bad thing, and the fact that you still love that person but also understand different places would be best for both of you. Writing songs became therapeutic. It sucks being a songwriter and having a girlfriend as it's like having a diary that they can read!

Having the project in *OutBlak Adventures* of writing my own song about my coming out made me realise how much support I had from family and the project group. The friendships continued to grow, especially with Violet, Kym and Naomi. From then on the whole group was my support group. This is my song 'Coming Out' that I wrote:

We sat down at the table
I was feeling a little unstable
My mother told us some bad news
That her life was nearly through

It's not easy coming out
My whole future was in doubt
Now I'm living my life free
With my girl and family
I didn't know what to say
Then I told her I was gay

I knew at such a young age
I thought something was wrong
So many questions I'd asked why
So then I thought I'd rather live a lie

It was my first ever live solo performance. I was scared.
Having Naomi as a musician/performer was extra support as
we both played guitar and sang, and she helped me get my voice
just right. I hadn't thought of being a solo artist but that's where
it started and later the gigs started rolling in. I've become a
stronger person being around Aboriginal queer events. It was
pretty much the only positive in my life at that stage. Now I feel
comfortable holding my girlfriend's hand at the Spirit Festival,
a big event I've performed at. I am also part of Blak Lemons,
a lesbian support group that Violet started at the Health In
Difference Conference when we did the show there.

Raymond Zada

Theatre can be a great way to escape from our lives and be
engulfed in a world of fantasy. It also allows us to create a space
where we can stand up and talk about things we may never
normally have the opportunity to bring up. *OutBlak Adventures*
fits squarely within the latter type of theatre.

After the success of our 2009 performance of *Queer Gifted
and Blak* during the Feast Festival, we were understandably on
a high and it was suggested we could tour the show to regional
South Australia so more people could hear our stories. We were

all very enthusiastic about the idea and perhaps, deep down, we were thinking it probably wouldn't happen.

When Margie Fischer let us know we'd got funding to do the regional tour, it all became very real. Initially we had planned our tour to include the Far West Coast and Eyre Peninsula but, by the time we factored-in rehearsals, travel time, and budget, we had to limit the tour to four regional centres: Murray Bridge, Barmera, Whyalla, and Port Augusta. Our final performance would take place in Adelaide during the Feast Festival.

Our publicity had the tag line: 'This show has been a hit in Adelaide and Sydney. Now we're taking our biggest step ... we're bringing it home to family and friends.' For all of us, this was absolutely the case, at least one performer had family and friends in each of the locations we would visit.

Performing to audiences in Adelaide and Sydney was relatively easy. Adelaide offered the advantage of us having a group of supportive friends in the audience, while the Sydney audience would mostly be strangers and we were there to talk about our successful show. For the regional tour, there was no telling who we might see in the audience when we walked out on stage to share our stories.

For me personally, my hometown of Port Augusta was going to be my biggest challenge as my dad and my older brother lived there. My dad was going to be away for work on the date we were due to perform. However, my older brother and his family would still be in town – along with a heap of cousins. The thing that made it most challenging is the fact that my older brother is the one member of my immediate family who I never actually came out to. In 1992, he was living in Queensland when I was coming out and it wasn't something I wanted to do over the phone. As these things go, there was never really a 'right' time to tell him and, eighteen years later, I found myself on a trajectory to arrive in my hometown to talk about it on stage!

He had met my boyfriends and I had no doubt he knew about my sexuality but I'd never come out to him like I had with my parents and three other siblings. In my performance I shared my coming out story with the audience and, at each venue, each show brought me one step closer to standing on stage in Port Augusta and not knowing if my brother would be at the show.

Touring with the others was great fun. We had all really bonded during rehearsals and enjoyed each other's support as we prepared to embark on our journey together. Most of us grew up in country areas and I don't think any of us could ever have imagined that one day we'd be driving back into town to stand up on stage and talk about our sexuality.

Our first performance was at the Town Hall in Murray Bridge. It went well and there was some small comfort knowing we were only forty-five minutes from Adelaide. It didn't seem too much like we were driving out into the country.

The shows weren't just challenging for the performers; we were very open about what we shared and nothing was taboo. Naturally, we were sensitive about the topics we raised but any discussion around sexuality and coming out generally touches on suicide too.

A crucial part of the tour was having the opportunity to hang out with audience members after each performance. We provided food and drinks at each venue and it was a great opportunity to talk more about the things we mentioned in our stories. This was particularly important around the issues of suicide and acceptance, and the feedback we received assured us that what we were doing was important and appreciated.

One week later, we were on our way to Barmera. Then, for the third Saturday in a row, we were back on the bus driving to Whyalla. My nerves about performing in Port Augusta were rising with each week and on this particular Saturday we drove right through Port Augusta to get to Whyalla. I was pleased we were driving straight through as I wasn't ready to get up on stage in my hometown.

Bizarrely, my twin brother had been living in Whyalla and had moved to Perth only a month or so before. I had already come out to him and could have coped with him being in the audience but I'm not sure his conservative girlfriend would have been prepared for our show's content.

In two weeks' time, we would be performing our final show of the tour in Port Augusta. I decided I would drive to Port Augusta to visit my family during our weekend off, to talk to my brother about the show and to put up some tour posters. I visited my Nan and mentioned I'd be back the following week to do a show. I was intentionally vague about the content. I went down the main street with my posters but could only bring myself to put up one poster on the notice board inside Woolworths. It didn't look too conspicuous amongst all the other notices.

That night, I phoned my brother to say hello and drop by. That's when he told me something I wasn't expecting – he wasn't in town! So I found myself in a position I didn't want to be in. I was all psyched-up to visit him and tell him about the show and its content but, just like eighteen years ago, it wasn't something I wanted to do over the phone. We chatted for quite a while and I managed to avoid any mention of the show. I wasn't sure I could get away with slipping back into town the following week to do the performance but I was willing to give it a try.

After I hung up from our call, I thought my plans had gone to shit. Then my phone rang; it was brother again. His first words were: 'Oh, by the way, we're coming to see your show next week.' We both laughed and I said: 'Okay.' I was elated. The months of worrying about performing in Port Augusta were forgotten and I grabbed the rest of the posters, jumped in the car, and drove down the main street. I stuck up posters anywhere I could get away with it. It was late on a Saturday night, so I took my time putting up ten posters along the street. Even writing about it makes me beam.

Getting onto the bus with the others to drive to Port Augusta the following weekend, I remember being excited to be heading home. I had my usual nerves about getting up to perform but I was pleased my brother and his wife would be in the audience.

Backstage I had a peek out to the audience – there he was, sitting with his wife and his two children. Suddenly, I ran through everything I talk about in my performance to decide what I should take out. My niece was thirteen and my nephew was ten. I was comfortable with talking about my sexuality in front of them but how was I supposed to talk about myself wanting to commit suicide when I was their age?

In the end, I didn't censor myself and I presented my story as I had at each previous performance with the big difference being when I got to part about my brother. On that afternoon, eighteen years after I first came out, my brother went from being the only member of my immediate family who I hadn't come out to, to being the one member of my family who knew my entire coming out story and what it was like for me growing up. It felt amazing to be able to share that with him.

After the performance, my brother came up to hug me and tell me he loved me. It was the perfect end to the tour and was great preparation for our final performance in Adelaide where my Mum lives. I was ready to let her know about the show.

My mum and my best friend both feature prominently in the early part of my coming out story, so it was great to have them both in the audience for the final show. Neither of them knew what it was like for me growing up and my suicidal ideation was something I had never talked about prior to my performance the year before.

Mum and I had always been very close but we grew apart a little after she found out I was gay. Everything got back to normal after the first twelve months and sharing my story through the performance has brought us even closer together.

OutBlak Adventures allowed each performer to create a space where we could speak freely and without interruption. It was an opportunity to talk about things we had never previously been able to bring up, and it highlighted the diversity of our coming out stories as well as the similarities. We were able to discuss taboo topics because they were wrapped safely in the context of theatre.

Kym Wanganeen gave our acceptance speech at the Ruby Awards and he finished by saying: 'Kamungka Nudlu Kuma Nendi', which is Kaurna meaning 'Together we become one' – and that is the legacy of the *OutBlak Adventures* tour for all the performers.

'Words are like Weapons, They Wound Sometimes': Andrew Bolt, Gay White Men, and an Out and Proud Gay Black Man

Dr Mark McMillan

A gay white man with a law degree? Just the kind of Aboriginal who needs a special handout.[1]

That is what I read under the heading 'Aboriginal man helped', as I sat at my desk in Tucson, Arizona, on 19 August 2009. I was undertaking doctoral studies at the University of Arizona's James E. Rogers College of Law. The College is a place that has some of the planet's most distinguished Indigenous legal scholars. I was first drawn there in 2003, and the following year completed my Master of Laws in Indigenous Peoples Law and Policy. I then returned to the Jumbunna Indigenous House of Learning at the University of Technology, Sydney (UTS), vowing to return to Tucson – and the Law College – at some point to complete the doctoral program. I was able to achieve this when I won a Fulbright Scholarship in 2009.

Tucson is a long way away from where I grew up, and from where I secured my identity as a Wiradjuri person and as a gay man. Bear with me, as it was not that simple coming to grips with me being a gay man. The little town of Trangie is my home and it is where I derive a sense of self. Trangie is seventy-two kilometres west of Dubbo, thirty-three kilometres west Narromine, and one hundred kilometres east of Nygan. It has a population of around one thousand people.

Tucson by contrast has close to a million people. It is in the state of Arizona, located in the American south west, and is known as the site of the most continuously inhabited places in the United States of America – of white people. Argh! I hate this often [mis]quoted piece of information about Tucson because it is not true: Tucson and its surrounds have been continually inhabited by Native American tribes since time immemorial. Tucson is famous also for the amazingly beautiful mountain ranges that surround it and the aeroplane graveyard that is the resting place of many retired aircraft. My most enduring memories are the saguaro cactus and the Santa Catalina Mountains.

It was one of the days when I was sitting at my desk overlooking the Catalina Mountains. And, like most days, I had Cher 'playing' on my computer. This day I was actually listening to 'If I Could Turn Back Time'. Some of the lyrics of that particular song are now part of the title to this chapter: 'words are like weapons, they wound sometimes'. As an aside, I actually used the song (and video) to Cher's 1973 song 'Half Breed' in my doctoral dissertation public defence. Cher has a particular place in my world – and it is not just because I am gay, or that somehow loving Cher is a measure of 'gayness'. If that is true, then I am gayest of gays! But the irony of listening to *that* song at *that* moment, and of then using it years later as the basis for talking about my gayness, is not lost on me. Now, *that* song is indelibly etched in my mind, connecting place and time forever with Andrew Bolt's two articles, the subsequent court case, and my life as a gay Wiradjuri legal academic.[2, 3]

Back to the first article. Of itself, its heading was fairly benign. What shook me to my core was that I was looking at – after the heading – a colour picture of me. Yes, me! Me! Can you imagine how surreal that is: to be sitting at a desk, in another country, and then there is an article written *about* you.

I did not just stumble onto an image of me, or an article about me. I do not spend hours of the day 'googling' myself – which I have recently found is actually a 'thing'. It is known as 'ego surfing'! Who knew? Not me. It is a bit like Todd Carney and 'bubbling', it is a 'thing'. But alas, no! I was not doing any errant ego surfing. I had received a phone call from my Mum. Her words were, 'What the fuck did you do?' Clearly, I had no idea what she was talking about when she launched into her tirade. However, Mum was not angry with me; she was being protective of me. Like many black fellas of a certain age, there is tendency to assume that whatever you have done, or that if people are having a go at you, that somehow you brought this all on yourself. Hence, 'what the fuck did I do?' was the easiest way into the conversation by Mum. It worked. She had my attention. Mum explained that someone she knew had called her after reading about me in the *Daily Telegraph* – the daily 'newspaper' from Murdoch's News Limited stable in Sydney. The *Daily Telegraph*, apparently, syndicates Andrew Bolt's blog and his *Herald Sun* articles.

Mum was also a bit upset because the picture used by Andrew Bolt was taken when I received the Fulbright Indigenous Scholarship from the Australian-American Fulbright Commission in 2009. Mum had come to the awards ceremony in Hobart. She cried as she witnessed what a big deal it was to receive this scholarship. After I had been presented the award on the stage, Mum said to me, 'I am very proud of you, and Nan would be proud too'. This was *huge* for me. Mum was proud, and I had made her that way. It seems so small as I repeat it here, but I can tell you that it is something I will remember for the rest of my days. We are a little Aboriginal family from Trangie, and there I was on stage getting an award that neither Mum nor I had ever heard of growing up.

Mum got really pissed off that Mr Bolt had used the official photograph from the Fulbright Commission because Mr Bolt was sullying a 'life event' for her and me, and for my son. Mr Bolt's commentary complained that I had received the Fulbright Indigenous Scholarship:

> A gay white man with a law degree? Just the kind of Aboriginal who needs a special handout. (Hmm. I wonder which Aborigines missed out on this scholarship, thanks to McMillan's entry. Maybe the judges could explain.) ... It's some feat when Fulbright's affirmative action – an indigenous scholarship – ends up leaving this year's intake of Fellows looking just as white as ever.[4]

This little snippet of the article really, really upset my Mum. She was perplexed that Mr Bolt not only questioned my 'blackness' but also took shots at my sexual orientation – and very publicly. You see, my sexual orientation and my acceptance of it was a protracted and a very personal issue. Especially with my Mum. Like any mother, she was troubled by my 'coming out' – for herself, for my then wife, and ultimately for my son. I will get onto this a bit later. Mum now was pissed off that I was being outed in a way whereby I was not controlling it for myself or my family.

Back to 19 August 2009 and what these three sentences by someone who never had (and still has not) met me say about being queer and black in Australia.

Mum saw straight through Mr Bolt's words. She asked me whether Mr Bolt was saying that I was not black enough to win an Indigenous scholarship? Or that gay white men who hold law degrees can never suffer from anything (disadvantage, depression, etc.)? Because – according to my Mum's interpretation of what Mr Bolt was saying – if you are a white homosexual male, then you are at the top of the heap. And my

Mum, like all mothers who endure their children's struggles with accepting their sexual orientation, was being made to relive my struggles and her struggles of my *finally* accepting that I am a gay man. Not a gay 'white' man – just a gay man.

Mum also observed Mr Bolt's suggestion that I had won the scholarship at the cost of a 'deserving, disadvantaged, heterosexual black man'. And Mr Bolt was calling on the judges to explain my 'whiteness' and 'sexuality' because surely this was a mistake: a gay white lawyer was surely taking the piss out of the Fulbright Commission? My Mum wondered if any scholarship – anywhere – was allowed to interrogate someone's sexual orientation and use that as the basis of determining whether someone 'deserves' the scholarship?

You can see that my Mum is a really smart woman. Value add that, she was now a really pissed off black woman. Mama bear wanted blood for the hurt to her cub. All this was still happening even though I still was yet to look at the article. So with my Mum offering the sweetest encouragement for me and my son (who was with me in the USA), she was also trying to explain her protection mechanisms. I still smile that she wanted to really seek redress and retribution in a particularly black way on someone who she was never likely to meet.

Mum hung up and I was worried. I was worried because this 'thing' must be big if my Mum was calling me from Australia offering protection. I was worried because Mum was clear that my sexual orientation was being publicly consumed – without my participation. This means that I was not in control of who, what and where. Who was making comments? What would be the implications to me and my son? And where and how the fuck was I supposed to respond to this very public intrusion – and now demand – around my 'gayness' and 'whiteness' and my 'aboriginality'. So, I tried to read the article.

I felt physically sick when I first read the article. It was not making any sense. In that moment, life was not making any sense. I have never been on Andrew Bolt's radar – or so I thought. What had I done? How did I offend him? When did I offend him?

I must have read the article twenty or thirty times. For the life of me, I could not (and still can't) work out what was Andrew Bolt's message. What was his point? The article that started it all off contained two images: the first was a head and shoulders shot of me taken at Jumbunna Indigenous House of Learning at UTS, and the second was a group photo of the 2009 Fulbright scholarship recipients (including someone who is obviously a man who has dark skin colouring standing in the middle of the back row):

> It is wonderful to see a rare and wonderful opportunity like this being offered to someone from a race that faces so much discrimination and poverty just because of the colour of their skin:
> ... Mark McMillan has received the 2009 Fulbright Indigenous Scholarship sponsored by the Department of Education, Employment and Workplace Relations. Mark, who is a senior researcher at Jumbunna Indigenous House of Learning, University of Technology, Sydney, will go to the University of Arizona's James E. Rogers College of Law to undertake the newly established Doctor of Juridical Science in the Indigenous Peoples Law and Policy Program.
>
> McMillan has also been chosen by Reconciliation Australia [RA] as the face of *Which One of These Men is Aboriginal?* – its campaign to break down racist preconceptions that so hurt other members of his community of white Aborigines.
>
> RA lists his other qualifications: *A 40-year-old Wiradjuri man, Mark hails from Trangie, NSW. A law graduate from the ANU in Canberra, Mark also has a Masters of Law from the University of Arizona and will finish his doctorate – also at the University of Arizona – in 2010. Mark is Senior Researcher at*

the Jumbunna Indigenous House of Learning Research Unit at the University of Technology and is a Board member of the Trangie Local Aboriginal Land Council, Metro Screen and the NSW Mental Health Association. He is a proud father of an 11-year-old son, a proud gay man, rugby player, partner and active member of his community.

A gay white man with a law degree? Just the kind of Aboriginal who needs a special handout.

(Hmm. I wonder which Aborigines missed out on this scholarship, thanks to McMillan's entry. Maybe the judges could explain.) ...

It's some feat when Fulbright's affirmative action – an indigenous scholarship – ends up leaving this year's intake of Fellows looking just as white as ever ... And, no, that's certainly not Mark in the middle of the back row [in the group photo]. Mark is Aboriginal, you see ...

McMillan describes the agony of *not* being discriminated against for being Aboriginal: *I am a blonde-haired, blue-eyed, fair-skinned Aboriginal Australian. Every time I look in the mirror, that's what I see ... As a child, I grew up expecting everyone to be like me, to look like me – with the blonde hair and blue eyes.*

Clearly, my naive ideas about how Aboriginal people were 'supposed' to look were wrong. But being Aboriginal and fair and blonde was normal to me and I grew up in a world where I was treated 'normally'. Along the way however, I noticed that not everyone was receiving the same brand of treatment and that made me angry. It has taken a while to let go of that anger ...

Impeding my growth from that young person into the adult I wanted to become was the profound issue of identity. I was a 'white' black man ... I was becoming a victim.

Racism sure has come a long way in this country if the problem now is that some people aren't black enough.[5]

Hopefully, you will get a sense of why I am confused. Not about who I am or my sexual orientation, but about why

I irked Andrew Bolt so much that he would write this article about me (and a second article about me and other 'fair skinned Aborigines' distributed two days later)? Why was he so upset that I had received an award? An award that I applied for, that I was interviewed for, and then I was granted. I had to tell a group of people my life story and explain to them why such an award would benefit other Aboriginal and Torres Strait Islander people and communities. You see, that was a condition of the application. I had to talk about how – if I received the award – it would be of benefit to the Aboriginal and Torres Strait Islander community. It was easy to talk about because that is how I grew up: being part of an Aboriginal family and community. I did not have to make anything up or embellish, because it is how it is! The Federal Court of Australia has now ruled that I am indeed, an Aborigine.[6] This came about as a result of Mr Bolt's articles.

According to Mr Bolt, my Fulbright Scholarship is not an award any more – it is a handout. By an extension of this logic, all prestigious academic awards are – in fact – handouts. From his article, does Mr Bolt infer that there are not enough Aboriginal people to earn and compete for such awards? To extend his logic that Fulbright scholarships are now 'handouts', is Mr Bolt suggesting that Fulbright awards to non-Indigenous recipients must also be viewed as handouts? And, that all award winners are not receiving such awards for the recognition of their potential and excellence? Instead, that what they were awarded was a handout? Could the same be said of Rhodes Scholarships? Handouts? I am not sure that the recipients of these kinds of awards would actually be happy that their achievements have been denigrated in this way. Is Mr Bolt arguing that not only is the scholarship a handout – but also that it should only be 'handed out' to blacks (as in the black physical colouring of a person's skin) – who meet *his* threshold of disadvantage and colour? Quite the combination isn't it? Now throw into the mix sexual orientation as being a criterion in Mr Bolt's concept of 'deserving'.

So, being awarded a prestigious scholarship brought suspicion to me being black, and derided me from being gay and having a law degree. All of these factors combined – for Andrew Bolt – suggest that I cannot be Aboriginal. Or if I am Aboriginal, then I am gammon, that my family is gammon and that my community is gammon.[7] Mr Bolt never talked with me before this article. He never talked with anyone from my family or anyone who knows me or my family or my community. People from Trangie know me and my family. Why? Because we are in the community! People from Trangie know our history, because we are part of theirs and they are part of ours. They might be able to tell you stories of how we grew up in Trangie. It was a terrific way to live. I love Trangie, its people and where it sits in place on Wiradjuri country.

But back to my Aboriginality and Mr Bolt's invisible digs at my blackness. Well, you know what? Fuck him! Because ... I am! I am a proud Wiradjuri man. That is what I am, and that is who I am. Because, as the Federal Court has said:

> By their pleadings both Mr Bolt and HWT have admitted that each ... Mr McMillan ... are of Aboriginal descent; that since each was a child, at the times of publication of each of the Articles, and at present, each person did and does genuinely self-identify as an Aboriginal person and did and does have communal recognition as an Aboriginal person.[8]

I am also a gay man. I believe that it was being brought up black that instilled in me the resilience to face and accept that I am a big poof. That I can own it! And that I can be proud of it. Not be proud of it to show off – but being proud of it so that my son can see that you have the right to be you. That every person has the right to exist as they are, free from discrimination and

harassment because as – Lady Gaga says – I was 'born this way'.
I was born black and so I was born gay. Being born black was
never an issue for me. As I have stated publicly in 2008 (and
these are my words – words that Mr Bolt used to denigrate
me by taking some of these words out of context so as to serve
his purpose of having a shot at me; my Aboriginality and by
denigrating my sexual orientation[9]):

> Growing up with a strong sense of social justice was not
> something that ever needed to be explained in the abstract.
> We shared the experiences common to many people from
> disadvantaged backgrounds, and our grandmother was very
> insistent that all people were treated not just equally, but well.
> I knew that I was Aboriginal from a very young age although,
> in our household, Aboriginality was never discussed as being
> something special or anything less than ordinary. It was just
> who we were, both as individuals and as a family. I never looked
> at my family members and thought, 'Wow, you look really
> Aboriginal.' Or, 'Gee, you look really white!' ...
>
> [With respect to my understanding of identity, I said:] To say
> that I was incapable of explaining what was happening to me
> and within me is not really the case. It would be more exact to
> say that I simply didn't know what was happening to me. Every
> human transition from young person to adult, then to more
> mature adult, etc., is a journey. And, impeding my growth from
> that young person into the adult I wanted to become was the
> profound issue of identity. I grew up in place where everyone
> knew I was Aboriginal / part of an Aboriginal family, but the
> moment I moved outside of that environment, I found I had to
> constantly explain away that aspect of my identity.
>
> How do you begin to explain to someone that you have
> started to question everything you ever believed about
> yourself because you are required to defend it so often? ... My
> insecurities about my identity not only hindered my ability
> to educate people about the diversity of Indigenous people,

but also fed a stereotype associated with minorities that I had always rallied against. I was becoming a victim. I was becoming someone else's label. To complicate things, I was also struggling with another aspect of my identity – something else which society tries to label and define; I was gay. I found this difficult because I couldn't relate on any level with the gay stereotype. I mean, I played sport for Christ's sake![10]

This is why the words of Mr Bolt actually stung me. Like nearly everyone I know who is same-sex attracted, coming to terms with your sexuality is an individual and unique journey. The individuals' journeys are – in nearly all cases that I know of or have been part of – quite traumatic. That journey is an ongoing one.

My particular journey to acceptance of my own sexuality was traumatic. It continues to be so because of the public intrusion into my queer understandings and knowing by people like Mr Bolt. The trauma around these public intrusions is due to their demand to associate my queerness and blackness as being one in the same identity. And, that I must account for one identity through the other. I am black and queer. Yes! But they are not the same identity. I will try and get to these by answering these questions: What is the connection between being black and queer – for Mark McMillan? Why did I have issues about being queer? Why did I fight against it for so long? How did I use the resilience developed through my Aboriginal identity to cope with and accept (eventually) my queer identity?

Being publicly challenged about your sexual orientation is, put simply, fucking awful. The only time that I have been so publicly attacked for being gay is by Mr Bolt. Even though he said in the Federal Court that he was not attacking nor making fun of my sexual orientation, the issue was: what did I feel? You can see from the snippets from his first article that he was saying I was 'white' not black – and a poof to boot. The public discussion about my sexual orientation is littered, not only in Mr Bolt's articles, but also from the media reporting of the trial itself. Mr Bolt was attacking me and the other Aboriginal people for being not 'black enough', however it was Mr Bolt's discussion of my sexual orientation that saw him lose his cool while in the witness box. Mr Bolt's reaction to being questioned in court over him referring to my sexual orientation when he was talking about Indigenous identity was reported in the *Age* newspaper:

> It took until 3.25pm on his second day in the witness box, but *Herald Sun* columnist Andrew Bolt finally lost his cool yesterday. As Herman Borenstein, SC, asked Bolt why he had appended the term 'gay' to his description of Aboriginal lawyer/academic Mark McMillan in a 2009 blog post, Bolt, who had remained implacably calm through almost eight hours of cross-examination, exploded. 'For you to first smear me with the Holocaust and now try to portray me as a gay bigot is an unforgivable travesty,' he fumed. Bolt denied any suggestion he was homophobic, saying the godfather of his children is gay.[11]

Mr Bolt connected my Aboriginality to my sexual orientation. No one else did that. He did it. Then he was outraged that a simple question was put to him: if Mr Bolt was talking about Aboriginal identity, why did he even utter a word about me being gay? What has my sexual orientation got to do with my Aboriginality? Clearly Mr Bolt was upset for being called out on it:

> 'I don't share your assumption that being gay is an insult,' [Andrew Bolt] told Mr Borenstein, who had in fact offered no view on homosexuality. Mr Borenstein did, however, say many people – 'perhaps even some *Herald Sun* readers' – were homophobic, and suggested describing Mr McMillan as a 'gay white man with a law degree' in a blog on August 19, 2009, was calculated to inflame prejudices of Bolt's readers.[12]

Bam! My sexual orientation was being talked about – very publicly – so as to incite the possibility of people being offended by my being gay. This is in addition to me being held up for ridicule for not being black enough to claim my Wiradjuri identity. To make matters worse, Mr Bolt suggested in another article that I am gender confused.[13] So now I am a gay white man who is confused about my gender identity – and it was raised in the Court. Justice Bromberg referred to this in his judgment, 'Mark McMillan winning the Black Women's Action in Education Foundation Scholarship originally intended to help educate black women, not white men.'[14] The disdain towards me for not being black enough, for being gay and gender confused, and more broadly for the assault on 'real' black people by corruptly 'scuffling at the trough' is apparent in Mr Bolt's description:

> And the man to the left, Sydney law academic Mark McMillan, has won one of our richest prizes for Aboriginal students – the Fulbright Indigenous Scholarship. If, studying the faces of these two 'Aboriginal' men you think this is surely the most amazing stretch of definition, you're wrong. McMillan has gone one better still: he's also won the Black Women's Action in Education Foundation Scholarship, originally intended to help educate black women, not white men. But that's modern race politics at our universities and anywhere else where grants and privileges are now doled out. Hear that scuffling at the trough? That's the sound of black people being elbowed out by white people shouting 'but I'm Aboriginal, too'. Hark! – is that a man's voice I now hear bellowing: 'And I'm an Aboriginal woman.'[15]

The reason that this matters is because this is what can happen when someone else makes comments about you with the express intention of making other people hate you on the basis of their homophobia and prejudices. How did I resist the urge to fight Mr Bolt about the gay smearing? Rather than just concentrate on fighting for Aboriginal identity? It is because my Nan, Mum and all my family taught us – yes, taught all of my family – that being Aboriginal is what we are. Or, more precisely – Wiradjuri. That makes you strong and you *must* be proud.

I have lived a life where I can accept that fact that I may look a certain way and act a certain way ... but I am Wiradjuri. I cannot change that as much as I cannot change the direction of the earth's rotations around the sun. So it was, that I entirely accepted who I am as a whole being – a queer black man. I could fight that fight because I accept what I cannot change in myself – nor do I want to. Being queer is part of what makes me a complete human being. Nan, Mum and my Aboriginality allowed me understand that it is okay to be gay because 'it is, what it is'.

Thanks Mum and Nan!

A Lore unto Themselves

Steven Lindsay Ross

The Big Bang Theory tells us that after the start of the universe, there was an amorphous cloud of atoms and particles. The catalyst for the coalescing of the gases and dust were very small differences in that early cosmic soup. If it wasn't for these differences and mutations, the universe would never have formed.

I find enormous comfort in this: that nature thrives on difference.

When you're Aboriginal, you're always reminded of your difference – from the sideways glance of a shop assistant to the excitable look of school children when you're delivering a Welcome to Country. When you're Aboriginal and gay, there are layers of difference and this can be challenging for some people.

Since the emergence of the marriage equality debate, there have been a number of squeaky conservative cogs who provide fodder for the media, and who see eye-to-eye with the conservative Coalition Government. These voices shudder at the thought of anything that challenges their notion of 'normal'. I'm thinking of the opinions of folks such as the boxer Anthony Mundine. In late 2013, he unleashed a homophobic rant on

Facebook following the screening of an episode of *Redfern Now* on ABC television. The particular episode that upset him had depicted the reverberations of grief, homophobia and racism when an Aboriginal man became a sole parent following the sudden death of his white male partner. Mundine posted:

> Watching redfern now & they promoting homosexuality! (Like it's ok in our culture) that ain't in our culture & our ancestors would have there head for it! Like my dad told me GOD made ADAM & EVE not Adam & Steve.[1]

His comments released a flood of memories for black LGBTI people like me, and gave room for more Indigenous people to express their homophobic beliefs.

Not only is anti-homosexual rhetoric cruel and demeaning, it is also increasingly out of step with mainstream Australia. In the case of Mundine, it was out of step with Aboriginal and Torres Strait Islander (ATSI) leaders and thinkers and with the wider community. Of course, diversity of thought exists in the ATSI community. And to that end, many Indigenous LGBTI people experience homophobia and transphobia in their own lives. Unfortunately, the perpetrators are often their own people or family.

I was about five years old, I reckon. My father – a Wiradjuri man – and I were getting out of our old family Valiant. We lived in what was called 'the new mission', in Macauley Street in Deniliquin, New South Wales. All the blacks had been moved to Deniliquin from Moonacullah Mission some twenty year earlier. The charming houses built for the Moonacullah Aborigines were fibro and had been erected on the fringes of town, not far from the sewerage plant. A stiff northerly breeze carried the smell of raw faeces into our street, and if there was an operational issue with the works, the town's sludge would come bubbling up into our bathrooms. This was not exactly a welcoming experience of assimilation. Deniliquin was, and still is, a pretty town on the Edward River (*Koletch*, in our Wamba Wamba language). Ever since I can remember, the sign coming into town announced that there were eight thousand people living there.

On this particular summer day, my father had been 'looking after me' ... I would sit in the corner of the local TAB while he bet on the horses. We arrived back in Macauley Street afterwards to discover he'd left the house keys inside. He ordered me to climb through the window to open the door, but I refused. His response was to abuse me and for the first time in my life I was called a 'poofter'. I didn't know what this word meant but, considering the tone of its delivery, I knew it couldn't be a good thing.

Over the following years I heard this word a lot more and figured out its meaning. Given my pre-pubescent romance with another boy, I soon knew that *I was this thing*. This was the prism through which I saw my early sexuality. In the community I lived in, I did get a sense that homosexuality was not a good thing within our mobs. And, of course, like all homophobia and all bigotry, these attitudes were designed to de-humanise me, to marginalise me, and to keep me down.

In 1978, my mother wisely left my father and moved to Sydney with my sister and me. Mum moved in some pretty funky and arty circles, and we were often at bohemian parties in Balmain. My sister and I would hide under my mother's skirt while mysterious white people drank and danced and ate exotic food. The host of these parties was known as Aunty Sharon, a redhead with striking features and a beak-like nose, who spoke beautifully and loved hugging us kids. She was my mother's boss and she lived in Waterview Street, Balmain, with her girlfriend. My mother never had to explain any of this to me and I lapped up the experience, as any curious child would. I loved our visits to Aunty Sharon, and the look and smell of her house. My favourite thing was to fall asleep cuddling her life-sized Wonder Woman cushion.

In hindsight, these were formative years that helped to empower my sexual identity and sense of self-worth. My mother never sheltered us from these influences. I suspect she knew all my life that I was gay; when I finally came out to her in 1991, she said: 'Surprise, surprise'. My mother is a proud Wamba Wamba and Muthi Muthi woman and she knows her culture, her ancestors, and the way forward for her people. She spent her life working for the mob and instilling her knowledge into future generations through environmental work, weaving and storytelling. My father, on the other hand, is highly colonised: a former boxer, welfare-oriented, and a tragic figure of a man who was never there for any of his children. When I came out to my father, he told me he used to bash people like me. Whenever we fought, homophobic insults were not off limits.

I have seen this prejudice in other families in Deniliquin, too – we must have been a queer little community, given how many gay and lesbian relatives I have. One experience that springs to mind is that of my cousin Henry, who is transgender. Henry blossomed into Violet during her teen years. Not knowing how to deal with this change, her brothers were brutal and violent. Violet moved to Newcastle and rarely returned home. Small country towns are not the most hospitable places for young black kids, let alone young black LGBTI kids. Despite all this, there remained a staunch set of sisters, nieces, nephews and cousins who adored Violet, kept in regular contact and resisted, berated and belittled those small-minded brothers. This group also provided powerful protection for the rest of us LGBTI kids growing up. Hopefully, the prejudice of the old uncles dies with them. We were lucky enough to have Elder LGBTI people guide us through our childhood and coming-out phases.

Research and reports on the mental health of ATSI peoples

are confronting. The National Aboriginal and Torres Strait Islander Social Survey in 2008 found that thirty-three percent of young people aged 18–24 years reported high or very high levels of psychological distress.[2] This is more than twice the rate of fourteen percent for other young Australians.[3] Additionally, there was a total of 2,643 hospitalisations in 2008–09 for mental and behavioural disorders in Indigenous young people aged 12–24 years; this was three times the rate for non-Indigenous young people. Particularly concerning are the high rates of suicide amongst younger ATSI peoples. The highest age-specific rate of suicide for males was among 25–29 year olds, and for females was among 20–24 year olds.[4] As most people appreciate, suicide has enormous and intergenerational traumatic effects on families, communities and cultures.

For ATSI GLBTIQ peoples, the impact of colonisation and homophobia can have a double impact, thus bringing more pressure to bear upon mental health wellbeing. There has been some excellent work undertaken by the Australian Federation of AIDS Organisations (AFAO) in the late 1990s which produced the National Indigenous Gay and Transgender Consultation Report, authored by Gary Lee and Timothy Moore in association with AFAO's Indigenous Gay and Transgender Committee. This report found that isolation and discrimination can hinder testing for sexually transmitted diseases including HIV/AIDS. Importantly, the report also initiated an essential dialogue about perceptions of gayness in Indigenous communities.[5]

Since that time, mental health has emerged as a vital issue nationally and internationally, but there is a dearth of research and therefore a lack of meaningful policy responses. The advocate Dameyon Bonson has highlighted the importance of research and support for black GLBTIQ peoples particularly around mental health. In an article published in the *Guardian* in 2015, he stated:

People who identified as Indigenous and LGBTI suffered higher rates of depression, often self-medicated on alcohol and drugs and, in the worst cases, took their own lives ... International research tells us that Indigenous LGBTI people are up to forty-five times more at risk of suicide than the general population.

We don't have a clear picture of what the figures are in Australia because the research doesn't exist. As someone who is Aboriginal and working in suicide research, I realised that I had also become complacent to the fact that there is no health promotion material out there tailored towards this community, and we need to change that.[6]

Bonson has organised crowding funding and media coverage around mental health and suicide prevention for ATSI GLBITQ peoples, and he is promoting ongoing research and support by speaking at conferences. Clearly, more needs to be done in this field, and appropriate State and Federal – as well as community responses – need to be developed.

Homophobia and transphobia still find fertile ground in our communities. If anything good came from Mundine's incendiary comments, it was the chance for collective self-reflection by Aboriginal LGBTI peoples, along with their families and supporters. For every person who supported Mundine, there were dozens more who spoke out against his narrow-mindedness, promoting the loving acceptance of gays, lesbians and trans people in our community. Mundine's rant also encouraged support and advocacy for black LGBTI peoples in local and broader representations. The best example was an open letter by Black Rainbow, (a national coalition of ATSI gay, lesbian, bisexual, sistergirl, transgender and intersex peoples), that was published in the *Koori Mail*. The twenty-six signatories to this letter canvassed how the process of invasion has led some Indigenous people to adopt the distortions arising from colonisation and also to confuse some imported religious beliefs with those of Aboriginal and Torres Strait Islander cultures:

> We are a group of strong and fabulous Aboriginal and Torres Strait Islander lesbian, gay, bisexual, sistergirl (transgender) and queer people who would like to highlight our existence and the positive roles we undertake in our communities. We would also like to congratulate the makers of the first episode of *Redfern Now*, and to respond to recent homophobic comments in the mainstream and social media.
>
> Our 'Black Rainbow' peoples are making excellent contributions in politics, sports, arts, land rights, health, education, justice, business, science, research, the bureaucracy, healing, community life, family life and most importantly, in cultural survival and restoration. We are your family members, community workers, advocates and leaders. We bring strength and love to our communities.
>
> For some in our communities, however, they seem to be hung up on the lies that 'homosexuality is a white man's thing', and 'there wasn't homosexuality in traditional cultures', so we would like to share a few home truths.
>
> 1. Homosexuality exists in all cultures and all peoples – always has, always will. There was same-sex attraction in pre-invasion Aboriginal cultures, just as there is now. It might not have looked like the same as the lives available to us today, but you can rest assured, wherever there were humans, there was a diversity of sexual and romantic expressions. It is not an aberration. It is natural. It is as old as humanity.
> 2. Any straight man or woman who is challenged by homosexuality is often not comfortable in their own masculinity or femininity.
> 3. The process of invasion has seen some Aboriginal and Torres Strait Islander individuals and communities adopt views that are more aligned with some fundamental parts of Christianity, Islam or other religions that actively promote discrimination toward same-sex attracted people.

Unfortunately, some of our own peoples are buying into colonisation's lie and confusing some imported religious beliefs with Aboriginal and Torres Strait Islander cultures.

4. When people say 'I have many gay friends and family, but it's not our culture', it's like a white person saying 'I have many Aboriginal friends, but I don't want them in my house or marrying my daughter'. You are being a bigot.

5. One of the ways in which white colonisation works is to keep 'minorities' like women, Aboriginal people, gays and lesbians, multicultural communities and people with disabilities separate. Some of our people say they fight against racism, but their hatred of gay and lesbian Aboriginal people plays into the hands of white male colonial power.

6. All teenagers question their sexuality as a normal, healthy but often painful part of adolescent development. Aboriginal and Torres Strait Islander people who are questioning, or coming to terms with their sexuality are already at a much higher risk of suicide than others. The inaccurate comments made by Anthony Mundine are harmful to the emotional wellbeing of our brothers, sisters and peers.

7. For anyone to suggest there is something evil about how people are born, they are giving the doubtful teenager another reason to consider suicide. Through this hate, they are choosing to put the blood of their own people on their hands.

8. It confirms that not every Aboriginal and Torres Strait Islander person is an expert on every aspect of their cultures, and the media should not give credence to everything any one person says on a matter.

9. We challenge Anthony Mundine, in the spirit of healing and understanding, to meet with some of us, away from the media, to work together to build a better community for our mobs and our future.

We would like to thank and celebrate the creators, cast and crew of *Redfern Now*, particularly Kirk Page and Andrew

Wills, for their brilliance and honesty in storytelling, art and production – your work makes our lives better.

We write this letter to remind everyone that diverse sexualities do exist in Aboriginal and Torres Strait Islander communities, have always existed, and will continue to flourish. We stand proud and strong and will not be swayed by bigotry.

This is a cause for which many of us have died, and so we honour them by continuing to thrive.

We acknowledge and thank our partners, families, friends and many allies for their love and solidarity.

Most importantly, we want to say to anybody from a diverse sexuality – whether lesbian, gay, bisexual, sistergirl (transgender), intersex, queer or unsure – that it's okay to be who you are. There'll always be people trying to tell us we don't belong but we can take comfort knowing our cultures make us a part of something much bigger and stronger than even our loudest oppressors.

We are united, we stand strong and we reclaim our rightful places in our cultures.[7]

Gregory Phillips, who coordinated the development of the open letter, also stated:

Most importantly, we take this opportunity to send a message to anybody in our respective communities – be they lesbian, gay, bisexual, sistergirl, transgender, intersex, queer or unsure – we want to let them know that it's okay to be who you are. There'll always be people trying to tell us we don't belong but we can take comfort knowing our cultures make us a part of something much bigger and stronger than even our loudest oppressors. We are united, we stand strong and we reclaim our rightful places in our cultures.[8]

The responses from Phillips and other black GLBTQI peoples highlight the strength, resilience and intelligence in our communities. There are those who do who lack that support;

physical and mental health is undermined by homophobia and by a lack of understanding in our communities and in the broader Australian society.

The contrast between my mother's open-hearted embrace of my sexuality and my father's hateful reaction made me contemplate the idea raised by Mundine about the place of homosexuality in so-called 'traditional' Aboriginal culture. There are indications from some cultures around the world that diverse sexuality is an integral part of 'traditional' Indigenous life – for example, the sistergirls of the Tiwi Islands, or the Two-Spirit movement found among some Native American cultures.

There is also a logical and reasonable approach to this argument: Aboriginal people have been in Australia for more than 60,000 years in what many anthropologists describe as a triumph of survival and mathematics. Given the overwhelming evidence that homosexuality is biological, it is logical to assume that homosexuality would have been a part of such a social equation. It is estimated that there have been four billion Aboriginal people In Australia since the dawn of time. Four billion, and not one gay person? That just defies belief.

Some argue that our culture would have oppressed such behaviour. This raises some interesting questions, as well as some colonial mythologies. Which traditional Aboriginal culture is being referred to here? When white people colonised Australia, there were hundreds of Aboriginal cultures. To know the mores and values of every single Aboriginal culture would be a major feat of anthropological prowess – one of which I doubt Mundine and his ilk are capable.

This argument also ignores the major diversity between groups, and indeed within them. This is why a homogenous approach to government policy doesn't work, and why a consensus on constitutional reform will probably never work. We are as diverse as any other ethnicity and this must be acknowledged to really move forward. This idea of 'traditions' is also dangerous because it glues us to the past, rendering us immovable and static. It also sets up a system of haves and have-nots – those who have maintained their 'traditional' culture, and those who have lost it. All cultures change, and Aboriginal people would not have survived for so long had they not been adaptive and dynamic.

As for gay people being accepted in Aboriginal communities, I know a dozen or more black LGBTI people who are strong and powerful leaders in their communities. Some have led their mobs to successful native title consent determinations – a role that is built on trust. A native title case would include holding secret knowledge of sacred sites, family histories and land management practices, not to mention being entrusted to negotiate on behalf of thousands of claimants. This responsibility would not be given lightly. It is a position that involves trusting a person's character. The fact that LGBTI people have been entrusted in these processes speaks volumes for the support we have within our communities.

Of course, there will be narrow-minded people in our communities, too. We may dislike the Fred Niles, George Pells or Tony Abbotts of mainstream culture, but we are not surprised that those voices exist in a liberal democracy. There are narrow-minded Indigenous people. There are also Indigenous fundamentalists, climate-change deniers, racists and misogynists. When I think of these people, or when I hear their bullshit in the media, I think of my accepting, unsurprised mother. I think of my sisters fighting for my rights, and defending my cousin Violet, and I remember the embrace of that Wonder Woman cushion.

Part Three

Looking Out of the Mirror –
Essays

Dual Imperatives: Decolonising the Queer and Queering the Decolonial

Oscar Monaghan

Introduction

As a queer, mixed-race Indigenous person of colour, the question of how to resist the dual forces of heteronormativity and settler colonialism is central to my survival. I cannot separate the queer parts of me from the Aboriginal; nor can I separate the Aboriginal from the Chinese or Indian or, for that matter, the Anglo. I cannot bracket the queer when I am doing decolonising work (and I have never been asked to), and I cannot bracket the brown and black and *Indigenous* when I am resisting the heteropatriarchy (although I have been asked to). These fights are not the same fight, but they are intertwined; work in one can undo work in the other, and I am uninterested in work that liberates some while reinforcing the oppression of others. That they are intertwined, however, gives us scope for productive alliances: our resistance to settler colonialism can open spaces foreclosed by the colonial regime of gender and sexuality, and our resistance to the heteropatriarchy aids our decolonial work by highlighting the gendered and sexual dimensions of colonialism.

In this essay I bring together existing scholarship in the fields of Native/Indigenous, Queer Studies and Settler Colonial Studies to think about the necessity of a productive alliance at queer and Indigenous intersections.[1] In the first section, I briefly discuss the difference between colonialism and settler colonialism to better enable us to think about the logics at play in the Australian context. In the second section, I look at the relationship between settler colonialism and sexuality and gender, paying particular attention to the way native sexualities have been displaced and 'settler sexualities' imposed.[2] In the third section, I draw on scholars like Jasbir Puar, who complicates the ways we think about the relationship queer people can have with the state, to consider how queer political projects can reify the settler state and participate in imperialism.[3] In the fourth section, I nod to the possible alliances that emerge between Indigenous and Queer activisms when we take seriously the imperatives of both.

Before I proceed further, it is necessary to make some preliminary remarks about terminology. I use the term 'Indigenous' throughout this essay to refer to the peoples, 'communities, clans, nations and tribes' who are 'Indigenous to the lands they inhabit, in contrast to and in contention with the colonial societies and states that have spread out from Europe and other centres of Empire.[4] This term is not without its controversy and, as with any umbrella terminology, there is the risk of homogenising the diverse peoples who fall within its ambit.[5] I use it here in recognition of its political utility; Gayatri Spivak deployed the concept of strategic essentialism to 'express the utility for political consciousness-raising endeavours of placing a simplified and definable boundary around an identity category, thus rendering it recognisable and enabling mobilisation around it'.[6]

I. Colonialism and settler colonialism

Colonialism and settler colonialism are both expressions of imperialism, and both are characterised by a relationship of domination. However, though related, the two are discrete phenomena that establish distinct systems of relation. As Lorenzo Veracini notes, our analysis must attend to this difference as the distinction between the two 'create[s] different conditions of possibility for different patterns of relationships'.[7] By centring the distinction in our anti-colonial and decolonial work, we remain vigilant that decolonisation is not the same as settler decolonisation,[8] and that *settler colonialism* 'has been in many ways remarkably resistant to decolonisation'.[9]

Colonialism has multiple formations. Tuck and Yang define it primarily as exogenous domination – a relationship of 'spatial separation' and exploitation.[10] The metropole (the coloniser) expropriates and extracts 'fragments of Indigenous worlds, animals, plants and human beings' in order to create wealth for the metropole.[11] Veracini adds that a necessary distinction is maintained between coloniser and colonised, as colonialism imports a 'drive to sustain the *permanent* subordination of the colonised' that requires the categories of 'coloniser' and 'colonised' to exist.[12] The existence of the two categories enables the continual extraction of Indigenous resources for profit and first-world building; the successful colonial relationship is one that exists in perpetuity.

Settler colonialism is what emerges when the 'settlers come with the intention of making a new home on the land, a homemaking that insists on settler sovereignty over all things in their new domain'.[13] The settlers' interests in the lands and lives of Indigenous peoples extend beyond 'the selective expropriation of profit-producing fragments' – their interests are totalising and annihilating.[14] In the settler colony, there is 'no spatial separation between the metropole and colony'.[15] Indeed, the settlers seek the collapse of that category in pursuit of two complementary imperatives: (1) to establish and maintain control over Indigenous territories for the purposes of settler homemaking and the production of capital,[16] and (2) the disavowal of Indigenous claims to territory.[17] Thus, unlike the successful colony, which yearns to exist always, the successful settler colony is one that ceases to exist as the distinction between Indigenous and Settler is elided in order to facilitate the assertion of settler sovereignty.

We can see that the logic of colonialism is one that centres the colony-metropole relationship, whereas settler colonialism seeks to erase it in order to facilitate the nativisation of the settler state and the disavowal of Indigenous claims to territory.[18] The 'nativisation' or 'indigenisation' of the settler state is predicated on not just Indigenous dispossession, but Indigenous disappearance – and it remains an essential element of settler colonial desires. The terms denote not just a displacing or replacing desire, but, somewhat ironically, a desire for an *originary authority* that dissipates Indigenous claims to sovereignty and territory. The true desire is perhaps not for either the dispossession or disappearance of Indigenous peoples, but that they were never there (to be disappeared) in the first place. Of course, such a wish only makes sense in the context of an Indigenous presence, and this is one of the ways that the ongoing survival of Indigenous peoples provokes such a fundamental anxiety for the settler state. Writing in the U.S. context, Philip Deloria explains: 'Americans wanted to feel a natural affinity with the continent, and it was the Indians who could teach them such aboriginal closeness. Yet, in order to control the landscape they had to destroy the original inhabitants.'[19] The desire to be Indigenous to the land sits with the need to destroy that which is Indigenous. Patrick Wolfe describes the settler-colonial desire to disappear the native as the 'logic of elimination'. This eliminatory logic 'not only refers to the summary liquidation of Indigenous people … it strives for the dissolution of native societies,' so that the new settler society can be erected on the 'expropriated land base'.[20]

2. Settler colonialism and sexuality and gender

Gender and sexuality are significant sites around which settler colonialism has mobilised to dissolve Indigenous societies. Indigenous genders and sexualities have been (and are) used by settler colonial regimes to justify colonial occupation, territorial acquisition, and continue to serve as key locations for the 'promulgation of European modernity by settlers'.[21] Summarising a subset of Indigenous feminist and queer scholarship in the area, Scott Lauria Morgensen notes that this literature 'teaches that heteropatriarchal colonialism has sexualised [I]ndigenous lands and peoples as violable, subjugated indigenous kin ties as perverse, attacked familial ties and traditional gender roles ... all to transform indigenous peoples for assimilation with or excision from the political and economic structures of white settler societies'.[22] We can see, then, that the elimination of the native is carried out through the imposition of the colonial heteropatriarchal regime of gender and sexuality and the attendant settler colonial regulation of sex and gender.[23]

Michel Foucault's work around sexuality tells us that sexuality is 'an especially dense transfer point for relations of power'.[24] Critiquing Foucault, Ann Laura Stoler extends his argument to show how sexuality is a 'dense transfer point for specifically *imperial* power'.[25] The centrality of sexuality to colonial power relations helps explain its importance to settlers and Indigenous peoples alike: the former mobilised around sexuality to visit a vicious sexual colonisation upon Indigenous peoples, and the latter resisted that sexual colonisation despite the settlers' harsh modes of enforcing it. Colonialists viewed the diverse gendered and sexual practices of the Indigenous peoples they encountered as proof of a deviance and depravity that justified colonial intervention,[26] and 'the tendency or tactic of Europeans to see sodomy everywhere ... enabled a devastating two-fisted excuse for murderous violence and a complicated homoerotics of genocide'.[27]

To understand the way the settlers sought to displace Indigenous genders and sexualities, we must look at the genders and sexualities produced through settler colonialism. The settlers did not merely bring with them an inherited and unchanged system of sex and gender, they found themselves changed by their participation and investment in the settler colonial project. Scholars like Cole Harris and Louis Hartz highlight the ways European colonisers were forced to adapt to the new lands they had settled: the expanses of land provided a backdrop of extreme physical and social isolation that produced strong nuclear families,[28] and the experience of etching new societies into the landscapes meant that 'certain strands of European life were discarded while others were amplified in processes of settlement and colonisation'.[29] Colonisation was thus *generative*: the sexualities and genders of the settlers were produced through settler colonisation, and through social norms and laws relating to marriage, consent, and sexual relations.[30]

'Settler sexuality', a term coined by Morgensen, describes 'a white national heteronormativity that regulates Indigenous sexuality and gender by supplanting them with the sexual modernity of settler subjects.'[31] Settler sexualities, like all sexualities, are the products of their social and discursive contexts.[32] In the settler colonial context, sexual modernity was conditioned in part by the imperatives driving the settler colonial project: to eliminate the Indigenous populations, and to nativise the settler for the ultimate purpose of acquiring land. The link between gender, sexuality and land is borne out in various settler colonial contexts, such as the United States and Canada, where land 'available' to settlers was only accessible by married couples and single men (married couples were entitled to 160 acres and unmarried men 80 acres),[33] while unmarried settler women had no entitlements to land at all.[34] Tying the promulgation of the colonial family (married, nuclear and heterosexual) to the acquisition of land encouraged the literal spread of the settlers' gendered and sexual formations across Indigenous lands. These gendered formations were structured by the heteropatriarchy and they inscribed the domination of men over women into the settler colonial landscape, thereby imposing a social structure that was as alien to Indigenous societies as the Europeans invading their lands.

Indigenous systems of gender relations were specifically targeted in this modernising project; colonialists found the lack of patriarchal domination as primitive and perverse as the diverse genders and sexual practices they encountered. Linda Tuhiwai Smith explains how colonialism devastated Indigenous gender relations as 'family organisation, child rearing, political and spiritual life, work and social activities were disordered by a colonial system which positioned its own women as the property of men with roles which were primarily domestic'. Prior to colonial occupation, Indigenous women from many different Indigenous societies claimed a different relationship: 'one embedded in beliefs about the land and the universe, about the spiritual significance of women and about the collective endeavours that were required in the organisation of society'. Traditional roles for many Indigenous women across different Indigenous societies involved complete inclusion within many aspects of social and political life.[35] Indeed, scholars like Andrea Smith argue that 'it has been through sexual violence and through the imposition of European gender relationships ... that Europeans were able to colonise Native peoples'.[36]

3. Queer praxis and settler colonialism

The logic of elimination is present even in counter-cultural spaces, structuring queer communities, projects and activisms. Most contemporary queer projects are implicated in settler colonialism – at the very least erasing the settler colonial present, and at most, actively and violently deploying racist and colonialist frames. Cameron Greensmith and Sulaimon Giwa argue that, while Indigenous people (and their genders and sexualities) are granted some degree of inclusion within LGBTQI spaces and services, this does little more than obscure the 'ongoing settler-colonial violence required for modern Queer formations to exist.'[37] In this section I look at the way queer demands for recognition from, and inclusion within, the state and its institutions reify the settler state's power and therefore represent an investment in settler colonialism.

Settler homonationalism is a theoretical framework increasingly deployed in queer theory, Native/Indigenous studies and settler colonial studies. It provides a useful framework to understand the way nationalisms and racialised sexualities intersect.[38] In her monograph *Terrorist Assemblages: Homonationalism in Queer Times*, Jasbir Puar uses the term 'homonationalism' to explore the way the relationship between queer subjects and the nation-state is changing. Specifically, Puar argues that where queer subjects were previously 'figures of death (i.e., the AIDS epidemic)', they are increasingly 'becoming tied to ideas of life and productivity (i.e., gay marriage and families)'.[39] Morgensen extends Puar's analysis 'at the intersections of queer and Native studies' to examine the 'the racial and national formation of sexual modernity.'[40] In doing so, Morgensen coined the term 'settler homonationalism' to describe the way contemporary queer politics align with settler colonialism.

Settler homonationalism as a frame enables us to destabilise and unsettle 'the production of normalised citizen-subjects within disruptions of heteronormativity'.[41] Although queer political projects may disrupt heteronormativity by making visible a queer presence, unless they contain critiques of settler colonialism, racism, classism, etc., they produce and uphold homonormativity.[42] Homonormativity nourishes and maintains heteronormativity 'while promising the possibility of a demobilised gay constituency and privatised, depoliticised gay culture anchored in domesticity and consumption.'[43] This homonormative undercurrent can be explicit or implicit. It is explicit in queer appeals for inclusion within the military – such appeals are little more than queer requests to participate in a violently imperialist and classist institution. It is implicit in the queer appeal for same-sex marriage: an appeal built upon assimilationist narratives that centre (and thus serve) class-privileged, monogamous queer people, whilst erasing the needs of Indigenous queer people, queers of colour, disabled queers, working class queers, and trans people. It is an appeal for recognition from a racist, colonialist, classist, ableist and queerphobic state premised on the normalising logic of homonormativity. Implicit manifestations of homonormativity are present even in events like Pride parades, where participants are expected to have a certain level of class privilege and a concomitant capacity to consume.[44]

4. Potential sites of alliance

In this section I highlight what I see as sites where a productive alliance is possible between Indigenous and queer activisms. I begin by foregrounding a discussion of decolonisation.

Recall the discussion in the first section regarding the distinction between colonialism and settler colonialism. The lack of 'spatial separation' between coloniser and metropole raises obvious difficulties for decolonising work.[45] This is complicated further, in certain settler colonial contexts, by the imperialism wrought by settler nations – the most infamous example being the United States.[46] Eve Tuck and K. Wanye Yang explain:

This means, and this is perplexing to some, that dispossessed people are brought onto seized Indigenous land through other colonial projects. Other colonial projects include enslavement … but also military recruitment, low-wage and high-wage labour (such as agricultural workers and overseas-trained engineers), and displacement/migration (such as coerced immigration from nations torn by U.S. wars or devastated by U.S. economic policy). In this set of settler colonial relations, colonial subjects who are displaced by external colonialism, as well as racialised and minoritised by internal colonialism, still occupy and settle stolen Indigenous land.[47]

This reminds us that the category of 'settler' is not confined to people who are White or of European descent. The interplay of the global and local 'exponentially complicates what is meant by decolonisation, and by solidarity, against settler colonial forces.'[48] It is essential that we foreground these complications whilst we do our decolonising work as these multiple oppressive logics intertwine.

I follow Tuck and Yang in asserting that 'decolonisation is not a metaphor', but I also believe that it is crucial to remember that Indigenous sovereignty and nationhood has never been premised on ownership of territory, but on Indigenous custodianship of and relationship with land.[49] Patricia Monture-Angus explains: 'Sovereignty, when defined as my right to be responsible … requires a relationship with territory … What must be understood is that the Aboriginal request to have our sovereignty respected is really a request to be responsible.'[50] Andrea Smith notes that the Indigenous peoples groups at the 2009 World Social Forum asserted 'that all peoples are welcome on their lands, but they must live in a different relationship with land'.[51] Though I agree with Morgensen when he says that queer settlers must 'displace desires for a history or future on stolen land,'[52] I wonder what possibilities might lie in collective imaginings for a restored Aboriginal responsibility for land and a reconfigured relationship to land for us all.

Broadly speaking, queer people and Indigenous people alike have suffered under the heteropatriarchy. As Morgensen makes explicit, 'if we understand heteropatriarchy on stolen land to be a settler-colonial project, then arenas for conforming to settler rule will extend beyond those typically marked by anti-colonialism and will foreground gendered and sexual spaces'.[53] This struggle against the heteropatriarchy ought properly be conceived as a struggle against social domination in all its forms – including the social domination entailed through narrow definitions of nation which are premised on 'a closely bounded community and ethnic cleansing.'[54] As glimpsed above, Indigenous notions of nationhood tend to prioritise social systems based on reciprocal responsibilities and 'interrelatedness', and therefore do not require a social system based on heteropatriarchal domination.[55] Queer and Indigenous struggles which centre the state and articulate themselves within state-centric logics (i.e., politics of recognition) are reinscribing the state's power over their lives.[56] Glen Coulthard, critiquing an Indigenous politic of recognition, appeals to Indigenous activists 'to shift their focus from seeking recognition from the settler state to seeking recognition from each other as well as other oppressed communities'.[57]

There are genuine parallels and intersections between queer and native struggles, and it is here that I find scope for a productive alliance. Both queer people and Indigenous peoples are confronted daily with imperatives to assimilate. In many ways, though, I take Puar's point that queers are increasingly being accommodated within the folds of the state and granted a kind of sexual citizenship, both queer people and Indigenous peoples are populations the state would like to disappear to the extent that they cannot be assimilated and brought within the White, colonial, capitalist nation. There are shared histories and ongoing realities of gender and sexual variance being used as justification for regulation and control, and the desire for body sovereignty and gender self-determination echo Indigenous struggles for sovereignty over our bodies, our lands, and the right to self-determination. I am not saying they are the same fight, but they are part of *a* fight against a social logic that our lives and bodies are not our own.

Conclusion

I live on land that is not my own, far from the lands of my many ancestors; this land continues to care for and nurture me. The Gadigal People of the Eora nation, like so many other First Nations peoples, continue to survive and resist the ongoing settlement of their land in a myriad of ways. It is here that I do gender and sex and love in a way that the settler state deems perverse, and it is here that the settler state marks me out for death as both Indigenous and Queer. It is here, also, that I have come to find my liberation to be inextricably bound up at the intersection of Queer and Indigenous.

I see the act of decolonisation as a necessarily queer process that provides us space within which to imagine the possibilities beyond the gender binary and outside the confines of heteronormativity. This does not mean forgetting that 'queer' as a term and as a frame is epistemologically an invention of the modern West, nor does it mean affixing the label 'queer' to pre-invasion Indigenous sexualities and genders. The queering we do is not undertaken with a view to arriving at some idealised Indigenous authenticity; rather, it is as much about naming the settler state as heteropatriarchal and White as it is about recovering subordinated histories and recognising that the sexual and gendered formations found in those histories was neither heteronormative nor queer. Similarly, I believe our queer political goals must extend beyond envisioning exclusionary futures on stolen lands. We must denaturalise settlement from within queer projects,[58] 'question the colonial origins and uses of sexual minority and Queer identities ... and challenge the colonial power of settler states and global institutions'.[59] A queer praxis that centres an analysis of settler colonialism is necessarily one that contains a critique of state power and social domination; when we denaturalise settlement, we denaturalise the social control required to institute the state as an inherently exclusionary, colonialist and racist institution.

I cannot separate, nor am I torn between, the queer and the Aboriginal. It is not merely that I refuse to bracket any one aspect of myself whilst working towards liberation and sovereignty; it is that liberation itself demands we confront the sites where oppressions intersect.

Stranger in a Strange Land: Aspiration, Uniform and the Fine Edges of Identity

Sandy O'Sullivan

Displaying complexity in the identities of Aboriginal women has been an important and challenging discourse in positioning who we are.[1] For Aboriginal lesbians, inhabiting overlapping and multifarious identities across sexualities, genders, cultures and communities has been rarely framed outside of individual experience.[2] Further these identity markers have sometimes operated to further pathologise, or to measure disadvantage or difference in the depiction of a racialised body.[3]

In 2006 I completed a PhD in Performance Art that focused on the conflations of gender and sexuality and their impact on my Aboriginal body.[4] As a performer I was interested in the resulting externally imposed manifestations inscribed on the body, and the experience and trajectory in regulating response, reaction and performativity. In focusing on my own body rather than a group study of Aboriginal lesbians, the work allowed an individual journey that neither spoke for community, nor made large statements about the impact of these conflations. The research was performed into an exhibition that explored anecdotes of gender misidentification, misunderstandings about sexuality, and ideas about what constitutes both the absent and present Indigenous identity. The performances rendered a panoptic view of identity revealed to encourage an audience to consider how external indicators inform their perceptions of identity.[5, 6]

While this and other work that explores individual experiences can provide a lens into the everyday experiences of Aboriginal lesbians, what value does an individual story hold? What do our singular stories and journeys tell others about who we are as a community, and whether we form a community? In the context of this book, can our individual stories demonstrate a larger understanding of the complex diversity of our queer Indigenous selves? Some of these questions are educed here as a means to exploring the difficulty of providing research into who we are as a community, and of the risks when we do not.

Uniform/Conform/Perform

In the early 1980s I worked at a laundromat. It was long hours and hard work but at fifteen and with little education or experience, it paid well. In my spare time I worked at a music store for a dollar an hour. It was poor compensation but I wanted to be a musician and my boss allowed me – very slowly – to pay off my first instrument – a banjo – that I was sure I needed if I wanted to be a rock star.[7]

This is the experience of an Aboriginal lesbian. And it is not.

In addition to the work being physically demanding, I discovered an unspoken contract that required me to conform, behave and dress in particular ways; a confusing implicit code many young people learn when they enter the workforce. I also learned that these requirements were more compelling and restrictive because I had no educational qualifications and few skills. Beyond the physical uniform of conformity, the identity markers over which I had less control and saw as disadvantages in my presentation, were soon managed in a way that I believed would make me more *palatable*. As a fair-skinned Aboriginal person, it would only be through disclosure that random work associates would learn of my Aboriginality; this could be *managed*. Across my teen years and my twenties, I identified as heterosexual, though I frequently had to convince others of this as my gender presentation frequently had people assuming I was a lesbian. In fact, I constantly had to come out as straight.

While these early identity markers were constrained by what was possible for me to manage and alter, I hoped that my attempts at 'passing' transcended fundamental cognition in others. In spite of my own interventions across and in the framing of my body, my heterogeneous identity was intact, still multiple and faceted – an internalised imbrication of elements over which I had no control. Being unfamiliar with my own lack of power position, as a measure to avoid challenge, I learned – as many do – to adopt both a literal and figurative uniform of conformity.[8] This experience was an early reinforcement that I felt on the outer edge of society, not just as an Aboriginal – Wiradjuri – woman with very little education but as someone who manifested a confusion of gendered and sexual difference in multiple ways. Most problematic in this body management was control over my gender presentation. I performed masculinity in ways, I came to realise, over which I had very little control.[9] These differences raised obstacles – or perceived obstacles – in gaining work, in social contexts, and in being able to perform what I, and sometimes others, saw as a contemporary Aboriginal woman in the 1980s.

As a response to this failure to engage and perform the expected and accepted body, I opted out of failure as both an act of aspiration and of desperation. I became, with the skills I had available, some *thing* that I believed would allow me to manifest and be rewarded for the differences over which I had little control: I became a musician and performer.[10] Performance *of* difference allowed me to apply what I imagined was my strongest cultural, if not social, capital to leverage success over failure without engaging in the unattainable areas of conformity.[11]

This is the experience of an Aboriginal lesbian. And it is not.

To say that sexuality is a difficult conversation in Indigenous Australian contexts is to assume that we enact our Indigeneity in a bubble of conscious performativity. It further assumes that individuals can, or desire to, disentangle our sexualities and gender identities from our Indigeneity, from our individual selves, and from our relationships and communities. For many years there existed a common rhetoric within informal community discussion that alternative sexualities and non-dyadic gender performance were manifestations of Western influence on our traditional Aboriginal cultures, and that in deep time these manifestations either never existed or were managed out of our population.[12, 13] This history was often explained to me when I was younger – in fact so often that I have come to realise it may have been an act of others managing my problematic performance; of presenting a warning. This has been soundly challenged previously in Australia and internationally.[14] This book continues that legacy of context and historical correction. However, the ideas of a cultural disconnect from diverse sexuality manifested a time in my life where I believed I had little choice but to select sexuality and gender over culture. That is, my more present and visible marker of identity was unable to be erased, while I perceived my ethno-cultural identity at the time – to my eternal shame – as a remnant to overcome.

The process of addressing this disconnect, and the broader unifying of our bodies through our sexuality, gender and Indigeneity, is reflected in the seminal essay 'Peopling the Empty Mirror: The Prospects for Lesbian and Gay Aboriginal History'.[15] While the essay demonstrated how much this problem of unification played on the minds of many Aboriginal queers leading up to the 1990s, the Aboriginal authors described their multifarious identities and insisted on their inclusion and belonging in our communities. It, unsurprisingly, became one of the earliest texts that discussed other measures of diversity within our communities, as well as the acceptance and understanding that accompanies people of mixed heritage, diasporic and dispossessed peoples, and people who were removed from families and communities.

It was through a recent re-reading of 'Peopling the Empty Mirror' that I learned a late lesson in the power of multiple stories gathered in one place and their capacity to form a complex framework, while maintaining individual thoughts around our diverse identities. This re-reading informed my current major research project where I would explore representations of First Peoples and our capacity to include our diverse identities and perspectives.

Displaying untidy communities: Orderly and intemerate
In 2010 I began a review of 450 museums across multiple countries. Funded by the Australian Research Council, the brief was to examine the capacity of museums of national significance to engage and represent First Peoples. The process involved asking museum professionals what worked in this process of representation, and how they engaged with the communities that they represented. In some cases these were contemporary communities with relationships to the museum and often engaging in their own curatorial processes. In others, the community only existed in deep-time, and the knowledge was from either the archaeological record or from stories handed down through to other communities.

A part of the brief was to consider the perceived accuracy and value of these representations, and to understand what they provided back to the First Peoples community and what story they told to the broader community? Central to this was whether they were representing Indigenous communities as contemporary, robust and diverse? Several hundred of the museums were under the control of First Peoples' communities, and typically their brief was to represent their own nation or group. While many inclusions of First Peoples' representations in mainstream museums deliver snapshots of community life, the museums managed by communities often displayed a broader range of ideas with a container of representation less rigidly defined by a need to show uniqueness, and a greater emphasis on the everyday, contemporary life and the history of the community. Diversity, while more variously presented in museums with Indigenous control, is still informed by the political and social perspectives and focus of the community's desired presentation. With influences ranging from conservative to progressive, at times the desire to present a united identity results in diversity being oversimplified and under-explored.

At one museum that represents a First People whose contemporary communities now believe only exist in deep time, there was an object displayed with wall text indicating it was a fertility idol. More than 6,000 years old, the figurative carving unusually has a penis and breasts, is curvaceous, and has a squared jaw. To a differently-cultured visitor not of their time, it appeared to be a representation of both genders, and the curator reinforced this idea. When asked what this might mean about the culture, or even why their unusual characteristics weren't included on the wall text, the curator explained that it would be too confusing for the museum visitor, as the curatorial team could provide no definitive answers. Interestingly, I had not asked why there were no displayed theories as to what it meant to the First Peoples, but rather why the object's differently gendered body was not described to a museum visitor. While this could present a complexity that cannot be contained or reasoned within a broader culture that expects ordered gender delineation, it is interesting that the perception was that a visitor would find gender – a characteristic that most people are acutely aware of at a very early age – confusing.

Across many of the visited museums there was a dearth of representation on genderplay, gender variance, and sexualities beyond reproductive or family formation, with an often intemerate approach to identity. In contrast to the representations being teased out in multiple mainstream exhibition spaces, its absence appears to support a homogenising and moderating of difference. Academic Alex Wilson of the Opaskwayak Cree Nation theorises that ontological revisions warp a view of gender and sexuality by promoting binary management of girls and boys, and men and women, aligned with the imposed Christian cultures strongly inscribed within the project of colonisation. Wilson explains that in her own language there are no words that define gender, nor words that articulate differences in sexuality.[16] If a brief of the social history museum is to exhibit the unique cultural contributions of First Peoples and Nations, then moving beyond reductive echoes of a limiting colonial view must reflect the real characteristics of our potent and complex cultures: we must be able to demonstrate an untidy and unknowable society and social order.[17] To move beyond tidy commodification by others or by ourselves, as a base expectation of the representation of body, we must further insist on seeing the multiplicity of our sexualities and gender identities that existed, exist and may be imagined in the future. It will be a measure of our capacity to be dealt with as living cultures.

The social history museum has a difficult problem in relocating whole-of-community representations of First Peoples, and not only because of the aggregate nature of these reductive views: collecting often results in objectification and difference through a describable, diminishing form.[18]

Beginning with the colonial 'elephant in the room', it is necessary to acknowledge community concerns that museums may not be trusted to represent, when their project has been so aligned with colonial ideas of collection, categorisation, display, and even the acquisition of our ancestral remains.[19]

Reparations and repatriations have started a more informed and even relationship between museums and First Peoples' communities, but it has been demonstrated through the research of this project that community-run or managed processes result in a more robust diversity, where individual stories are not woven to frame the broad culture, but to represent a range of views, practices and ideologies within that culture. In the newly-designed *Bunjilaka Aboriginal Cultural Centre* at the Melbourne Museum, the lived experience of individuals within their local communities is displayed with stories, ideas and a complex diversity that includes stories from queer and gender-diverse community members.[20] Co-curated by Woromi woman Genevieve Grieves and the Yulendj Group of Elders, and supported by the Director of Bunjilaka and Yalukit Wilam woman of the Boon Wurrung Caroline Martin, the permanent installation forms a journey that begins in deep time and delivers the visitor to a contemporary community that is diverse, not fragmented, yet representing a range of views and beliefs. Interwoven in many of the hundreds of individual contemporary stories available to the visitor, are queer and gender diverse peoples, each discussing their contribution to both the Aboriginal and Queer communities. Spaces like *Bunjilaka* are demonstrating the power of these stories in truly representing our communities and the diversity of our lives. We are not ordered, intemerate or capable of being reduced to a time capsule of a singular identity. The museum that acknowledges this will be more interesting, more engaging and will have the support and input from actual, Indigenous people.[21]

Performing identity/performing erasure

I left school for the first time at thirteen. I attempted to go back a few times, and finally was working fulltime by fifteen unable to grasp the fundamentals of reading and cognition. In contrast for the last twenty-three years I've been a university-based academic, for the last seven years a full-time researcher, and I have a range of qualifications including a PhD. And it all happened because of uniforms. And gender. And sexuality. And Indigeneity.

This is the experience of an Aboriginal lesbian. And it is not.

Throughout the 1980s and '90s, I continued to work as a musician and performer, sometimes subsidising my work with 'real' jobs in offices. There was an identity disconnect between that aspect of my work-life and the performance work. At night I would be either playing punk or folk, or performing my Elvis act, the latter usually at a conservative club in the outer suburbs. Unlike many of my contemporaries my act wasn't lip-synched, and it was after one particular moment of performing Elvis that I realised that most of the audience didn't get the 'joke'. In fact, I may not have even performed the 'joke', but when an elderly patron came up to me and told me what a nice young man I was, I realised that it was entirely possible that they thought I was just a very short, curvaceous man and I got an insight into how that 6000 year old idol felt.

I had not yet 'come out', but even so I understood that there was something different about my sexuality. I held strongly to the idea that my off-stage gender performance continued to be problematic, and at that stage I still had few employment or education skills to aspire to other kinds of transgressions. This, combined with a realisation that my onstage gender performance was probably too quirky and that I was over-invested in an idiosyncratic approach to performance, meant that I would never have success beyond eking out a living. The office work I was doing to fill the void of time and money was life-sucking to me. I met many interesting people, but was still required to conform in ways that left me feeling like a failure.

As it turned out, the suppression wasn't just about the very present gender identity but one that affected cultural connection in ways I had yet to understand. That none of this speaks to Indigeneity is no omission in the writing, but also in the lived experience of that time of my life when I imagined I escaped my cultural identity. Of course I hadn't really escaped my Indigeneity; that doesn't happen. Aboriginal People are, as Aunty Mary Graham says, 'not alone in the world'.[22]

Performance as escape: The safe and welcoming university

From my late teens to my early twenties, and with a great deal of help, I learned to become a voracious reader. I had aspirations of learning formally, perhaps taking on a high school certificate. When I was in my mid-twenties, I found out that I could enrol in a theatre program at the University of Wollongong on the basis of my performance, and that I would be given support to learn to write essays. When I attended the audition, it became clear that my gender presentation and, in fact, my on-stage gender performance was welcomed and seen as innovative. For the first time I understood that I might find a way to genuinely leverage my cultural capital. This sounds like the plot to a fantasy movie of misfits finding their non-conformist place. But I also encountered unexpected moments that I wasn't prepared for in the suppression of my cultural identity. I attended university mostly with people younger than myself who had just completed high school, had lived mostly middle-class lives, and who, for the most part, imagined performance as a viable if difficult profession. For me it remained a desperate act of belonging. My mind was expanded, beyond arts training, I began to learn about the context of art and in a lot of ways I corrected knowledge that had never flowed in my own life. Where my fellow students – most of them younger and with an uninterrupted education – understood the terminology being used, for me it was foreign and frightening. As I progressed in my education it became liberating to realise that I could learn and that my life could be improved through this learning. This journey helped me to consolidate and interrogate my own gendered identity, and to relax into feeling less of a level of resistance. It led rather inevitably and not long after finishing my degree, to coming out as a lesbian: a relatively painless process since I had spent the majority of my life to that point explaining to people that I *was not* a lesbian.

If I had once used performance as an escape from my life, through exploring my body I discovered more about perceptions of gender and sexuality across the broader community. And then there would be these moments that would happen, I would get past them and move on. As someone who had never done well in education, learning how to analyse and think through problems was a gift, and I was incredibly grateful to all of my lecturers and at a fairly present level I idolised them. So when, early on in my degree, I mentioned to one of my lecturers – a non-Indigenous academic who had worked in remote communities – that I was Aboriginal, she took me aside and explained that I should be very careful about saying that, because it could be very offensive to Aboriginal people. I had no language then to challenge this; she was right. She had to be right because she was right about everything else. This same process happened a couple more times over the journey of my degree. My life was becoming ordered and better in a lot of ways. I was becoming someone who could aspire to do more, be more, and be anything – just not Aboriginal. It was one of the things I learned over my mind-expanding creative arts degree, if you can believe that.

This is the experience of an Aboriginal lesbian. And it is not. Where at first I had thought the intellectual work was the necessary evil that accompanied my arts training, it proved to assist me in developing a mechanism for understanding performative identity, and led me into a career as an artist and educator. This identity work has underpinned much of my critical research and teaching for more than twenty years. From representation in museums to arts practice, I have been interested in how individuals and communities are supported, encouraged, permitted or restricted from expressing themselves; how others describe and define them; and the fine edges of identity that are extricated, engaged, overlapping and combined to form our broader community. But at the beginning of this journey, I was still forgetting something.

It was some time after finishing my degree that I learned how to embrace and be proud of my Indigeneity, although it came at a cost. I had been an artist for a number of years, and had taught art, media and performance – transcending my earlier, failed education and succeeding in ways beyond my imagination. Over the same period, there had been major changes to the broader community's understanding of Indigenous Australians that was led, in no small part, by a requirement for the whole of Australia to consider its role in decimating Indigenous communities. The *Bringing Them Home* report produced a comprehensive review and recommendations for supporting families, individuals and communities who had been damaged by the Government crime that formed the Stolen Generations. Included throughout the anecdotes, stories and reports from people affected by this action, were extensive commentary on the fine and overlapping edges of identity, community disconnections, rejections, and the difficulty of belonging – all framed as key challenges to healing. In reading the report and in hearing these stories, I was devastated by how the lives of our Peoples had been destroyed and how so much of it was on the basis of a form of racial correction.[23] I came to realise how wilfully ignorant I had also been, how complicit in an internal act of colonisation I was, and how my own cognitive distortions left me both cultureless and bereft. And of course they didn't, because Aunty Mary Graham's words resonate: we are all connected.[24] It was through these connections that I was given many lifelines to help me find a way back to culture and belonging.

While the university had provided me with a place to learn and subsequently to teach about identity, I realised that it had not been a culturally safe place. I reflected, as will some of you reading this, that the lecturer I had encountered years before, had a narrowed view of identity and belonging, and indeed of Aboriginal Peoples. Over time, I've been supported in developing a voice to challenge these ideas through the work of Aboriginal theorists writing about identity and the academy, including Aunty Mary Graham, Aileen Moreton-Robinson, Karen Martin, Martin Nakata, Victor Hart, Lester-Iribinna Rigney, Judy Atkinson, Lynette Russell and, thankfully now, too many to name. I have found a language to understand how a seemingly-supported journey of education can be intentionally scuttled by those who seek to police the boundaries of belonging and to create silos of identity. And I have realised my own complicity in that journey. By understanding that my earlier empowerment had come at a cost, I realised that I had a responsibility to myself and others to correct this mistake. And through talking to community, to my family and to my communities of practice, I began the project of reintegrating my self.[25]

Unification/balance/uniform

There is a complexity to Aboriginal Peoples that deserves attendance, and we must be at the forefront of insisting on that complexity. We can be anything, everything, and the composite that we enact. When I began my PhD in the early 2000s, I explicitly anticipated connections and disconnections between the identity markers of gender, Indigeneity and sexuality. The more interesting provocations emerged from how these areas connected to form a real person. In 2004 I released a music CD, *Felt Up*, that was an attempt at a humorous connection back to all of these identity processes.[26] After a live performance of the songs, I was talking to some people in the audience who asked me why none of them were about Aboriginality. I was happy to report that even if they couldn't tell from their hearing, *all* of the songs were about being Aboriginal, and all of the songs were Aboriginal. Every song I make is an Aboriginal song, because I'm an Aboriginal woman. The capacity to focus on aspects of my identity, and to recognise and celebrate them as part of the whole, has been the greatest benefit to this journey of unification.

Twenty-five years after I re-started my education, I am now a Senior Indigenous Researcher at Batchelor Institute of Indigenous Tertiary Education, working through the disciplines of art and performance on cultural reproduction and representation and performed identities. A little while ago I was talking with colleagues about the recent practice of academics dressing like business people, and I joked that if they had looked like this when I first auditioned to go to university I may not have seen it as a rebellious salvation. Personal revelation does not always align with a broader knowledge of cultural practice, and it was only through the discussion that I realised – for the first time – that the uniform I had to wear when I first entered the workforce at fifteen, was not literal but a figurative uniform of singular conformity.

When I first entered the workforce more than thirty-five years ago, I never imagined I could be accepted for who I am, and be offered the chance to work in an area that I love. This was not my journey alone; I have benefitted from the work of the people who came before me, and of my ancestors with whom I have reconnected. While I would not impose this on others, I know my responsibility is to be multifarious, complex and inextricable in my identity representation, and to ensure that others are not made to feel – in our own country – like strangers in a strange land.

This is the experience of an Aboriginal lesbian. And it is not.

The Border Made of Mirrors: Indigenous Queerness, Deep Colonisation and (De)fining Indigenousness in Settler Law

Alison Whittaker

This is where the border begins, and my hand is reflected against it. I am curly and racially-ambiguous in the williwilli-stricken rural summer, and my mother drops me to school on photo day.

I had known I was Gomeroi since my birth but my mother never told the school. She feared that the institutional cruelty she, her parents, cousins and brothers had felt in the drought plains of north-west New South Wales would set me aside, bring me shame, and wound me. I had it set in my mind to prove her wrong. I marched up to the photographer demanding to be in the group picture of Indigenous students. I argued myself into that picture, stamping my feet and citing kin relations, family history and cultural practice. I was red-faced, fast-hearted in the second row when the shutter snapped; my hand brushed that of a girl two grades ahead of me. This, I recall thinking to myself, was probably not something to march up and yell at the photographer.

Thus began my mismatched relationship with identifying myself as Aboriginal before institutions. These institutions had the power to grant me or deny me access to community, integrated selfhood, and the service base with which I could combat my own disenfranchisement.

For Indigenous queers on or from the rural fringe, such vulnerability arising from a terse historical and contemporaneous context is an exercise of systemic failings, lateral manifestations of colonial policy, and widespread disenfranchisement from our own communities and ourselves.

Introduction: Suspicion, resentment and authenticity

In 1999, then Social Justice Commissioner Dr William Jonas wrote of the legal exactitude with which this interplay between Indigenous peoples and identification is disputed as a symptom of 'the suspicion and resentment with which some non-Indigenous people regard the assertion by Indigenous people of their status as Indigenous'.[1]

There, too, are lateral manifestations of the suspicion and resentment of which the Social Justice Commissioner speaks. These are particularly apparent as Indigenous communities, spurred on by the three-tiered test of identification at law, turn to arbitrate their peripheries through settler legal tests of imagined cultural, social, anthropological and racial authenticity, impacting and excluding queer Indigenous persons and diasporas.[2] The necessary counterpart of this is the critical impact of settler legal demarcation of Indigenous persons as deep methodological colonisation.

There is some value in interrogating the meeting of Indigeneity, queerness and rurality, both as an exercise of examining the performance of settler law on the Indigenous legal and discursive subject, and as a means of better understanding Indigeneity as lateral policing of the 'authentic'. It has been suggested that 'the practice of creating and imbuing racial categories with seemingly impermeable boundaries has underpinned a range of colonial practices'.[3]

And so, this chapter attempts to do just that by picking apart the queer context, precedent and epistemological impact of underpinning Indigenousness in colonial law. This is a difficult task given cavernous gaps in the existing literature and jurisprudence.

Pinning down the Indigenous legal subject – from sixty-seven models of fraught colonial identification to the less troubling but deeply colonial three-tier model – is a contested site.[4] The current three-tier model operates by defining Indigenousness as heritage, self-identification and community-identification. It seems progressive, but is functionally and contextually problematic.

Deep colonisation, learned lateral hostility, white queerness

To better understand the test with its relationship to queer and trans Indigenous persons, we must turn to lateral contexts within which queer Indigenous identities operate.

The existence of queer identities in Indigenous communities is widely-discussed, and teases apart a hegemonic component of conceptualising or deconstructing Indigenousness at large and, more specifically, the colonial assumption of 'primitiveness'.[5] This cannot be thoroughly recounted in a mere book chapter as relevant Indigenous histories and social re-castings are oral and diffuse, and the hegemonic sidelining of Indigenous queerness draws its epistemological power from the abjection of Indigenous gender and sexualities, and from the casting of those traits as that of the primitive 'other'.[6]

As the dominant settler moral narrative has shifted to one of white homonormative citizenry and rights,[7] so the counterposed settler image of the Indigenous subject was also epistemologically shifted in order to fit the colonial assumption of 'primitiveness'. Now, the Indigenous sexual and gendered subject is imbued with compulsorily heterosexual and cisgendered traits, and our culture is tempered with settler assumptions of both 'original' and contemporaneous queer antagonism.[8]

Settler queer frameworks have been criticised by Robinson, a Mi'kmaq scholar, who asserts that pan-queer and -trans narratives ignore the sexuality and gender framework of First Nations, who have their own linguistic frameworks for dealing with sexual and gender diversity.[9] Critically, Monaghan notes about the Australian context that queer decolonisation concerns 'recovering subordinated histories and recognising that the sexual and gendered formations found in those histories was neither heteronormative nor queer'.[10] Indigenous persons were forced to ingest and perpetrate queer antagonism and self-loathing, and they later were chastised by liberal homonormativity (and settler proscriptions of pan-queerness and -transness) for having done so.[11] Indigenous queers are conceptually pushed to the peripheries of what our communities might recognise as their own.

The assumption that queerness then emerges from progressive whiteness necessarily assumes the malevolent normativity and queer antagonism of the bush, where the 'messianic' touch of progressive liberal whiteness is less salient. Such imaginings are problematised not only by the prevalence and presence of Indigenous queer persons in regional and rural areas, but by persuasive auto-ethnographic rumblings that 'queerness' in Australia did not move from the queer, white metropole, but existed, rooted deeply in Indigenous groups.[12] Such disputes on whether Indigenous queerness either exists or emerges from these white liberal centres of enlightenment are arguably part of policing of the periphery of Indigenousness. This entrenches the lateral and colonial unseeing of Indigenous ways of being that see queerness attributed to the 'enlightened' brush of whiteness.[13]

Clark describes this as symptomatic of the tension between imagined barbarism and queer antagonism within 'traditional' culture, and ongoing assimilationist pressure to reject that imagined 'barbarism' for what is supposedly the fruit of Western liberal civilisation.[14] In this context, due to the impact of white legal lenses attempting to demarcate the authentic Indigenous person, there remains some tension between performing 'authenticity' and the scope within which that 'authenticity' can include queerness, erroneously regarded as the product of Western liberalism.[15]

These structures, pitfalls and hostilities play some part in the way that Indigenous persons are said to identify one another at law. The peripheries of authenticity derived by white colonial law are comprised of mirrored borders to Indigenous-specific services and to self-affirmation. The scholar Deborah Bird Rose refers to such competitive and crudely-Indigenised processes within colonial legal systems as deep colonisation, where 'colonising practices are embedded within decolonising institutions which may conceal, naturalise, or marginalise continuing colonising practices'.[16]

The process by which Indigenous persons are subjected to crudely legalistic versions of cultural identification practice has forced 'talking up' to white gazes, and all the administrative burden with which it comes. In playing up to this concealed, naturalised gaze, Indigenous communities tighten the aperture of their communities, as if these ways of knowing are our own, in manners which are deeply aspirational and practicable, rather than legalistic, and thus are beyond formal appeal.[17]

This deep colonisation, cumulating with the cultural and epistemic effects of competitions of authenticity, leaves queer Indigenous subjects with few places to turn for affirmation. Many, like myself, compartmentalise these elements of ourselves. We perform white queerness in the metropolis, fearing the settler colonialism of white queer liberalism; and we perform heterosexuality and cisgenderedness in the rural fringe, fearing that those who love us would perceive queerness to be a change in our fundamental being brought by the brush of metropolitan whiteness. Being ideologically weaponised in such a way against our communities to artificially evidence their backwardness is a dimensional cruelty that denies the patterns of both learned queer antagonism and cultural self-loathing. It reinforces the unlearning which has pushed us to the peripheries of collective selfhood.[18] The law exacerbates this by formalising and administrating that process.

Modelling challenges

'The law' has been dealt a complex hand of how to adopt broad identification for members of hundreds of pluralistic and localised societies whom have been scarred and dehumanised by attempts to identify them. It is difficult to sympathise with its conundrum compared to the complex hand dealt to Indigenous persons who are wounded by such policy historically and contemporaneously, and who agitate for better-practice models under the same institutional proviso that their identity must be validated. This entails cultural cut-corners and costs.

Formal legal identification suggests not only the assenting white gaze in order to authorise it, but also an unshakable colonial-ness to identification itself – one that rejects spoken-ness and collective reciprocity.[19] It is difficult to imagine a reform within settler law, other than its abstention from modelling Indigenous identification, which would counter these questions of colonial authorisation and its operational burden.

The law answers this, then, with an attempt at under-standing the communal base of Indigenous identification, as one which is related to Country and Kin. This is a crude, problematic translation at law which enforces settler objectives of demarcation whilst performing unengaged 'decolonising' epistemology. It exacerbates the operational and aspirational communal policing of Indigenous queers outlined above through subtly naturalising grotesquely-mirrored traditional practices for the benefit of settler legal demarcation.[20]

White colonial identification seeks to examine that which it has impacted by its policies through a lens demanding evidence of connections which it has itself made difficult to prove. This necessarily neglects those for whom the impact of colonial frameworks means an actual or discursive separation from Country and Kin. With increasing population shifts from predominantly-Indigenous rural communities to the metropole, the uprooting of populations from groups that might discharge one or several evidentiary burdens in identification presents some concern.[21] Utilising white law as gatekeepers to formal identification – and thus to necessary services and policy – can entrench the disenfranchisement of these queer Indigenous diasporas.

At law

The jurisprudence and experiential frameworks behind and emerging from each of the three Requirements provide more specific reflections on the aspirational impact of settler identifying law. The three-tier test emanates from common law interpretation of race,[22] and intervention in particular statute.[23]

The law considers Indigenous identification in three tiers:

- that a person be of Aboriginal and/or Torres Strait Islander heritage (the 'Heritage Requirement');
- that they identify as Aboriginal and/or Torres Strait Islander (the 'Individual Identification Requirement'); and,
- that they be accepted as Aboriginal and/or Torres Strait Islander in their community or former community (the 'Community Requirement').

The means by which Indigenous identification is evidenced varies by purpose and jurisdiction.[24] Commonly, it may be evidenced by a Confirmation of Aboriginality certificate or a statutory declaration attesting the three tiers.

This test derives greater impact than the sum of its parts alone. Additional impact is made through the policy enabled by identification, and the comparative weight given to each criterion, which varies case-by-case.[25]

The law is flavoured by how it is enacted. Its practical evidentiary components, limitations incurred by certifying bodies, and resource restrictions have an operational impact. Due to the lack of formal appeal options for these non-legal elements, they can have an unsupervised, naturalised gatekeeping impact which prevents us from accessing identification that, when coupled with the substantial legal and material burden facing marginalised identifiers, can also prevent us from attempting to access identification.

The Heritage Requirement

The Heritage Requirement has been clarified as a 'technical rather than real criterion for identity', and 'a social, rather than a genetic, construct'.[26]

Despite the Heritage Requirement's general lack of dispute in day-to-day use since the 1990s, its discursive impact likely operates in unspoken practice, without contestation in appellate bodies. This discursive impact, in addition to deliberate informality in most identification processes, leaves us without a clearly-accessible formal appeals process (or instead with prohibitive, settler evidentiary processes in appellate courts). This legal inaccessibility is not assisted by the diffuse presence of the three-tier test in the common law, and in its peppering through statute.

Contestations of the Heritage Requirement in the 1990s saw complications emerge concerning the theoretical positioning of heritage in the three-tier test, particularly where documentation was unavailable due to invisiblising colonial impact.[27] Notoriously, the Tasmanian Aboriginal Centre was known for strongly-emphasising heritage through reassessing claims of identification on the basis of 'known' Aboriginal surnames or other proof of direct lineage.[28]

When disputes arose in a trial electoral roll for Indigenous persons, rules introduced under the Aboriginal and Torres Strait Islander Commission (Regional Council Election) Amendment Rules 2002 (No 1) mandated, in the case of an objection to Indigenous identity, that a verifiable family tree, archival or historic documentation would be required to prove heritage.[29] Photographs and family folklore 'will not normally be sufficient'.

Aside from counter-intuitive proof requirements arising from disputed Indigenousness, these rules erroneously anticipated good faith documentary rigour from state agencies and white anthropology. In discounting traditional and make-do documentation in the face of that anthropologic and state violence, such rules move away from the autonomous epistemological intent (howsoever grotesquely-mirrored) of the three-tier test, and position identification once more in its blood-quantum roots, which Behrendt suggests have continued in the courts' undue focus on descent.[30]

In day-to-day practice in small Indigenous identifying bodies, there is an operational rebuttable assumption of heritage, particularly where the individual uncontroversially fulfils the Community Requirement. In my own experience working informally on an ad hoc basis with queer and dislocated Indigenous persons seeking identification, this is a less reliable operational assumption when the identified subject is queer. The epistemic colonial impact of counter-posed white sexual ethics outlined above, may see communities not perceive queer individuals' familial or kin heritage relationships to be known to them or, alternatively, perceive them to be 'inauthentic' or gammon. Additionally, demographic trends with the movement of queer Indigenous populations may dislocate identifying subjects from communities that could raise that operational assumption of community knowledge.

The Heritage Requirement does not strictly require the tracing of biological lineage, but operationally, in requiring case-by-case assumptions or documentary proof, misunderstands some Indigenous familial, community and kin relations. It causally attributes lineage to constructs of strict maternity and paternity, and misunderstands ambiguities between individual blood relationships in its proofing requirements upon contestation. The Heritage Requirement is also problematised by queer Indigenous relationships and traditions, which undermine lineage requirements that have biological, 'maternal' and 'paternal' bases.

The Heritage Requirement is similarly problematic in its violent administration of trans Indigenous persons, who, in evidencing heritage, may be confronted by the same hurdles they face in administrative documentation under settler legal systems.[31] These resist the use of anything other than assigned/birth/'dead' names and genders coercively assigned at birth, and deny them recognised authenticity as whole persons in their true gender in the eyes of the law. Despite its rare testing and utilisation, and a general in-practice assumption in favour of persons who seek to identify, anticipation of failing lineage requirements, and a distrustful history with proving lineage evidence to administrative bodies, are prohibitive gatekeepers for some queer and trans Indigenous persons.

The Individual Identification Requirement

An Individual Identification Requirement in part, turns to questions raised within contestation of the Heritage Requirement, that of an individual identifying with a communal whole, self-knowledge and self-perception,[32] and of culturally-significant constructs of individual esteem in Indigenousness.

Individual Identification Requirements are, however, naturally contingent on the relative willingness of individuals to identify themselves as Indigenous persons. These have limited legal contestation, except when considering the scope of particular non-judicial inquiries.[33] In the social context outlined above, this contingency is operationally flawed for marginalised Indigenous groups.

Although it is tempting to refer to individual identification as a potential unshackling of Indigenous queer persons from institutions that may interrogate their authenticity, Indigenous identification is understood to be reciprocal: our self exists only with reference to the whole. Individual Identification Requirements exist in this test as a formal mimicking of 'informal' identification; an Indigenous person making themselves known to the community, and the community knowing them as Indigenous in turn.

Both Community and Individual Requirements are concomitant, and critically relational. At law, the contextual and shifting balance between the requirements on a case-by-case basis requires consideration of the relationship of those requirements. Whilst not necessarily evidencing them in each instance, legal identification relies on the interplay of each of the three elements.

Although identification of all three elements through a statutory declaration on behalf of the individual is possible, it is only an evidentiary possibility and does not itself constitute an individuated model. Intriguingly, where an individual, less-formalised approach is taken in Census identification, there is an observed increase in persons identifying as Indigenous.[34]

To untether community and selfhood is to undermine the relational nature of presentation and acceptance, and individualises queer Indigenous persons by rejecting these Indigenous cultural practices (howsoever crudely and harmfully imitated by the law) in favour of an individual liberal identity rights model that does not wholly represent enmeshment or community.[35]

In a contextual framework which counterposes Indigenousness and queerness against each other, Indigenous queer persons may silo components of themselves in individually presenting for identification. Regional queer persons may seek to remove themselves from the perceived rural impact of queer antagonism, an epistemological and demographic phenomenon in itself,[36] so there is little shock that, coupled with Indigenous migrations to the metropole, there is an Indigenous queer dislocation which is unable to find legal affirmation. In doing so, we are impacted by geographic gaps in proofing and presentation requirements and are robbed of our whole access to community and identity in metropolitan diasporas.

In practice, this means that many queer and trans Indigenous persons simply do not attempt to identify themselves as Indigenous at law, both due to self-dismissal, and from the fear of lateral rejection as 'inauthentic', based on their queerness or transness, or barriers posed by physical relocation from homelands. That the law acts as the gatekeeper for these processes prevents Indigenous persons on the fringe from approaching the gate at all and, thus, from expanding the jurisprudence around this area of law on appeal.

The Community Requirement

The Community Requirement is problematised as an element of identification policy as it fails to account for the impact of its inquiry and legal and historical gaze upon the subjects it seeks to evaluate. Some of these failings emerge from the origin of the inquiring lens; can a community truly be said to identify their own if they must do so on terms which are imposed by statute and homogenised, rather than recognising and working alongside the local differences of communal and kinship identifications?

In the specific terms of Indigenous queer peoples, some problematic elements emerge instead from the discursive factors discussed above. Where an assent of identification must be unanimous, these learned structures can make tremendous exclusionary impact with a small number of actors.

These factors are exacerbated also by the material context within which queer Indigenous persons relocated from rural communities to metropolitan communities, based on both learned queer antagonism within their original communities, and on racism within queer communities which frames the metropole as enlightened queer white Utopia.[37] In metropolitan areas, rural/queer Indigenous diasporas are thrust into a context within which they cannot often find the communal assent required, due to their isolation or relative newness to those groups. Where formal identification is the gatekeeper to combatting that isolation or newness, there are few avenues by which queer Indigenous persons can place their feet in communal, Indigenous grounds, and receive critical support from community.

Where acceptance from the queer community is forth-coming, but not from the Indigenous community, it is easy to imagine queer Indigenous subjects becoming increasingly marginalised by their Indigenous status, and increasingly internalising questions of their inauthenticity in the Indigenous community. Acceptance within the queer community may also be limited by the invested settler colonialism of the queer community,[38] leading to increased individuation and isolation of Indigenous persons.

The material impact of colonisation changes the way

dislocated Indigenous queers form community altogether. We can enmesh in community through distinct ways than growing up, daily interaction or strict knowledge of groups.[39] To understand this necessary plurality and dislocated communality, one must consider divergent models of performing community, including those of cultural practice, relational and affect-based identification, historic grounding, re-learning ancestry, and even more periphery interaction. Evaluating how a community may then seek to identify its own when its own have been driven to the borders by colonisation, is necessarily complicated.

This complication exists throughout diasporas and, despite being a question of evidence, it is also a question of concomitant individual identification. Technically, it might also be a question of whether the subjective identification of an individual by the community is legally or epistemologically possible, or should instead be viewed with an imagined objective lens or standardised evidentiary criteria and onus.[40] The deep colonisation of Indigenous epistemological approaches to identifying their own in order to fit a colonial lens is in many ways a root cause of this dilemma.

Conclusion

Investigating the fraughtness of any legal model is frequently met with questions of what could, ideally, stand in its place. Attempts to refine the law as it currently stands appear to me to be futile, as expanding jurisprudence only emerges from the lateral contestation of authenticity at law – a process which deeply wounds those parties concerned. Legislative reform is undermined by paternalistic and theoretical interests of the parliaments which enact them. Even the most progressive models under settler colonial law necessitate the competition of Indigenous parties before one another and a white legal gaze, something which inevitably manifests in a deep colonising impact.

An alternative is to allow diffuseness in Indigenous identification or, as Maddison suggests, legislating instead for the explicit protection of Indigenous identity.[41] Permitting the adaptation of varying models by communities in an autonomous sense loosens the prescriptiveness and exclusionary evidentiary hurdles facing Indigenous identifiers, and particularly those driven to the fringe of Indigenousness at law as it currently stands.

This operative looseness is what permitted me to find my way into that school picture and now into the grooves of the community on Eora land within which I have re-nested. That spokenness, that reciprocity, is a cultural legal framework which resists the untethering of my queerness from my Aboriginality and the violent fragmenting of the self. Instead, it accepts the wholeness of queer and trans Indigenous selves, both in law/policy, but for me, more critically, in the loosely-bordered pores of a surviving and resisting mob.

Are We Queer? Reflections on 'Peopling the Empty Mirror' Twenty Years On

Maddee Clark

'Peopling the Empty Mirror' takes up as a project the charting of a history of homosexuality in pre-contact and early contact Aboriginal culture. A group of seven authors calling themselves the 'Gays and Lesbians Aboriginal Alliance' establishes grounds for the writing of specific kinds of Aboriginal lesbian and gay histories from what it terms 'a coalitionist politics'.[1] In this essay, I respond to some of the themes presented in both 'Peopling the Empty Mirror' and in emerging queer Indigenous scholarship, situating these in the Australian present and within my own experiences. In particular, I want to continue to push open the discussion the essay started about approaching Aboriginal queer history writing. Specifically, I want to investigate aspirations for a queer politic around settler colonialism as well as the idea of 'coalition politics' from the position of Aboriginal, feminist, trans and queer experience.

Tracing queer Aboriginal histories

The project of history making has played an essential part in the creation and legitimation of the occupying settler state. The creation of linear and discreet histories continues to be part of the colonial ontological assertion of progress and nationhood. In response, Aboriginal people are forced to create and articulate histories from positions of marginality. In white settler written histories we still appear as a plot device. Bain Attwood put this simply:

> Since 1788, European representations have undoubtedly undergone considerable change but basic forms of Aboriginalist knowledge and power have not altered [rendering] Aborigines as inert objects who are spoken for by others ... Aboriginalism essentialises its object of study: Aborigines are manufactured in ontological or foundational terms as an essence which exists in binary opposition to non-Aborigines.[2]

Attwood here points towards the displacement of Aboriginal voices in historical construction by 'European positivist' discourse. Following Kevin Rudd's apology to the Stolen Generations in 2008 and the rise of reconciliation discourse in Australia, Intervention-era history writing has revised its relationship with Aboriginal people and our perceived humanity to a degree, but ultimately continues to invest in the legitimation of settler neutrality, presence and life. Aboriginal sexual histories are often written by settlers with an anxious investment in believing that white settlement is justified, largely peaceful, and necessary. We are constructed as genderless, savage, straight, and without sexual agency, needing to be controlled and managed by outside forces.[3] Throughout settler colonial Australian history and continuing today, this history expresses itself through state regulation of Aboriginal labour, economics, sexual activity, family relationships, consumption (or perceived over-consumption and over-indulgence), and personal lives. Our sexual lives have been silenced and managed right down to their intimate details.

Australian historical texts also inevitably invest in the sexual politics of the frontier. For example, Inga Clendinnen's *Dancing*

With Strangers re-imagines first contact between settlers and Aboriginal people in Eora country. The book reads with a heavy investment in settler sexual morality and legitimacy which Philip Morrissey has described as an uneasy response to the 'troubling and disturbing fact' of Aboriginal presence and sovereignty.[4] Clendinnen refers to Aboriginal people as 'Australians' and 'original immigrants', and the chapter 'Australian sexual politics' refers solely to the accounts of diaries of colonists such as Watkin Tench in imagining widespread, standard and culturally endemic sexual violence and savagery. Of the newcomers, she writes:

> What was not at all standard was the British response to sexual encounters or, more correctly, their lack of response … It is true that some British men beat, raped, even killed women, especially convict women … But British violence was typically expressed by fists and feet, and tended to happen when the perpetrator, and the victim too, were in private and in drink.[5]

British sexual violence is almost entirely erased in Clendinnen's account, and what violence she does admit is mitigated by the drunkenness of both victim and perpetrator and the privateness of the offences. Her use of the term 'original immigrants' to describe Aboriginal people demonstrates an anxious negation of Aboriginal sovereignty, as she attempts to equalise British 'migrancy' with Aboriginal presence.

Monstrous and sexually violent images of Aboriginal men (and of Aboriginal women as silent and victimised) have dominated much of political and historical discourse on Aboriginal people in recent years. Shino Konishi and Leah Lui-Chivizhe write that the 2007 introduction of the Intervention was driven by the 'assumption that Aboriginal people's moral deviance would be writ large on their bodies'.[6] Controls on perceived Aboriginal 'over-consumption' and excessive desires were placed which, as has been shown in practice, has led to extreme curtailing of already limited resources in remote communities, immense increases in poverty and ultimately, forced movement.[7] The sexual invasiveness of the movement was normalised to the extent that the government was planning to impose mandatory health checks 'tantamount to assault' in order to 'identify ... any effects of abuse'.[8] The simultaneity with which the state has asserted large-scale and assaultive control over Aboriginal people's bodies while maintaining the construction of sexual savagery, passivity and uncontrollable lust of Aboriginal people is a testament to the dangerousness of those dominant histories.

The authors of 'Peopling the Empty Mirror' note while making their exploration into anthropological accounts of what they term 'homosexual practices' in Aboriginal societies that there are complications to trying to glean information about Aboriginal sexual behaviour from records of settlers with an interest in justifying colonisation.[9] More recently, critiquing the strategies of 'ethno-history', Konishi notes that European historical records on Indigenous peoples and their sexual behaviours must all be read as myths written by people with heavy imperial investments into the representation of sexual savagery:

Emphasis [should be] placed on contextualising these in terms of European representational practices and conceptions of the 'other', as well as imperial interests. [It should be] acknowledged that traveller's accounts cannot be unravelled or read against the grain to reveal an ethnographic truth. Instead of combing the sources for ostensibly truthful depictions, attentively examine the nature of the representational practices that the Europeans deployed in their descriptions of the New World, and ... resist speaking for and about indigenous peoples.[10]

There is emerging a clear need for critical and autonomous histories of Aboriginal sexuality to be written and discussed by Aboriginal people. However, the idea that our history has a linear progression with a starting point, or needs one, can be read as a legacy of the social mechanisms of history writing that have informed the settler colonial state. We don't need to be able to construct ourselves in written historical accounts in order to consider ourselves real and whole. The urge for a linear historical recovery of gay Aboriginal identity attempts to make cultural links that don't necessarily reflect the sexual complexities of our lives.

Unnameable bodies, unnameable desires

The use of naming to assert power over individuals, places, countries, landmarks, and sexual identities is at the forefront of my mind while I navigate queer settler communities. Tony Birch has discussed the 'race war' that erupted in the late 1980s over the renaming of features of Grampians national park in Victoria. The various objections to the suggested changes to reflect local Koori place names cited the threat to Scottish pioneers, complained that 'Aboriginal names all ... sound the same, and in most cases, the spelling looks the same ...[and are] totally unpronounceable to modern day black and white', and not acceptable unless they were further anglicised to be 'easily recognisable'.[11]

More recently, a proposal to rename a suburb of Ballarat after a local Aboriginal warrior, Mullawallah, was ditched after opposition from residents 'on the grounds that it was multi-syllable, hard to pronounce and spell'.[12] One resident suggested a local creek or reserve could be named after Mullawallah instead. Writing on country near Lake Corangamite, Victoria, where many buildings, creeks, camping spots and houses have Aboriginal language names, Bruce Pascoe writes, 'There seems to be a compulsion to remember the original name even while trying to forget how the property came under white ownership ... it's eerie to have the names and almost none of the people'.[13] Birch writes:

> To name spaces is to name histories and also to create them. The process is accepted as natural, representing a given ... Indigenous names themselves do not constitute a threat to white Australia. Houses, streets, and whole cities have Aboriginal names. This is an exercise in cultural appropriation, which represents imperial possession and the quaintness of the 'native' ... it is when names are restored to recognise earlier histories and cultures that the threat to ownership occurs[14]

I feel caught between the gaps of my language when I'm asked by people who mean well how I identify. The places that my tongue and my memory can't reach feel painfully obvious to me. Naming queer Aboriginal behaviours, feelings, relationships, identities, and states of being is an attempt to make them legible and intelligible; readable. When I'm fucking strangers, queers, straight men, lesbians, friends, past lovers and current ones, I believe that sometimes some of them think of and fetishise me as a woman with a particular kind of sexuality and a particular kind of body. This makes me feel misread, misgendered, legible in ways I don't consent to and can't access. I feel fluid and elusive as well as completely contained in words, and am aware of the ways I can make my body change its meaning across all the contexts I can put it in. I love the anonymity of anonymous hook-up cultures, and I have come to appreciate the differently gendered ways I can express my sexuality in all of them. I sometimes fantasise about my sexual and romantic encounters as collisions between two discreet and mutually impenetrable people who have an empty space between them where they overlap like a Venn diagram. We're both occupying a space but having different experiences within it, experiences which we can't really share. I feel fragmented, refracted, but not whole.

I think about the writing of a history of queer Aboriginality, and of representing that history and naming that history as queer or LGBTI. I wonder about the problem of legibility, and the trappings of writing or reading a history with intentions to reveal something you or someone reading you can recognise. I am conscious that history is written both to exclude and silence Aboriginal narratives and histories, and also to inhabit and perform settler fantasies of settler neutrality and innocence. I am aware that I also read history with a hopeful agenda. Queer, trans, brothaboy and sistergirl mob often discuss our lives with a hope to decolonise them and to recover our authentic selves and pasts. While we dream and imagine what our lives would be like without the forces of colonialism defining us within and outside our communities, we can't think of this simplistically nor set ourselves up to fail by chasing an idealised past or an untouched 'pristine, native state'.[15]

Randolph Bowers touches upon the complexities of simultaneously belonging to a tradition of First Nations knowledge and to the Euro-American academic structure. The tensions and challenges of producing dialogue from such a conflict are evident, and he is hesitant to resolve them simply:

> Some of this tension between worldviews is expressed overtly and covertly ... I do not apologise for the apparent contradictions this may create. As a person of mixed cultural origins, I admit a certain degree of confusion is warranted – and that this process of dialogue through the literature is a necessary step towards mutual clarification.[16]

Aileen Moreton-Robinson considers the utility of marginality and multiplicity as a location to produce a necessary 'creative space for developing the conceptual tools required to expose the social situatedness of knowledge production and the different realities that are produced and experienced'.[17] Moreton-Robinson critically distinguishes between the post-colonial and the post-colonising in order 'to signify the active, the current and the continuing nature of the colonising relationship that positions us as belonging but not belonging'. She explicates that the term 'post-colonial nation' is ahistorical and amnesiac within Australia's context, in which the settlers did not 'go home' and colonialism continues.[18] Moreton-Robinson disrupts the assumptions made in the application of post-colonial theory to Australia that there is a linear progress into post-colonial space which can be analysed alongside with the post-colonial histories of other countries that came under European colonial rule. Thus, she challenges the assertions that the colonial era itself was a discreet historical event. Referencing her, Henk Huijser analyses the appropriateness of applying post-colonial theory in Australian contexts, and asserts that:

> Resisting the impulse to create sameness (as opposed to equity) can help illuminate the powerful forces that try to do precisely that, as part of a restricting but politically dominant form of nation building.[19]

Similarly, Brydon notes that 'the very breadth of post-colonialism's reach has aroused concerns that the concept may prove unduly homogenising, overly ambitious, ahistorical, and thus complicit with the very relations of inequality that it ostensibly seeks to protest against'.[20] Moreton-Robinson's project of disrupting a unifying post-colonial discourse with a new way of studying difference and multiplicity is dynamic and potentially productive. It also encourages me to find methods to read, write and articulate an Aboriginal queer history while moving away from the urge to homogenise, or to make similarities out of differences.

Coalitions and collisions

I want to explore this homogenising urge within post-modern 'post-colonial' queer theories about Indigenous people more deeply. Not long after beginning this piece, I watched Matthew

Warcus' film *Pride* in which he documents the political alliance between London-based activist group Lesbians and Gays Support the Miners (LGSM) and striking Welsh miners during the 1984–85 British miner's strike. I had an incredible feeling of *deja vu* during the final scene of the movie. The members of London LGSM show up at the 1985 London Pride march with their home-painted, pro-miner banners only to be told by an organiser that they are not to march with political banners, and to move to the back of the march. Only the positive and simple material is to be out in front, while the overly-political content is to be out of sight. The campaigners are marked as the ugly and unfriendly side of the Pride movement. In 2011, I witnessed an incident at the Melbourne Pride march in St Kilda which mirrored this scene almost word-for-word; the only difference was that the issue under contention was not solidarity with miners, but queer refugees and asylum seekers living under the mandatory detention laws in Australia. Upon arriving with home-made banners, badges, and signs with pro-refugee slogans, myself and a group of (largely non-white and gender-diverse) student activists were called socialists and asked to leave. When we argued, a white cisgendered gay man shouted at us that we were not welcome and were too political. We were forced to move to a back section of the march.

Rea Saunders, writing in *Peopling the Empty Mirror*, explores the problems of coalition organising in environments where inevitable racial and gendered power dynamics come into play:

> We have to confront honestly our own racism, sexism, homophobia, and classism and acknowledge the difference between us … coalition politics can only be effective if all people involved are at an equal level. I am not interested in coalition politics where men still run things.[21]

Damien Riggs is one of several settler scholars who consider the ways that white settler queers have historically been encouraged to invest in the white Australian nation via their possessive investment in settler colonialism:

> Thus every time the government threatens to curtail our rights, we reaffirm our possessive investment by conforming to the 'aspirational practices' which suggest we can have 'equality with' the white heterosexual majority. In contrast to this, I would propose that maintaining such investments perpetuates a disavowal of Indigenous sovereignty.[22]

Going beyond the idea that coalitions *could* be run with everyone on an equal playing field – in order to develop what is referred to as 'coalition politics' in *Peopling the Empty Mirror* – queer Australian discourse must begin to articulate the relationship between settler colonialism and LGBTIQ identities, subjectivities and histories. Queer Australia must begin to understand not only racism and homonormativity within the LGBTIQ community, but also the underlying relationship between sexuality and the racialised white nation, and how that relationship has travelled through all of frontier and post-federation history and into the present.

This is particularly relevant to such themes as Indigenous people in government policy over the last twenty years or to asylum seekers and refugees.

For example, around the time of the 2011 Melbourne Pride confrontation, it was reported that a number of claimants in Australia seeking asylum based on LGBT persecution were being asked questions by authorities assessing their claims about whether or not they enjoyed listening to Madonna and Elton John, or reading Oscar Wilde, and about how and how often they had sex, and whether they were members of any public LGBT organisations. Such questions were often accompanied by highly invasive requests for 'evidence' in order to fulfil the official requirements for assessing claims based on persecution because of their sexuality. Jennifer Millbank's 2011 study noted that 'in an alarming number of cases tribunal members used highly stereotyped and westernised notions of 'gayness' as a template against which the applicants were judged'.[23] This brings into question the implication of western sub-cultural assumptions on what it means to experience being lesbian or gay. It also reveals the ways in which ambiguous cultural norms around homosexuality could become a means for the white nation to further articulate its borders in times when border protection is publicly politicised. The impact of the dialectical relationship between sexuality and nation in Australia since what is now commonly referred to as the formal end of the white Australia policy in the 1970s requires more investigation within queer politics. In particular, queer scholars must consider how policies around reconciliation, multicultural tolerance, mandatory detention, intervention, native title, and so on, reflect this relationship.

Scott Lauria Morgensen believes that the relationship between sexual identity formation and colonialist nationhood needs to be clarified. He argues that sexual modernity was formed within the colonies and exported back to Europe, and that this could not have taken place without the processes of colonisation or the interactions Europe had with the sexualised 'Other':

> In light of colonial histories, Europe is Western only to the extent that it is metropolitan – a center of colonial empires – which means neither Europe nor Western cultural legacies will be understood before studying their formation in colonial and settler societies ... Modern sexuality arose in the United States amid the colonial conditions of a settler society. Terrorising violence marked Native peoples as sexually deviant populations to be subjected to a colonial education of desire, while agents and

beneficiaries of sexual colonisation became subjects of settler sexuality. Settlement and its naturalisation then conditioned the emergence of modern queer formations.[24]

The settler imaginary has constituted sexual identities through an appropriative and reactive relationship with colonised peoples globally. Similarly, queer settler imaginaries often create analogies out of racism, racial marginalisation, migrancy, diasporic experience, and colonisation in order to narrativise themselves, constituting white settler queer identities through a repossession of the racialised other.

Nicolacopoulos and Vassilacopoulos theorise that Australian identities are defined through their 'problematic condition of seeking to embody one's will exclusively in something that is already an embodied being':

> If we reflect on white Australia as a product of the history-making that manifests the white nation's occupier being as a whole, [then] the essentials of a short history become visible in terms of two distinct targets for the annihilation of Indigenous sovereign being, namely the bearer of the question of our true origins as well as the question itself.[25]

In performing their assessment of the ontological roots of White Australia, Nicolacopoulos and Vassilacopoulos characterise all of settler Australian society as effectively a nervous reaction to Aboriginal sovereignty. This recognition is a testament to the power and inextinguishable nature of Aboriginal sovereignty: all assertions of Australian identity and belonging are produced in fear of the unspeakable truths about illegal occupation and the immovable reality of Indigenous belonging and ownership. Indigenous people are not only the ghostly imaginary of a fearful and anxious white national subject, we are the presence which destabilises white occupation and legitimacy, and this denaturalises the settler by their being present in our corporeality. Indigenous sovereignty others the settler presence in Australia, and forces it to perform its identity over and over. Queer settler identities in Australia could therefore be read as dependent upon the position of marginalisation that Indigenous people live in under colonialism.

Some scholars argue that settler colonialism 'queers' themselves colonise populations through the establishment of settler normativity and homonormativity. For example, in their discussion of settler homonationalism, Greensmith and Giwa write that under nationalistic settler colonialist projects, 'racialised subjects are excluded from White articulations of queerness and are simultaneously made Queer (monstrous, feminised, and abnormal)'.[26] This subsuming of queered-ness with othered-ness and race, as feminised and abnormal, is startlingly simplistic and could be read as unduly homogenising. I don't buy that processes of racism and colonialism are analogous to being 'queered' – or perhaps I want to clarify and complicate what queering can mean in relation to settler colonialism.

I'm cautious about the homogenising effect of describing the relationship between Indigenous people and the settler colonial state as one which 'queers'. I'm also wary of other comparisons that are crudely drawn between migration, diaspora and queer or trans experience, or between gay marriage and interracial marriage. Many queer and trans settlers with an interest in Indigenous knowledge and Indigenous activism, when I've asked them to explain how their interest was sparked, have answered that they are interested in Indigenous perspectives because they also identify with the 'marginalised' culture, being outside of 'normal' society themselves. I wonder what this comparison means when looking at some of the ways queer agency is defined against the middle class institution of family, and against reproduction, monogamous heterosexuality, and marriage. Since colonisation, Aboriginal people have been subjects of eugenicist state violence, and largely are unable to access the middle class or the institutions of family which western queer discourse has sought to undermine.[27] Arguments about the homonormative, sexually conservative and classist limits of same-sex marriage show only a shallow engagement with the ways that Aboriginal people have experienced family, eugenics, separation, and racialised sexual violence. I don't think the framework of 'queering' as a lens from which to understand the experiences of Aboriginal people living under sexualised colonisation can capture all of the complexity and the violence of the sexual and intimate relationship of settlers to Indigenous peoples. This framework may, in some ways, misunderstand the formations of those relationships from early frontier times to the present. These relationships take place at all levels: personal, governmental, discursive, and sexual.

I most value the kinds of collaboration which are able to happen without that homogenising instinct. Here, I mean the types of relationship-based and cultural building which I've experienced in racial and feminist activism where the differences between people are undeniable and unresolvable, and no-one attempts to make them legible or translatable. We are able to acknowledge each other's subjectivities and to share work which interests and heals us both. For me, the intricacies and intimacies of relationships are what drives movement building, rather than a forced solidarity which is based on a presumption of sameness, or worse, empty networking. Politics of solidarity and similarity in practice feel and look performative and clumsy. It's consumptive but not sustaining. Much of the work happens in private. Many of the affinities I've established are not systemic, and nor do they allow for unilateral movement or wholescale 'solidarity', or for shared identity.

Discussions on Queer and Indigenous subjectivities need to now push this conversation about the common ground between the movements a little further. This is not to negate the idea that LGBTQ settlers and Indigenous people both suffer in comparable and interlocking ways under the conditions of settler colonialism and heteropatriarchy but, rather, to complicate it. It is important to investigate where and when we can draw parallels, solidarity and common interest in the ways we experience marginalisation, as well as recognising when that 'comparison' subsumes, homogenises, appropriates, erases, or colonises.

Notes

Acknowledgements

1   Wendy Dunn/Holland, Maureen Fletcher, Dino Hodge, Gary Lee, E.J. Milera (John Cross), Rea Saunders and Jim Wafer (The Gays and Lesbians Aboriginal Alliance), 'Peopling the Empty Mirror: The Prospects for Lesbian and Gay Aboriginal History', in *Gay Perspectives II: More Essays in Australian Gay Culture*, ed. Robert Aldrich (Sydney: University of Sydney, 1994), 1–62. http://alga.org.au/files/Peopling-the-Empty-Mirror.pdf

2   For example, see Wayne King, *Black Hours* (Sydney: Angus and Robertson, 1996); and, Carolyn D'Cruz, 'Black Power and Gay Liberation: An Interview with Gary Foley', in *After Homosexual: The Legacies of Gay Liberation*, eds Carolyn D'Cruz and Mark Pendleton (Perth: UWA Publishing, 2013), 65–74.

3   Kathy Triffitt, 'A Story to Tell: Rodney Junga Williams, 18 February 1962–24 November 2011', *Talkabout* 176, March–April 2012, 11–14. http://issuu.com/positivelifensw/docs/176medium

4   Steven Lindsay Ross, 'A Lore unto Themselves', *Archer* 2, winter 2014, 77–81.

5   Dino Hodge, *Did You Meet Any Malagas? A Homosexual History of Australia's Tropical Capital* (Nightcliff, Darwin: Little Gem, 1993).

6   Lynn Gehl, 'A Colonized Ally Meets a Decolonized Ally: This is What They Learn', 15 March 2014, https://unsettlingamerica. wordpress.com/2014/03/15/ a-colonized-ally-meets-a- decolonized-ally-this-is-what-they-learn

7   Damien W. Riggs, 'Possessive Investments at the Intersections
    of Race, Gender and Sexuality: Lesbian and Gay Rights in a
    "Post-Colonising" Context', http://www.damienriggs.com/blog/
    wp-content/uploads/2013/09/Possessive-investments.pdf

8   Barbara Baird, 'In Relation to a White Father', *Critical Race and
    Whiteness Studies* 1, no. 2, 2011, www.acrawsa.org.au/ejournal

9   Gabi Rosenstreich and Sally Goldner, 'Inclusion and Exclusion:
    Aboriginal, Torres Strait Islander, Trans and Intersex Voices at
    the *Health in Difference Conference 2010* ', *Gay and Lesbian Issues
    and Psychology Review* 6, no. 3, 2010, 139–49.

Introduction: Looking In to the Mirror

1   Roland Barthes, *Image, Music, Text* (London: Fontana Paperbacks,
    1984), 165.

2   Andrew Gorman-Murray, 'Gay and Lesbian Public History in
    Australia', *Public History Review* 31, 2004.

3   Clive Moore, *Sunshine and Rainbows: The Development of Gay
    and Lesbian Culture in Queensland* (St Lucia, Qld.: University of
    Queensland Press, 2001), 51–53.

4   For example, Peter A. Jackson and Gerard Sullivan, eds,
    Multicultural Queer: Australian Perspectives (New York: Haworth
    Press, 1999); and, Garry Wotherspoon, *City of the Plain: History of
    a Gay Sub–Culture* (Sydney: Hale and Iremonger, 1991).

5   Rebecca Jennings, 'Lesbians in Sydney', *Sydney Journal* 2, no. 1,
    June 2009.

6   Ibid.

7   Wendy Dunn/Holland, Maureen Fletcher, Dino Hodge, Gary
    Lee, E.J. Milera (John Cross), Rea Saunders and Jim Wafer (The
    Gays and Lesbians Aboriginal Alliance), 'Peopling the Empty
    Mirror: The Prospects for Lesbian and Gay Aboriginal History',
    in *Gay Perspectives II: More Essays in Australian Gay Culture*, ed.
    Robert Aldrich (Sydney: University of Sydney, 1994), 1–62.
    http://alga.org.au/files/Peopling-the-Empty-Mirror.pdf

8   I am appropriating the term 'perverse' and attaching meaning to
    it from my Queer-Aboriginal philosophical position, rather than
    accepting its definition in a negative or pejorative sense. My use
    of the term 'perversities' infers both queering Aboriginality *and*

Aboriginalising queer – a kind of simultaneous interplay with infinite potential to expand categorisation.

9   Jon Willis, 'Heteronormativity and the Deflection of Male Same-sex Attraction among the Pitjantjatjara People of Australia's Western Desert', *Culture, Health and Sexuality* 5, iss. 2, January 2003, 137–51, 137.

10 Geza Roheim, *Children of the Desert: The Western Tribes of Central Australia* (New York: Basic Books, 1974).

11 Dino Hodge, *Did You Meet Any Malagas? A Homosexual History of Australia's Tropical Capital* (Nightcliff, Darwin: Little Gem, 1993).

12 Robert Reynolds, 'Writing Queer Cultural Histories', *Critical inQueeries* 1, no. 1, September 1995, 69–83.

13 Robert Aldrich, *Colonialism and Homosexuality* (New York and London: Routledge, 2003), 218.

14 Dunn/Holland et al, 'Peopling the Empty Mirror', in *Gay Perspectives II*, ed. Aldrich.

15 Chris Finley 'Decolonizing the Queer Native Body (and Recovering the Native Bull-Dyke): Bringing "Sexy Back" and Out of Native Studies' Closet', in *Queer Indigenous Studies: Critical Interventions in Theory, Politics, and Literature*, eds Qwo-Li Driskill, Chris Finley, Brian Joseph Gilley and Scott Lauria Morgensen (Tuscon: University of Arizona Press, 2011), 32–42, 33.

16 Driskill et al, *Queer Indigenous Studies*; Mark Rifkin, *When Did Indians Become Straight? Kinship, the History of Sexuality, and Native Sovereignty* (Oxford and New York: Oxford University Press, 2011); Daniel Heath Justice, Mark Rifkin and Bethany Schneider, 'Introduction', *GLQ: A Journal of Lesbian and Gay Studies* 16, iss. 1–2, 2010, 5–39.

17 Franz Fanon, *The Wretched of the Earth* (New York: Grove Press, 1963), 36.

18 Marie Battiste, 'Research Ethics for Protecting Indigenous Knowledge and Heritage: Institutional and Researcher Responsibilities', in *Handbook of Critical and Indigenous Methodologies*, eds Norman K. Denzin and Yvonna S. Lincoln (Thousand Oaks, CA: Sage Publications, 2008), 497–511, 508.

19 Driskill et al, *Queer Indigenous Studies*.

20 Rifkin, *When Did Indians Become Straight?*, 7.

21 Linda Tuhiwai Smith, *Decolonising Methodologies: Research and Indigenous Peoples* (Dunedin: University of Otago Press, 1999), 1.

22 Beth Blue Swadena and Kagendo Matua, 'Decolonising Performances: Deconstructing the Postcolonial', in *Handbook of Critical and Indigenous Methodologies*, eds Denzin and Lincoln, 31–44.

23 Driskill et al, *Queer Indigenous Studies*; Jessica Hutchings and Clive Aspin, eds, *Sexuality and the Stories of Indigenous People* (Wellington, Aotearoa New Zealand: Huia Publishers, 2007).

24 Andrea Smith, 'Queer Theory and Native Studies: The Heteronormativity of Settler Colonialism', in *Queer Indigenous Studies*, eds Driskill et al, 43–65.

25 Linda Tuhiwai Smith, *Decolonising Methodologies*, 65.

26 Smith, 'Queer Theory and Native Studies' in *Queer Indigenous Studies*, eds Driskill et al, 47.

27 Yvonna Lincoln and Norman Denzin, eds, *The Handbook of Qualitative Research*, (Thousand Oaks, California: Sage Publications, 1994), 575.

28 Stephen Kemmis and Robin McTaggart, 'Participatory Action Research: Communicative Action and the Public Sphere', in *The Handbook of Qualitative Research*, eds Lincoln and Denzin, (3rd ed., 2005), 271–330.

29 Laurel Richardson and Elizabeth Adams St Pierre, 'Writing: A Method of Inquiry', in *The Handbook of Qualitative Research*, eds Lincoln and Denzin, (3rd ed., 2005), 959–78.

30 Qwo-Li Driskill, '(Asegi Ayetl): Cherokee Two-Spirit People Reimagining Nation', in *Queer Indigenous Studies*, eds Driskill et al.

31 Rangitunoa Black, 'Mana Takatapui', in *Sexuality and the Stories of Indigenous People*, eds Hutchings and Aspin.

32 Crystal Johnson and Jason De Santis in conversation with the author, Adelaide, November 2010; and, Jason De Santis in conversation with the author, Darwin, August 2012.

33 Stephen Gilchrist, 'From Tiwi with Love: Bindi Cole', *Artlink* 30, no. 1, 2010, 74–77.

34 Noel Pearson, 'Contradictions Cloud the Apology to the Stolen Generations', *Australian*, 12 February 2008; Troy-Anthony Baylis, 'Sandra Saunders: Shaker-Maker', in *Deadly: in-between heaven and hell*, exhibition catalogue, National Aboriginal Cultural Institute – Tandanya, Adelaide, 28 February–25 March 2012.

35 Elizabeth Kerekere, 'Takatapui – Where Worlds Collide', in *Sexuality and the Stories of Indigenous People*, eds Hutchings and Aspin, 38.

36 Rifkin, *When Did Indians Become Straight?*, 7.

37 Finley 'Decolonizing the Queer Native Body', in *Queer Indigenous Studies*, eds Driskill et al, 32.

38 Amartya Sen, *Identity and Violence: The Illusion of Destiny* (New York: W.W. Norton & Co, 2006).

39 Hetti Perkins and Clare Williamson, *Blakness: Blak City Culture!*, exhibition catalogue, Australian Centre for Contemporary Art with Boomalli Aboriginal Artists Co-operative, Melbourne, 1994.

40 Lincoln and Denzin, 'The Seventh Moment: Out of the Past', in *The Handbook of Qualitative Research*, 1057.

Kungakunga: Staying Close to Family and Country

1 Oopoonga is Tiwi for marijuana.

2 Crystal Johnson, 'Indigenous Report', *GayNT* 1, iss. 3, 2000, 22.

3 Cyril Johnson, 'Indigenous Report', *GayNT* 1, iss. 1, 2000, 14.

4 http://mindoutconference.net

5 http://www.anzpath.org/events/biennial-conference

6 https://www.youtube.com/watch?v=O1P9gmiXOss

7 http://sistersandbrothersnt.com

Pigeon-holing Trauma: Situating Demoralisation

1 Henry Morgenthau III, 'The Negro and the American Promise', Boston Public Television, USA, 1963. http://www.pbs.org/wgbh/americanexperience/features/bonus-video/mlk-james-baldwin

2 Miggaloo means ghost, and now is a variable term referring to people of European persuasion.

3 Dhari is a traditional Torres Strait headdress mostly made of white feathers. It occupies the centre of the Torres Strait Islander flag and is worn when performing traditional dances and ceremony.

4 W.E.B. Du Bois, *The Souls of Black Folk* (Chicago: AC McClurg & Co, 1903).

5 Australian Federation of Aids Organisations, *Anwernekenhe 2: Report of the Second National Indigenous Australian Gay Men and Transgender Peoples Conference* (Sydney: AFAO, 1998), http://www.afao.org.au/__data/assets/pdf_file/0004/4657/Indig_anwernekenheii.pdf

6 Nickname for Brisbane, referencing Las Vegas.

7 Big Mother or Eldest Aunty.

8 Nickname for Brisbane, referencing Disney Land.

9 When I grew up *only* my family were considered my 'Elders', although I was taught to respect *all* elderly people.

10 Stolen Generation is well known now, however, there are lost people who will never recover their Indigenous identity. Hidden are those who continue to hide their Indigenous identity to the public for fear of losing what they have gained because of Whiteness.

11 Palawah is a collective term for Tasmanian Aboriginals, akin to Murri in Queensland.

12 Anangu people are one of the Central Australian tribal groups. Tjukurpa is the word Pitjantjatjara-speaking Anangu use to describe Dreaming, the force which unites Anangu with each other and with the landscape.

13 http://www.livingpositivevictoria.org.au/poslink/Poslink_Issue_050.pdf, page 3.

My Totem is Tawny Frogmouth

1 'Brotherboys Yarnin' Up – Kai and Dean', https://www.youtube.com/watch?v=fTtiYD8GmXQ

My Story, Your Story, Our Story

1 http://www.abc.net.au/news/2007-08-13/indigenous-community-mourns-loss-of-aunty-mary/638300

2   *Green Weekly*, 25 October 2009, https://www.greenleft.org.au/ node/42661

3   www.coomaditchie.org.au/coomie-story.html

4   http://redfernoralhistory.org/Organisations/ AboriginalMedicalService/tabid/208/Default.aspx

5   http://www.wollongong.nsw.gov.au/services/community/pages/ aboriginal.aspx

6   https://bundjalungelderscouncil.wordpress.com

7   http://en.wikipedia.org/wiki/ History_of_Gold_Coast,_Queensland

8   http://en.wikipedia.org/wiki/The_Castro,_San_Francisco

9   James Kinsella, *Covering the Plague: AIDS and the American Media* (New Jersey :Rutgers University Press, 1989).

10 John D'Emilio, *Making Trouble: Essays on Gay History, Politics and the University* (New York: Routledge, 1992).

11 Albert Holt, *Forcibly Removed* (Broome, WA: Magabala Books, 2001).

12 Michael Marmot, 'Social determinants of Health Inequalities', *The Lancet* 365, no. 9464, March 2005, 1099–1104.

13 Peter Read, *Tripping Over Feathers: Scenes in the Life of Joy Janaka Wiradjuri Williams: A Narrative of the Stolen Generations* (Crawley, WA: UWA Publishing, 2009). Also, Samia Goudie, 'Testimony', self-produced video, 1998.

14 Gaynor Marilyn Macdonald and Julie Marcus, *Two Steps Forward, Three Steps Back: A Wiradjuri Land Rights Journey: Letters to the Wiradjuri Regional Aboriginal Land Council on Its 20th Anniversary, 1983–2003* (Canada Bay, NSW: LhR Press, 2004).

15 Human Rights and Equal Opportunity Commission, The Royal Commission into Aboriginal Deaths in Custody, 1987–1991, http://guides.naa.gov.au/aboriginal-deaths-in-custody/index.aspx

16 Ronald Wilson, *Bringing Them Home: Report of the National Inquiry into the Separation of Aboriginal and Torres Strait Islander Children from their Families* (Sydney: Human Rights and Equal Opportunity Commission, 1997).

17 Susan Barrett, 'Reconstructing Australia's Shameful Past: The Stolen Generations in Life-Writing, Fiction and Film', *lignes 2*, 2005, 1–13, http://www.lines.fr/lines2/01barrett.pdf

18 Judy Atkinson, *Trauma Trails, Recreating Song Lines: The Transgenerational Effects of Trauma in Indigenous Australia* (North Melbourne: Spinifex Press, 2002).

19 Maria Yellow Horse Braveheart, http://www.historicaltrauma.com

20 Peter Read, *The Stolen Generations: The Removal of Aboriginal Children in New South Wales 1883 to 1969* (Sydney: Government Press, 1982), http://www.stolengenerations.info/index.php?option=com_content&view=article&id=75&Itemid=30

21 Erik Eklund, 'The "Place" of Politics: Class and Localist Politics at Port Kembla, 1900–30', *Labour History* 78, May 2000, 94–115.

22 Peter Read, *A Rape of the Soul So Profound: The Return of the Stolen Generation* (Sydney: Allen & Unwin, 1999).

23 *Koori Mail*, 18 November 1998, 17.

24 Yin Paradies, Understanding the Impact of Racism on Indigenous Child Health, 2009, https://www.youtube.com/watch?v=pehT4CFPnJQ

That Rope Pulls Along Many People

1 Information on the 2 Spirits program and support groups, gar-ban-djee-lum in Brisbane and Yupla Mipla Ahfla in Cairns, is available found at: www.qahc.org.au/2-spirits-promoting-healthy-aboriginal-and-torres-strait-islander-communities

2 Open Doors provides counselling and support services for LGBT young people aged twelve-to-twenty-four and their families who live in South East Queensland, http://www.opendoors.net.au

3 The name *gar'ban'djee'lum* means 'us mob' and was provided by Butchulla and Gubbi Gubbi Elders; *yupla mipla ahfla* means 'you, me, us' in Kriol spoken in northern mainland Australia.

4 Condoman and Lubelicious are part of a sexual health campaign using a variety of print and multi-media resources. An example of a radio advertisement produced in 2012 by 2 Spirits in collaboration with the Institute for Urban Indigenous Health

and 98.9 FM Radio can be viewed at www.youtube.com/
watch?v=aW3ckE314-o

5   'Our Story, Our Time, Our Future: 2014 International
    Indigenous Pre-conference on HIV & AIDS', Sydney,
    17–19 July 2014. Conference proceedings are available at
    indigenoushivaids2014.com

'Words are like Weapons, They Wound Sometimes'

1   Andrew Bolt, 'Aboriginal Man Helped', Blog, *Herald Sun*, 19
    August 2009, http://blogs.news.com.au/heraldsun/andrewbolt/
    index.php/heraldsun/aboriginal_man_helped

2   Ibid., and, Andrew Bolt, 'White fellas in the black', *Herald Sun*,
    21 August 2009, http://www.heraldsun.com.au/news/opinion/
    white-fellas-in-the-black/story-e6frfifo-1225764532947

3   I was one of the applicants in the Federal Court action brought
    against Mr Bolt and the Herald Weekly Times for breaching the
    Commonwealth's Racial Discrimination Act. Eatock v Bolt [2011]
    FCA 1103 (28 September 2011), http://www.austlii.edu.au/au/
    cases/cth/FCA/2011/1103.html

4   Bolt, 'Aboriginal Man Helped'.

5   Ibid.

6   Eatock v Bolt [2011] FCA 1103 (28 September 2011)

7   I use gammon in the sense of having a derogatory connotation.

8   Eatock v Bolt [2011] FCA 1103 (28 September 2011) at paragraph
    65.

9   According to Justice Bromberg of the Federal Court of Australia .
    Eatock v Bolt [2011] FCA 1103 (28 September 2011)

10 http://www.abc.net.au/indigenous/stories/s2371651.htm

11 Karl Quinn, 'Anti-gay claim enrages Bolt', *Age*, 31 March 2011,
    http://www.theage.com.au/victoria/antigay-claim-enrages-bolt-
    20110330-1cgf0.html

12 Ibid.

13 Bolt, 'White fellas in the black'.

14 Eatock v Bolt [2011] FCA 1103 (28 September 2011) at paragraph
    49.

15 Bolt, 'White fellas in the black'.

A Lore unto Themselves

1   http://www.abc.net.au/news/2013-11-01/
    anthony-mundine-aborigines-homosexual-gay/5063836

2   The 2008 National Aboriginal and Torres Strait Islander
    Social Survey (NATSISS) provides information on a range of
    demographic, social, environmental and economic indicators,
    including: personal and household characteristics; geography;
    language and cultural activities; social networks and support;
    health and disability; education; employment; financial stress;
    income; transport; personal safety; and housing. The survey
    collected information from approximately 13,300 Aboriginal
    and Torres Strait Islander adults and children living in private
    dwellings in remote and non-remote areas, including discrete
    communities. More information on the 2008 NATSISS is available
    from the Australian Bureau of Statistics, National Aboriginal and
    Torres Strait Islander Social Survey: Users' Guide, 2008 (cat. no.
    4720.0).

3   National Health Survey, 2007–08, p. 82. http://www.abs.gov.au/
    ausstats/abs@.nsf/mf/4363.0.55.001

4   Chris Holland with Pat Dudgeon and Helen Milroy, 'The Mental
    Health and Social and Emotional Wellbeing of Aboriginal and
    Torres Strait Islander Peoples, Families and Communities',
    2013 – A Supplementary Paper to National Mental Health
    Commission, *A Contributing Life: The 2012 National Report Card
    on Mental Health and Suicide Prevention*, Sydney: NMHC, 2012.

5   Gary Lee and Timothy Moore, *The National Indigenous Gay and
    Transgender Project: Consultation Report and Sexual Health Strategy*.
    (The combined consultation report [Lee is sole author] and
    strategy [Lee and Moore joint authors in association with the
    AFAO Indigenous Gay and Transgender Steering Committee] is
    known as the 'Green Document'.) Sydney: Australian Federation
    of AIDS Organisations, 1998. http://www.afao.org.au/__data/
    assets/pdf_file/0016/4660/Indig_report.pdf See also Gary Lee,
    Malaga to Malaga: Man to Man. 2nd ed. Darwin: Danila Dilba
    Biluru Butji Binnilutlum Medical Service Aboriginal Corporation
    and Northern Territory AIDS Council, 1996.

6 http://www.theguardian.com/australia-news/2015/feb/18/
   lgbti-indigenous-people-offered-a-rainbow-to-follow

7 'Homophobia in Our Communities', *Koori Mail*, 564, 20
   November 2013, 25.

8 http://www.samesame.com.au/news/10380/
   Black-Rainbow-challenges-homophobia

Dual Imperatives

1 Throughout this essay I refer to 'Indigenous studies', 'Aboriginal
   studies' and 'Native studies'; the latter is the term used in North
   America, while 'Indigenous studies' and 'Aboriginal studies' are
   used somewhat interchangeably in the Australian literature.

2 Scott Lauria Morgensen, 'Settler Homonationalism: Theorizing
   Settler Colonialism within Queer Modernities', *GLQ: A Journal
   of Lesbian and Gay Studies* 16, 2010, 105–131.

3 Puar is writing in the U.S. context about U.S. queer subjects;
   nonetheless the conceptual framework she provides extends to
   many other Western nations, including Australia.

4 Alfred Taiaiake and Jeff Corntassel, 'Being Indigenous:
   Resurgences against Contemporary Colonialism', *Government and
   Opposition* 40, iss. 4, 2005, 597–614.

5 Ibid., 599; there are about 350 million Indigenous peoples living
   within approximately seventy countries around the world.

6 Cameron Greensmith and Sulaimon Giwa, 'Challenging
   Settler Colonialism in Contemporary Queer Politics: Settler
   Homonationalism, Pride Toronto, and Two-Spirit Subjectivities',
   American Indian Culture and Research Journal 37, iss. 2, 2013,
   131, citing Gayatri Chakravorty Spivak, 'Subaltern Studies:
   Deconstructing Historiographies', in *Other Worlds: Essays in
   Cultural Politics*, ed. Gayatri Chakravorty Spivak, (New York:
   Routledge Press, 2006), 160–304.

7 Lorenzo Veracini, 'Introducing Settler Colonial Studies', *Settler
   Colonial Studies* 1, 2011, 2.

8 Ibid., 5.

9 Lorenzo Veracini, 'Settler Colonialism and Decolonisation',
   Borderlands 6, no. 2, 2007. See also Patrick Wolfe, 'Settler

Colonialism and the Elimination of the Native', *Journal of Genocide Research* 8, no. 4, 2006, 387–409.

10 Eve Tuck and K. Wayne Yang, 'Decolonization is not a Metaphor', *Decolonization: Indigeneity, Education & Society* 1, no. 1, 2012, 1–40, 4.

11 Ibid., 4.

12 Veracini, 'Introducing Settler Colonial Studies', 2 (emphasis in original). See also Albert Memmi, *The Colonizer and the Colonized* (London: Earthscan, 2003), 53.

13 Tuck and Yang, 'Decolonization is not a Metaphor',' 1.

14 Ibid., 4.

15 Ibid.

16 Ibid.

17 Oscar Monaghan, 'Legal Education in a Settler Context', *Dissent*, 2014, 27–30.

18 Veracini, 'Introducing Settler Colonial Studies', 2–3.

19 Philip Deloria, *Playing Indian* (New Haven, CT: Yale University Press, 1998), 5, cited in Tuck and Yang, 'Decolonization is not a Metaphor', 7.

20 Wolfe, 'Settler Colonialism', 388.

21 Scott Lauria Morgensen, 'Theorising Gender, Sexuality and Settler Colonialism', *Settler Colonial Studies* 2, iss. 2, 2012, 2–22.

22 Ibid., 4.

23 Ibid., 10.

24 Michel Foucault, *The History of Sexuality, Vol 1* (London: Penguin, 1978), cited in Richard Philips, 'Settler Colonialism and the Nuclear Family', *The Canadian Geographer* 53, iss. 2, 2009, 239–253, 242.

25 Ann Laura Stoler, *Race and the Education of Desire: Foucault's History of Sexuality and the Colonial Order of Things* (Durham: Duke University Press, 1996); and, *Carnal Knowledge and Imperial Power: Race and the Intimate in Colonial Rule* (Berkeley: University of California Press, 2002), cited in Philips, 'Settler Colonialism', 242.

26 Morgensen, 'Settler Homonationalism'.

27 Bethany Schneider, 'Oklahobo: Following Craig Womack's American Indian and Queer Studies', *South Atlantic Quarterly* 106, 2007, 606–7, cited in Morgensen, 'Settler Homonationalism'.

28 Cole Harris, 'The Simplification of Europe Overseas', *Annals of the Association of American Geographers* 67, 1977, 469–483.

29 Philips, 'Settler Colonialism and the Nuclear Family', 240, citing Louis Hartz, *Founding of New Societies* (New York: Harcourt, Brace & World, 1946).

30 Ibid.

31 Morgensen, 'Settler Homonationalism', 106.

32 Foucault, Michel. *The History of Sexuality, Vol 1.*

33 Philips, 'Settler Colonialism and the Nuclear Family', 243.

34 Ibid., 240.

35 Linda Tuhiwai Smith, *Decolonizing Methodologies* (Dunedin: University of Otago Press, 1999), 151.

36 Andrea Smith, *Conquest: Sexual Violence and the American Indian Genocide* (Cambridge, MA: South End, 2005), 139.

37 Greensmith and Giwa, 'Challenging Settler Colonialism', 130.

38 Morgensen, 'Settler Homonationalism'.

39 Jasbir Puar, *Terrorist Assemblages: Homonationalism in Queer Times* (Durham, NC: Duke University Press, 2007), see esp. preface, 4.

40 Morgensen, 'Settler Homonationalism', 105.

41 Greensmith and Giwa, 'Challenging Settler Colonialism', 133.

42 Ibid.

43 Lisa Duggan, 'The New Homonormativity: The Sexual Politics of Neoliberalism' in *Materializing Democracy: Toward a Revitalized Cultural Politics*, eds Russ Castronova and Dana Nelson (Durham, NC: Duke University Press, 2002), 179, cited in Greensmith and Giwa, 'Challenging Settler Colonialism'.

44 Kevin Markwell, 'Mardi Gras Tourism and the Construction of Sydney as an International Gay and Lesbian City', *GLQ: A Journal of Lesbian and Gay Studies* 8, no. 1/2, 2002, 81–99, 84.

45 Tuck and Wayne, 'Decolonization is not a Metaphor', 7.

46 Ibid.

47 Ibid.

48 Ibid.

49 Andrea Smith, 'Queer Theory and Native Studies: The Heteronormativity of Settler Colonialism', *GLQ: A Journal of Lesbian and Gay Studies* 16, no. 1/2, 2010, 41–68.

50 Patricia Monture-Angus, *Journeying Forward* (Halifax: Fernwood, 1999), 36, cited in Andrea Smith, 'Queer Theory and Native Studies'.

51 Smith, 'Queer Theory and Native Studies', 62.

52 Scott Lauria Morgensen, 'Unsettling Queer Politics: What Can Non-Natives Learn from Two-Spirit Organizing', in *Queer Indigenous Studies: Critical Interventions in Theory, Politics, and Literature*, eds Qwo-Li Driskill, Chris Finley, Brian Joseph Gilley and Scott Lauria Morgensen (Tuscon: University of Arizona Press, 2011), 134.

53 Morgensen, 'Theorising Gender, Sexuality and Settler Colonialism'.

54 Smith, 'Queer Theory and Native Studies', 60.

55 Ibid.

56 See Alfred Taiaiake, *Wasa'se: Indigenous Pathways of Action and Freedom* (Peterborough, ON: Broadview, 2005); Glen Sean Coulthard, *Red Skin White Masks: Rejecting the Colonial Politics of Recognition* (Minnaepolis: University of Minnesota Press, 2014); and, Jennifer Denetdale, 'Carving Navajo Naitonal Boundaries: Patriotism, Tradition, and the Dine Marriage Act of 2005', *American Quarterly* 60, 2008, 289–94.

57 Glen Sean Coulthard, 'Indigenous Peoples and the "Politics of Recognition" in Colonial Contexts', paper presented at the Cultural Studies Now Conference, University of East London, 22 July 2007; cited in Smith, 'Queer Theory and Native Studies'.

58 Morgensen, 'Settler Homonationalism'.

59 Morgensen, 'Unsettling Queer Politics'.

Stranger in a Strange Land

1 Aileen Moreton-Robinson, 'Whiteness Matters: Implications of Talking up to the White Woman', *Australian Feminist Studies* 21, no. 50, 2006, 245–56.

2 Images and video relevant to this essay can be accessed at http://www.sandyosullivan.com/stranger

3   Damien W. Riggs, and Martha Augoustinos, 'The Psychic Life of
    Colonial Power: Racialised Subjectivities, Bodies and Methods',
    Journal of Community and Applied Social Psychology 15, no. 6,
    2005, 461–77; and, T. Nicolacopoulos and G. Vassilacopoulos,
    'Racism, Foreigner Communities and the Onto-pathology of
    White Australian Subjectivity' in *Whitening Race: Essays in Social
    and Cultural Criticism*, ed. Aileen Moreton-Robinson (Canberra:
    Aboriginal Studies Press, 2004), 32–47.

4   S. O'Sullivan, *The Multifarious Identity: Intersections of Gender,
    Sexuality and Indigeneity*, PhD exegesis and artefact, Batchelor
    Institute of Indigenous Tertiary Education, Batchelor N.T., 2006,
    http://eprints.batchelor.edu.au/108

5   A.D. Schrift, 'Discipline and Punish', in *A Companion to Foucault*,
    eds Christopher Falzon, Timothy O'Leary and Jana Sawicki
    (Chichester, U.K.: John Wiley, 2013).

6   S. O'Sullivan, *Simulacra: Everyday Alone in Perspex, Colour and
    Light* in the exhibition, *The Multifarious Identity: Intersections of
    Gender, Sexuality and Indigeneity*, Watt Space, Newcastle, 2006,
    access at http://www.sandyosullivan.com/stranger

7   That didn't happen; it turns out banjos aren't exactly rock
    instruments.

8   D-O. Gougelet and E.K. Feder, 'Genealogies of Race and
    Gender, in *A Companion to Foucault*, eds Falzon et al.

9   E.L. Adams, 'Lesbian Folklore', in *Encyclopedia of Women's
    Folklore and Folklife*, eds Liz Locke, Theresa Vaughan and Pauline
    Greenhill (Westport, Conn.: Greenwood, 2009).

10 S. O'Sullivan, *Cartoon Physics*, promotional shot, Sydney, 1986,
    access at http://www.sandyosullivan.com/stranger

11 Pierre Bourdieu, 'The Forms of Capital', in *Education: Culture,
    Economy, and Society*, eds A.H. Halsey, H. Lauder, Phillip Brown
    and Amy Wells (Oxford: Oxford University Press, 1997), 40–58.

12 In contrast to the contemporary framing of the problematic term
    'pre-history', the term 'deep time' engages ideas of the written
    and known form as an emergence of connected cultural practice,
    and reflects a non-specific era substantially removed from the
    present. See, Amy Lonetree, *Decolonizing Museums: Representing*

Native America in National and Tribal Museums (Chapel Hill, U.S.A: University of North Carolina Press, 2012).

13 Wendy Dunn/Holland, Maureen Fletcher, Dino Hodge, Gary Lee, E.J. Milera (John Cross), Rea Saunders and Jim Wafer (The Gays and Lesbians Aboriginal Alliance), 'Peopling the Empty Mirror: The Prospects for Lesbian and Gay Aboriginal History', in *Gay Perspectives II: More Essays in Australian Gay Culture*, ed. Robert Aldrich (Sydney: University of Sydney, 1994), 1–62, 27–28; and, Jon Willis, 'Sexual Cultures: Some Notes on Indigenous Australian Sexualities', in *Perspectives in Human Sexuality*, eds Gail Hawkes and John Scott (South Melbourne: Oxford University Press, 2005) 119–41.

14 Dunn/Holland et al, 'Peopling the Empty Mirror'; and, Alex Wilson, 'N'tacimowin inna nah': Our Coming In Stories', *Canadian Woman Studies* 26, nos. 3/4, 2008, 123–99.

15 Dunn/Holland et al, 'Peopling the Empty Mirror'.

16 Wilson, 'N'tacimowin inna nah'', 193.

17 A.C. Bunten, 'The Paradox of Gaze and Resistance in Native American Cultural Tourism: An Alaskan Case Study', in *Great Expectation: Imagination and Anticipation in Tourism*, eds Jonathan Skinner and Dimitrios Theodossopoulos (New York: Berghahn Books, 2001), 61–81, see 63.

18 Ibid.

19 Lonetree, *Decolonizing Museums*.

20 Genevieve Grieves, (Lead Curator), *First Peoples*, exhibition, Bunjilaka Aboriginal Cultural Centre, Melbourne Museum, Australia, 2013.

21 Lonetree, *Decolonizing Museums*.

22 Mary Graham, 'Some Thoughts about the Philosophical Underpinnings of Aboriginal Worldviews', *Australian Humanities Review* 45, November 2008, 181.

23 Ronald Wilson, *Bringing Them Home: Report of the National Inquiry into the Separation of Aboriginal and Torres Strait Islander Children from their Families* (Sydney: Human Rights and Equal Opportunity Commission, 1997), see 41.

24 Graham, 'Some Thoughts about the Philosophical Underpinnings', 183.

25 I have struggled across this chapter with talking about my immediate family, my father's family, and their identity work. As one-sided as it would appear, I have come to the conclusion that theirs is not my story to tell. I would like to state, however, that I have always been supported and encouraged by them.

26 S. O'Sullivan, *Felt Up*, extract from audio CD, Independent Records, Inc., Sydney, 2004, access at http://www.sandyosullivan. com/stranger

The Border Made of Mirrors

1 Australian Human Rights Commission, *Social Justice Report no. 2/2000* (Sydney: AGPS, 1999).

2 S. Gorringe, J. Ross, and C. Fforde, *Will the Real Aborigine Please Stand Up: Strategies for Breaking the Stereotypes and Changing the Conversation*, AIATSIS Research Discussion Paper 28, (Canberra: AIATSIS, 2011). See also Elizabeth Povinelli, *The Cunning of Recognition: Indigenous Alterities and the Making of Australian Multiculturalism* (Durham: Duke University Press, 2002).

3 Michelle Harris, Bronwyn Carlson and E. Poata-Smith, 'Indigenous Identities and the Politics of Authenticity' in *The Politics of Identity: Emerging Indigeneity*, eds Michelle Harris, Martin Nakata and Bronwyn Carlson (Sydney: UTS ePress, 2013), 1–9.

4 Legal definitions of Aboriginality in Australian Law Reform Commission, *Essentially Yours: The Protection of Human Genetic Information in Australia*, ALRC Report 96, (Sydney: AGPS, 2003).

5 Ruthann Robson, 'Unsettled' in *Queer Theory: Law, Culture, Empire*, eds Robert Leckey and Kim Brooks (New York, Routledge, 2010), 190–206.

6 A. Smith, 'Queer Theory and Native Studies: The Heteronormativity of Settler Colonialism', *GLQ: A Journal of Lesbian and Gay Studies* 16, iss. 2, 2010, 41–68.

7 Damien Riggs, 'Unnarned Moral Authority' in *Priscilla, (White) Queen of the Desert: Queer Rights/Race Privilege* (New York: Peter Lang Publishing, 2006).

8 Scott Lauria Morgensen, 'Theorising Gender, Sexuality and Settler Colonialism', *Settler Colonial Studies* 2, iss. 2, 2012, 2–22.

9 Margaret Robinson, 'Two-Spirited Sexuality and White Universality', *Plural Space, Postcolonial Networks*, 2012 http://postcolonialnetworks. com/2012/06/02/two-spirited

10 Oscar Monaghan, 'My Queer Decolonial Project', *Honi Soit*, University of Sydney, 2014http://honisoit.com/2014/05/my-queer-decolonial-project

11 Robson, 'Unsettled'.

12 Troy-Anthony Bayliss, 'The Art of Seeing Aboriginal Australia's Queer Potential', *The Conversation*, 2014, http://theconversation.com/the-art-of-seeing-aboriginal-australias-queer-potential-25588

13 E. Kowel, 'The Politics of the Gap: Indigenous Australians, Liberal Multiculturalism and the End of the Self-Determination Era', *American Anthropologist* 110, iss. 3, 2008, 338–48.

14 Maddee Clark, 'Against Authenticity', *Overland Literary Journal* 215, Winter 2014, https://overland.org.au/previous-issues/issue-215/feature-maddee-clark

15 S. Maddison, 'Indigenous Identity, "Authenticity" and the Structural Violence of Settler Colonialism', *Identities: Global Studies in Culture and Power* 20, iss. 3, 2013, 288–303.

16 Deborah Bird Rose, 'Land Rights and Deep Colonising: The Erasure of Women', *Aboriginal Law Bulletin* 3, iss. 85, 1996, 6–13.

17 J. Bradley and K. Seton, 'Self Determination or "Deep Colonising": Land Claims, Colonial Authority and Indigenous Representation', in *Unfinished Constitutional Business: Rethinking Indigenous Self-determination*, ed. Barbara Hocking (Canberra: Aboriginal Studies Press, 2005), 32.

18 Aileen Moreton-Robinson, 'Patriarchal Whiteness, Self-Determination and Indigenous Women: The Invisibility of Structural Privilege and the Visibility of Oppression', in *Unfinished Constitutional Business*, ed. Hocking, 61.

19 S. Keenan, 'Bringing the Outside(r) In: Law's Appropriation of Subversive Identities', *Northern Ireland Legal Quarterly* 64, iss. 3, 2013, 299–316.

20 P. Wolfe, 'Settler Colonialism and the Elimination of the Native', *Journal of Genocide Research* 4, iss. 8, 2006, 387–409.

21 John Taylor and Martin Bell, eds, *Population Mobility and Indigenous Peoples in Australasia and North America* (London, New York: Routledge, 2004).

22 *Shaw v Wolf*, (1998) FCA 389; *Commonwealth v Tasmania*, (1983) 158 CLR 1.

23 *Aboriginal and Torres Strait Islander Commission Bill 1998* (Cth), clause 4(1); *Aboriginal Development Commission Act 1980* (Cth), the *Aboriginal and Torres Strait Islander Heritage Protection Act 1984* (Cth), the *Aboriginal Land Grant (Jervis Bay Territory) Territory Act 1986* (Cth).

24 *Attorney-General (Cth) v Queensland* (1990) 94 ALR 515.

25 *Gibbs v Capewell*, (1995) 54 FCR 503.

26 *Shaw v Wolf*, (1998) FCA 389.

27 AAT, *Re: Bruce William Patmore and Others*, Applicant, and *Independent Indigenous Advisory Committee*, Respondent, *Reasons for Decisions*, 18 October 2002.

28 J. Gardiner-Garden, 'Defining Aboriginality in Australia', Current Issues Brief no. 10 2002–3, Social Policy Group, Australian Parliamentary Library (Canberra: AGPS, 2003).

29 ATSIC, *Procedures for Tasmanian Pilot Indigenous Electoral Roll*, 2002, http://www.atsic.gov.au/events/elections_2002/tasmania/FAQ/default.asp

30 Larissa Behrendt, Consultation, *Essentially Yours* (Sydney: ALRC Report 96, 2003), 3 December 2002.

31 A.W. Lloyd, 'Defining the Human: Are Transgender People Strangers to the Law?', *Berkeley Journal of Gender, Law and Justice* 20, iss. 1, 2005, 150–95.

32 Povinelli, *The Cunning of Recognition*.

33 Royal Commission into Aboriginal Deaths in Custody, *National Report no. 5* (Sydney: AGPS, 1991).

34 Australian Bureau of Statistics, *Changing Propensity to Identify as being of Aboriginal and Torres Strait Islander Origin Between Censuses* (Canberra: AGPS, 2013), http://www.abs.gov.au/ausstats/abs@.nsf/Lookup/2077.0main+features52006-2011

35 S. Tascon. and J. Ife, 'Human Rights and Critical Whiteness: Whose Humanity?', *The International Journal of Human Rights* 12, iss. 3, 2008, 307–27.

36 A. Forsyth, 'Out in the Valley', *International Journal of Urban and Regional Research* 21, iss. 1, 1997, 38–62.

37 Riggs, 'Unearned Moral Authority'.

38 Damien Riggs, 'Possessive Investments' in *Priscilla, (White) Queen of the Desert: Queer Rights/Race Privilege* (New York: Peter Lang Publishing, 2006).

39 D.F. Martin, 'Rethinking the Design of Indigenous Organisations: The Need for Strategic Engagement', *Discussion Paper 248* (Canberra: Centre for Aboriginal Economic Policy Research, 2003).

40 K. Biber, 'Fact-Finding, Proof and Indigenous Knowledge', *Alternative Law Journal* 35, 2010, 208–12.

41 Maddison, 'Indigenous Identity'.

Are We Queer? Reflections on 'Peopling the Empty Mirror' Twenty Years On

1 Wendy Dunn/Holland, Maureen Fletcher, Dino Hodge, Gary Lee, E.J. Milera (John Cross), Rea Saunders and Jim Wafer (The Gays and Lesbians Aboriginal Alliance), 'Peopling the Empty Mirror: The Prospects for Lesbian and Gay Aboriginal History', in *Gay Perspectives II: More Essays in Australian Gay Culture*, ed. Robert Aldrich (Sydney: University of Sydney, 1994), 1–62. http://alga.org.au/files/Peopling-the-Empty-Mirror.pdf

2 Bain Attwood, 'Introduction', *Journal of Australian Studies* 35, 1992, xi

3 Troy-Anthony Bayliss, 'The Art of Seeing Aboriginal Australia's Queer Potential', *The Conversation*, 2014, http://theconversation.com/the-art-of-seeing-aboriginal-australias-queer-potential-25588

4 Philip Morrisey, 'Dancing with Shadows: Erasing Aboriginal Self and Sovereignty', in *Sovereign Subjects: Indigenous Sovereignty Matters*, ed. Aileen Moreton-Robinson (Sydney: Allen and Unwin, 2007), 66.

5 Inga Clendinnen, *Dancing with Strangers* (Melbourne: Text Publishing, 2003), 156.

6   Shino Konishi, Leah Lui-Chivizhe, and Lisa Slater, 'Indigenous Bodies', *Borderlands e-journal* 7, no. 2, 2008, 5, http://www.borderlands.net.au/issues/vol7no2.html

7   Ibid.

8   Ibid.

9   Dunn/Holland et al, 'Peopling the Empty Mirror', 27.

10 Shino Konishi, 'Wanton With Plenty: Questioning Ethno-Historical Constructions of Sexual Savagery in Aboriginal Societies', *Australian Historical Studies* 39, 2008, 357.

11 Tony Birch, ' "Nothing has Changed": The Making and Unmaking of Koori Culture', *Meanjin* 69, no. 4, 110.

12 Andrew Jefferson, 'Controversial Ballarat Suburb Name Mullawallah Could Become Beardington', *Herald Sun*, 11 December 2014.

13 Bruce Pascoe, 'Lake Corangamite' in *Convincing Ground: Learning to Fall in Love with Your Country* (Canberra: Aboriginal Studies Press, 2007), 73.

14 Birch, 'Nothing has Changed', 115.

15 Walter Mignolo and Michelle K., 'Decolonial Aesthesis: From Singapore to Cambridge to Duke University', *Decolonial AestheSis: Colonial Wounds/Decolonial Healings*, Social Text/Periscope, Summer 2013, http://socialtextjournal.org/periscope_article/decolonial-aesthesis-from-singapore-to-cambridge-to-duke-university

16 Randolph Bowers, 'Identity, Prejudice and Healing in Aboriginal Circles: Models of Identity, Embodiment and Ecology of Place as Traditional Medicine for Education and Counselling: A Mi'kmaq First Nation Perspective', *Alternative: An International Journal of Indigenous Scholarship* 6, iss. 3, 2010, 209.

17 Aileen Moreton-Robinson, 'The White Man's Burden: Patriarchal White Epistemic Violence and Aboriginal Women's Knowledges in the Academy', *Australian Feminist Studies* 26, no. 70, December 2011, 413.

18 Aileen Moreton-Robinson, 'I Still Call Australia Home,' in *Uprootings/Regroundings: Questions of Home and Migration*, eds Sara Ahmed, Claudia Castaĕda, Anne-Marie Fortier and Mimi Sheller (New York: Berg Publishers, 2003), 38.

19 Henk Huijser, 'Australian Idol versus Cronulla: Whither the
    Postcolonising Nation?', *New Zealand Journal of Media Studies* 10,
    iss. 1, 2007, 132.

20 Diana Brydon, 'Introduction' in *Postcolonialism: Critical Concepts
    in Literary and Cultural Studies*, ed. Diana Brydon (New York:
    Routledge, 2000), 26.

21 Dunn/Holland et al, 'Peopling the Empty Mirror', 27.

22 Damien Riggs, 'Possessive Investments at the Intersection of
    Race, Gender and Sexuality: Lesbian and Gay Rights in a "Post-
    colonising" Nation' in *Intersections: Gender, Race and Ethnicity in
    Australasian Studies*, eds Margaret Allen and Rajinder Dhawan
    (New Delhi: Prestige Books, 2007), 114.

23 Jenni Millbank, 'From Discretion to Disbelief: Recent Trends
    in Refugee Determinations on the Basis of Sexual Orientation
    in Australia and the United Kingdom', *International Journal of
    Human Rights* 13, no. 6, 2009, 322.

24 Scott Lauria Morgensen, 'Settler Homonationalism: Theorizing
    Settler Colonialism within Queer Modernities', *GLQ: A Journal
    of Lesbian and Gay Studies* 16, no. 1–2, 2010, 105–31, 110.

25 Toula Nicolacopoulos and George Vassilacopoulos, *Indigenous
    Sovereignty and the Being of the Occupier: Manifesto for a White
    Australian Philosophy of Origins* (Melbourne: re.press, 2014), 17, 84.

26 Cameron Greensmith and Sulaimon Giwa, 'Challenging
    Settler Colonialism in Contemporary Queer Politics: Settler
    Homonationalism, Pride Toronto, and Two-Spirit Subjectivities',
    American Indian Culture and Research Journal 37, iss. 2, 2013, 133.

27 Judith Halberstam, 'Queer Temporality and Postmodern
    Geographies', in *A Queer Time and Place: Transgender Bodies,
    Subcultural Lives* (New York: NYU Press, 2005), 1–22.

Glossary

Abo	a derogatory term for an Aboriginal person, no longer having widespread usage
AIDS	Acquired Immuno-Deficiency Syndrome
aboriginalism	a view of aboriginal cultures as being primitive and exotic, and having little to do with the modern world
Anangu	a general term which refers to Aboriginal people from Central Australia who belong to certain culturally-affiliated language groups, including Pitjantjatjara, Yukuntjara and Ngnangatjara
ATSI	Aboriginal and Torres Strait Islander
Blak	a term credited to Ku Ku/Erub/Mer visual artist Destiny Deacon, having been developed as a strategy of reclaiming colonialist language to create means of self-determination and expression; it has since become widespread in Aboriginal vernacular as a vehicle to express identity and subvert the racist notion that Aboriginal people are 'black', or rather are only identifiable as having 'black' skin

Brisneyland	a nickname for Brisbane, referencing Disney Land
Brisvegas	a nickname for Brisbane, referencing Las Vegas
brotherboy	a transman (also, brother boy and brotha boy)
cisgender	a person who is not transgender
colonialism	the policy or practice of acquiring full or partial political control over another country, occupying it with settlers, and exploiting it economically
deep time	the term 'deep time', in contrast to the contemporary framing of the problematic term 'pre-history', engages ideas of the written and known form as an emergence of connected cultural practice, and reflects a non-specific era substantially removed from the present
dhari	a traditional Torres Strait Islander headdress worn when performing dances and ceremonies
Elder	a respect title used to describe an older relative, now often used for any older or respected person
family	a person's relatives, usually meaning their extended family, and more recently including a person's adopted family of affiliation
gammon	a term describing a dishonest, false, untrustworthy or off-beat person or situation, with either humourful or derogatory connotation depending on the circumstance or region of use
gar'ban'djee'lum	a name meaning 'us mob' and provided by Butchulla and Gubbi Gubbi Elders for use by the QUAC 2 Spirits program

heteronormativity	the normalisation of heterosexual relationships and associated gender and sexual formations
heteropatriarchy	the dominance of straight men and the hierarchal and oppressive climate that results from that dominance
HIV	Human Immuno-deficiency Virus
homonationalism	the idea that homonormative ideologies replicate the same hierarchical ideologies as heteronormativity and nationalism
homonormativity	a gay politics that does not contest heteronormative assumptions and institutions
Koori	general term which refers to Aboriginal people from the south-eastern part of the mainland Australia, including Victoria and much of New South Wales
Kungakunga	the Luritja name for trans women
Kungarrakan	the fresh water people who are traditional custodians of Nungalakoo (Finniss River) in the Fitzmaurice region of the Northern Territory, extending from Laniyuk (Berry Springs) to Angurrulklpum (Batchelor township) and beyond into Purlugutj (Litchfield Park)
Laniyuk	the Kungarrakan name for the 'Berry Springs' region in the Top End of the Northern Territory, Laniyuk protects an important women's business story of female development from a child to young woman, and is accompanied by ceremony and song
miggaloo	ghost, now a used to describe a person of European descent
mob	family, tribe, social group or network of affiliated people

moolagoo   a word in some Aboriginal languages for 'cat' and sometimes used to describe a same-sex attracted person

Murri   a collective term for Queensland Aborigines

NAIDOC   National Aborigines and Islanders Day of Observance Committee, now more generally a term used for a week of annual celebration activities

Napanangka   the Warlpiri skin name for a woman in the kinship system of Aboriginal groups in Central Australia that determines how people relate to each other and their roles, responsibilities and obligations in regard to one another, ceremonial business and land

NTAHC   Northern Territory AIDS and Hepatitis Council

oopoonga   the Tiwi name for marijuana

O'Umma   Big Mother or Eldest Aunty

Palawah   a collective term for Tasmanian Aborigines

QUAC   Queensland AIDS Council

settler   a non-Indigenous individual or state whose presence in a colonised territory displaces Indigenous peoples

settler colonialism   a variant of colonialism where the coloniser does not leave the colonised territory and instead establishes a permanent settler state

settler normativity   the normalisation of the genocidal relations and institutions of settler colonialism that erases settler violence and Indigenous resistance

sistergirl   a trans woman (also, sister girl and sista girl)

Stolen Generations   children forcibly removed as young as possible from Indigenous Australians for the immediate purpose of raising them separately from and ignorant of their culture

	and people, and for the ultimate purpose of suppressing any distinct Aboriginal culture, thereby ending the existence of the Aborigines as a distinct people
tjukurpa	the word Pitjantjatjara-speaking Anangu use to describe Dreaming, the spiritual force which unites Anangu with each other and with the landscape
trans	a sistergirl / transgender woman or brotherboy / transgender man, but also a generalising term used to refer to any person who is not cisgendered, such as gender fluid people, genderqueer, agender, third gender, person with non-binary identity (also trans*)
Two Spirit	term arising from Cree First Nations People whose culture makes no distinction on gender, instead recognising that every living creature and everything that acts in and of this world is spiritually meaningful. Two Spirit identity may encompass all aspects of culture, gender, sexuality, community and relationship to the land; it also is a self-descriptor used by many Cree and other Aboriginal lesbian, gay, bi and tans people acknowledging them as spiritually meaningful people
wetji	the Kungarrakan title of respect given to grandmothers; also, the word for the White Egret which possess white feathers like the white hair of grandmothers
yimpininni	the Tiwi name for sistergirls
yupla mipla ahfla	a Kriol phrase spoken in northern mainland Australia meaning 'you, me, us' and used by the Queensland AIDS Council's 2 Spirits program

Select Bibliography

Jim Wafer and Dino Hodge

The ground-breaking essay 'Peopling the Empty Mirror: The Prospects for Lesbian and Gay Aboriginal History' was published in 1994 (see below for details). The authors – Wendy Dunn/Holland, Maureen Fletcher, Dino Hodge, Gary Lee, E.J. Milera (John Cross), Rea Saunders and Jim Wafer – called themselves the Gays and Lesbians Aboriginal Alliance. The essay supplied a comprehensive list of citations giving details of source material but did not include a list of references. The publication of the present book creates the opportunity to correct this omission, and also to include some of the major sources on sexuality and sexual identity of First Nations People that have been published in the intervening two decades.

The bibliography is divided into three main sections, two of which have a number of sub-categories. The first two sections pertain to sources published prior to the 1994 essay including sources discussed in the essay, while the third section identifies many (but not all) sources published from 1994:

- Sources with Specific Relevance to Aboriginal Homosexuality (prior to 1994)
  - Books, Journals and Reports
  - Newspapers, Newsletters and Ephemera
  - Audio-visual Material

- Background Sources (prior to 1994)
- New Sources (published from 1994)
  - Books, Journals and Reports
  - Newspapers, Newsletters and Ephemera
  - Audio-visual Material
  - Selected Internet Sites

The selected bibliography does not aim to include material cited in this book's essays.

SECTION ONE

Sources with Specific Relevance to Aboriginal Homosexuality (prior to 1994)

Books, Journals and Reports

'Aborigines and AIDS.' *National AIDS Bulletin* 3, no. 3 special issue (April 1989): 14–31 (ten articles, four with no author attribution).

Adam, Barry. 'Age, Structure, and Sexuality: Reflections on the Anthropological Evidence on Homosexual Relations.' In *Anthropology and Homosexual Behavior*, edited by Evelyn Blackwood. New York: Haworth Press, 1986, 19–33. See esp. 29–30.

Adams, Catherine and Ruth Carr. 'Mimi Pulka.' *National AIDS Bulletin* (December 1992/January 1993): 12–23.

Alexander, Ivor. 'AIDS: Controversial Coconuts.' *National AIDS Bulletin* 3, no. 3 special issue (April 1989): 26–27.

Ariss, Robert. 'No More "Blacks at the Back": Rodney Junga.' *Talkabout* 36 (September 1993): 12–14.

Avery, John. 'The Law People: History, Society and Initiation in the Borroloola Area of the Northern Territory.' PhD thesis, University of Sydney, 1985. See esp. 245–47, 250.

Bartlett, Ben. 'Central Australia.' *National AIDS Bulletin* 3, no. 3 special issue (April 1989): 18.

Basedow, Herbert. *The Australian Aboriginal*, Adelaide: F.W. Preece, 1925. See esp. 65.

___. 'Subincision and Kindred Rites of the Australian Aboriginal.' *Journal of the Anthropological Institute* 57 (1927): 123–56. See esp. 131–34.

Berndt, R.M., and C.H. Berndt. *A Preliminary Report of Field Work in the Ooldea Region, Western South Australia*. Sydney: Australasian Medical Publishing Co., 1945. See esp. 276–77. First appeared in *Oceania* as a series of articles in 1942–1943.

___. *Sexual Behavior in Western Arnhem Land*. New York: Viking Fund, 1951. See esp. 66.

Behrendt, Larissa. 'Everybody's business: The First National Aboriginal HIV/AIDS Conference.' *National AIDS Bulletin* 7, no. 3 (April 1992): 12–15.

Bell, Louise. 'Koorie Wirguls.' *Lesbian On The Loose* (July 1991): 11.

Blackwood, Evelyn, ed. *Anthropology and Homosexual Behavior*. New York: Haworth Press, 1986.

Bleibtreu-Ehrenberg, Gisela. 'Pederasty among Primitives: Institutionalized Initiation and Cultic Prostitution.' *Journal of Homosexuality* 20, nos. 1/2 (1990): 13–30. See esp. 19–20.

Brain, Robert. *Rites, Black and White*. Melbourne: Penguin, 1979. See esp. 179; cf. 139–42 and 178–81.

Burgmann, Verity, and Jenny Lee, eds. *Staining the Wattle: A People's History of Australia since 1788*. Melbourne: McPhee Gribble, 1988.

Close, Luke. 'Gay, Aboriginal and Proud.' *National AIDS Bulletin* 7, no. 3 (April 1992): 23.

Cook, Mark. 'Stories for Sharing – HIV/AIDS: An Understanding.' *Aboriginal and Islander Health Worker Journal* (c. 1990): 14.

Greenberg, David F. *The Construction of Homosexuality*. Chicago: University of Chicago Press, 1988. See esp. 35–36.

Grey, George. *Journals of Two Expeditions of Discovery in North West and Western Australia*. London: T. & W. Boone, 1841.

Hardman, Edward T. 'Notes on some Habits and Customs of the Natives of the Kimberley District, Western Australia.' *Proceedings of the Royal Irish Academy*, third series, vol. 1 (1888): 70–75. See esp. 74.

Harrasser, Albert. *Die Rechtsverletzung bei den Australischen Eingeborenen*, Stuttgart: Ferdinand Enke, 1936. (Supplement to *Zeitschrift für Vergleichende Rechtswissenschaft* vol. 50.) See esp. 61.

Herdt, Gilbert, ed. *Ritualized Homosexuality in Melanesia.* Berkeley: University of California Press, 1984. See esp. 5–6.

Hiatt, L.R., ed. *Australian Aboriginal Mythology.* Canberra: Australian Institute of Aboriginal Studies, 1975.

Hodge, Dino. *Did You Meet Any Malagas? A Homosexual History of Australia's Northernmost Capital.* Nightcliff, N.T.: Little Gem, 1993.

Japaljarri, Andrew Spencer. 'AIDS.' *National AIDS Bulletin* 3, no. 3 special issue (April 1989): 25.

Johnston, Craig, and Robert Johnston. 'The making of homosexual men.' In *Staining the Wattle: A People's History of Australia since 1788*, edited by Verity Burgmann and Jenny Lee. 87–99. Melbourne: McPhee Gribble, 1988. See esp. 89–90.

Jones, Ivor. 'Psychiatric Disorders among Desert and Kimberley Peoples.' *Australian Institute of Aboriginal Studies Newsletter* 3, no. 6 (1973): 17–20 and erratum. See esp. 180.

Kaberry, Phyllis. *Aboriginal Woman, Sacred and Profane.* London: Routledge, 1939. See esp. 257.

Karsch-Haack, Ferdinand. *Das Gleichgeschlechtliche Leben der Naturvölker.* Munich: E. Reinhardt, 1911. (Reprinted New York: Arno Press, 1975.)

Kearney, G.E., P.R. de Lacey, and G.R. Davidson, eds. *The Psychology of Aboriginal Australians.* Sydney: Wiley, 1973.

Klaatsch, Hermann. 'Some Notes on Scientific Travel amongst the Black Population of Tropical Australia in 1904, 1905, 1906.' In *Report of the Eleventh Meeting of the Australasian Association for the Advancement of Science.* Adelaide: Australasian Association for the Advancement of Science, 1908. 577–92. See esp. 581–82.

Lee, Gary. 'Dealing with HIV among Indigenous Peoples in Northern Australia.' *National AIDS Bulletin* 11, no. 5 (1991): 8, 30.

Leeden, A.C. van der. 'Thundering Gecko and Emu: Mythological Structuring of Nunggubuyu Patrimoieties.' In *Australian Aboriginal Mythology*, edited by L.R. Hiatt. 46–101.

Canberra: Australian Institute of Aboriginal Studies, 1975. See esp. 88–91.

Massola, Aldo. *The Aborigines of South-Eastern Australia as They Were*. Melbourne: Heinemann, 1971. See esp. 16.

Mathews, R.H. 'The Bora, or Initiation Ceremonies of the Kamilaroi Tribe, Part II.' *Journal of the Anthropological Institute of Great Britain and Ireland* 25 (1896): 318–39. See esp. 333–34.

___. 'Native Tribes of Western Australia.' *Proceedings of the American Philosophical Society* 39 (1900): 123–25. See esp. 125.

___. 'Phallic rites and initiation ceremonies of the South Australian Aborigines', *Proceedings of the American Philosophical Society* 39 (1900): 622–38. See esp. 636.

___. 'Notes on the Arranda tribe', *Journal and Proceedings of the Royal Society of New South Wales* 41 (1907): 146–63. See esp. 158.

Meggitt, Mervyn. *Gadjari among the Walbiri Aborigines*. Sydney: Oceania Monographs no. 14, 1966. See esp. 65.

Minutjukrr, Alec. 'History Story.' *National AIDS Bulletin* 3, no. 3 special issue (April 1989): 23–24.

Money, J., J.E. Cawte, G.N. Bianchi, and B. Nurcombe. 'Sex Training and Traditions in Arnhem Land. In *The Psychology of Aboriginal Australians*, edited by G.E. Kearney, P.R. de Lacey and G.R. Davidson. 395–416. Sydney: Wiley, 1973. See esp. 410.

Moodie, Rob. 'AIDS Education: Seeing it in a Different Way.' *National AIDS Bulletin* 3, no. 3 special issue (April 1989): 17.

Murray, S.O., ed. *Oceanic Homosexualities*. New York: Garland, 1992.

___. 'Age-stratified Homosexuality: Introduction.' In *Oceanic Homosexualities*, edited by S.O. Murray. 3–23. New York: Garland, 1992. See esp. 3–9.

Paterson, W. 'Notes Referring to the Kimberley Natives', in Richard Helms, 'Anthropology,' *Transactions of the Royal Society of South Australia* 16, no. 3 (1896): 237–332. See esp. 291–92.

Pilling, Arnold. *Homosexuality among Australian Aborigines*. Unpublished manuscript bibliography, Detroit: Wayne State University, 1983.

___. 'Homosexuality among the Tiwi of North Australia.' In *Oceanic Homosexualities*, edited by S.O. Murray. 25–31. New York: Garland, 1992.

Purcell, B.H. 'Rites and customs of Australian Aborigines', *Zeitschrift für Ethnologie* 25 (1893): 286–89.

Ravenscroft, A.G.B. 'Some Habits and Customs of the Chingalee Tribe, Northern Territory, SA' *Transactions and Proceedings and Report of the Royal Society of South Australia* 15, part 2 (1892): 121–22.

Róheim, Géza. 'Psychoanalysis of primitive cultural types.' *International Journal of Psychoanalysis* 13 (1932): 1–224. See esp. 51.

___. 'Women and Their Life in Central Australia.' *Journal of the Anthropological Institute of Great Britain and Ireland* 58 (1933): 207–65. See esp. 219, 226, 238.

___. *The Eternal Ones of the Dream: A Psychoanalytic Interpretation of Australian Myth and Ritual.* New York: International Universities Press, 1945. See esp. 122.

___. *Australian Totemism: A Psycho-Analytic Study in Anthropology.* London: Cass, 1971. See esp. 227; cf. 230.

___. *Children of the Desert: The Western Tribes of Central Australia.* New York: Basic Books, 1974. See esp. 243.

Roth, Walter Edmund. 'Notes on Government, Morals and Crime.' *North Queensland Ethnography Bulletin* 8 (1908, Brisbane). See esp. 7.

Rowse, Tim. 'Perspectives on the Cultures of Sexuality among Central Australian Aboriginal People' Unpublished paper, Menzies School of Health Research, Alice Springs, 1992. (Held in AIATSIS library as PMS 5238.)

Schmidt, Wilhelm. 'Sexualismus, Mythologie und Religion in Nord-Australien.' *Anthropos* 48 (1953): 899–924. See esp. 916–18.

Sergeant, Jill. 'Crossing the Barriers.' *Talkabout* 36 (September 1993): 18–20.

___. 'Out in the Country: Maryanne.' *Talkabout* 36 (September 1993): 15–17.

Smith, Iris. 'Sexuality and HIV.' *National AIDS Bulletin* 7, no. 3 (April 1992): 19–20.

Spencer, Baldwin, and F.J. Gillen. *The Arunta.* London: Macmillan, 1927. See esp. 470.

Stevens, M. 'A North Queensland Perspective.' *National AIDS Bulletin* 3, no. 3 special issue (April 1989): 19–20.

Stewart, Betty. 'I Am a Woman, I Am a Koori, and I Am a Lesbian.' In *What is Lesbian Discrimination?*, edited by Lavender for the Anti-Discrimination Board of New South Wales. 11–13. Sydney: Anti-Discrimination Board of New South Wales, 1990.

Strehlow, Carl. *Die Aranda- und Loritja-Stämme in Zentral-Australien* Frankfurt: Joseph Baer and Co., 1907–1920. See esp. vol. 4, part 1, 1913, 98.

Unattributed. 'Everybody's Business: The First National Aboriginal HIV/AIDS Conference.' *National AIDS Bulletin* 7, no. 3 special issue (April 1992): 12–25.

___. 'The HALT Team.' *National AIDS Bulletin* 3, no. 3 special issue (April 1989): 21.

___. 'Interview with Bernadette Hudson.' *National AIDS Bulletin* 3, no. 3 special issue (April 1989): 14–16.

___. 'The National Aboriginal Health Strategy.' *National AIDS Bulletin* 3, no. 3 special issue (April 1989): 28–31.

___. 'Primary Health Promotion.' *National AIDS Bulletin* 3, no. 3 special issue (April 1989): 21–22.

___. 'Report of the Working Panel on Aboriginals, Torres Strait Islanders and HIV/AIDS.' Consultation Paper no. 1, Department of Community Services and Health, Canberra, 1989.

van Reyk, Paul. 'Aboriginal Services: Are They Meeting the Need?' *Talkabout* 36 (September 1993): 21–23.

Newspapers, Newsletters and Ephemera
Collins, Deb. 'Performing in Tongues.' *Capital Q* (11 September 1992): 7.

Dunne, Gary. 'Double Trouble: An Interview with Tony Ayres.' *OutRage* 105 (February 1992): 47–49.

Dunne, Stephen. 'Stolen Property.' *Sydney Star Observer*, Mardi Gras Festival update no. 2 (12 February 1993): 18.

'GLAR Report.' *Gays and Lesbians Against Racism Newsletter* 9, Darlinghurst, Sydney (September 1992): 1.

Harari, Fiona. 'Politics on Parade.' *The Weekend Australian*, 27–8 February 1992, 20.

Harcourt, David. 'This Australia: What the Whites Don't Know about the Aborigines.' *The Bulletin* 93:4776 (9 October 1971): 46.

Lowe, Barry. 'Lowe-life.' *Sydney Star* 3, no.13 (29 January 1982): 7.

Mackinolty, Chips. 'Howe Urges Condoms in Jails.' *Sydney Morning Herald*, 3 March 1992, 7.

Magnusson, Tony. 'Pride and Prejudice: Death by Discrimination.' *Sydney Star Observer* 203, (19 February 1993): 23.

Audio-visual Material

Ayres, Tony, 'Double Trouble', produced by Diane Hamer and directed by Tony Ayres; a Big and Little Production for Channel Four (UK) and SBS (Australia); copyright Channel Four 1991.

CAAMA Productions, 'First National Aboriginal HIV/AIDS Conference: Everybody's Business', produced by CAAMA Productions and funded by the Department of Health, Housing and Community Services.

'Through Australian Eyes: *Mimi Pulka*', first screened in Australia on SBS television in December 1992.

SECTION TWO

Background Sources (prior to 1994)

Blackwood, Evelyn. 'Breaking the Mirror: The Construction of Lesbianism and the Anthropological Discourse on Homosexuality.' In *Anthropology and Homosexual Behavior*, edited by Evelyn Blackwood. 1–17. New York: Haworth Press, 1986.

Caminha, Adolfo. *Bom-Crioulo: The Black Man and the Cabin Boy*. San Francisco: Gay Sunshine Press, 1982. (First published 1895, English translation by E.A. Lacey.)

Dixon, R.M.W. *The Languages of Australia*. Cambridge: Cambridge University Press, 1980.

Dundes, Alan. 'A Psychoanalytic Study of the Bullroarer', *Man* (new series) 2, no. 2 (1976): 220–38. See esp. 233–36.

Fiedler, Leslie. 'Come Back to the Raft ag'in, Huck Honey.' In *An End to Innocence: Essays on Culture and Politics*, edited by L. Fiedler. 142–51. Boston: Beacon, 1955. See esp. 146.

Fry, Peter. 'Léonie, Pombinha, Amaro e Aleixo: Prostituição, Homossexualidade e Raça em Dois Romances Naturalistas.' In *Caminhos Cruzados*, edited by Carlos Vogt. 33–51. São Paulo: Brasiliense, 1982.

Jull, Peter. 'Aboriginal Self-government: Realities and Possibilities.' Unpublished paper distributed by the North Australia Research Unit, Darwin, 1992

___. 'Torres Strait Islanders and Aborigines: Participating in Australian Constitutional Renewal.' Unpublished paper distributed by the North Australia Research Unit, Darwin, 1992.

Liberman, Kenneth. *Understanding Interaction in Central Australia: An Ethnomethodological Study of Australian Aboriginal People*, Boston: Routledge, 1985.

Moraga, Cherríe, and Gloria Anzaldúa, eds. *This Bridge Called My Back: Writings by Radical Women of Color.* New York: Persephone Press, 1983.

Neumann, Klaus. 'A Postcolonial Writing of Aboriginal History.' *Meanjin* 51, no. 2 (1992): 277–98.

Ortner, Sherry B., and Harriet Whitehead, eds. *Sexual Meanings: The Cultural Construction of Gender and Sexuality.* Cambridge: Cambridge University Press, 1981.

Rosaldo, Renato. *Culture and Truth: The Remaking of Social Analysis.* Boston: Beacon, 1989.

Roscoe, Will, ed. *Living the Spirit: A Gay American Indian Anthology.* New York: St Martins, 1988.

Roscoe, Will. *The Zuni Man-Woman.* Albuquerque: University of New Mexico Press, 1991.

Thiele, Colin. *Storm-boy.* Adelaide: Rigby, 1974.

Trevisan, João S. *Perverts in Paradise.* London: Gay Men's Press, 1986. See esp. 103–5.

Warner, Michael. 'Introduction: Fear of a Queer Planet.' *Social Text* 29 (1991): 3–17.

White, Patrick. *Riders in the Chariot*. London: Eyre and Spottiswoode, 1961.

Whitehead, Harriet. 'The Bow and the Burden Strap: A New Look at Institutionalized Homosexuality in Native North America.' In *Sexual Meanings: The Cultural Construction of Gender and Sexuality*, edited by Sherry B. Ortner and Harriet Whitehead. 80–115. Cambridge: Cambridge University Press, 1981.

SECTION THREE

New Sources (published from 1994)

Books, Journals and Reports

Aldrich, Robert, ed. *Gay Perspectives II: More Essays in Australian Gay Culture*. Sydney: University of Sydney, 1994.

Ashburn, Elizabeth. *Lesbian Art: An Encounter with Power*. Roseville East, NSW: Craftman House, 1996.

Australian Federation of AIDS Organisations. *National AIDS Bulletin. Special Issue: Indigenous People and HIV* 12, no. 3 (1998), http://reconciliation.tripod.com/nab.htm

___. *Anwernekenhe 1: First National Aboriginal and Torres Strait Islander Gay Men and Transgender Sexual Health Conference*. Sydney: AFAO, 1994. http://ana.org.au/publication/ and www.afao.org.au/__data/assets/pdf_file/0003/4656/ Indig_anwernekenhe1.pdf

___. *Anwernekenhe 2: Report of the Second National Indigenous Australian Gay Men and Transgender Peoples Conference*. Sydney: AFAO, 1998. http://ana.org.au/publication/ and www.afao.org.au/__data/assets/pdf_file/0004/4657/Indig_ anwernekenheii.pdf

___. *Anwernekenhe 3: Third National Indigenous Gay, Sistergirl and Transgender HIV/AIDS and Sexual Health Conference*. Sydney: AFAO, 2002. http://ana.org.au/publication

___. *Anwernekenhe 4: Conference Report*. Sydney: AFAO, 2006. http://ana.org.au/publication

___. *Anwernekenhe 5: Conference Report, National Aboriginal and Torres Strait Islander Community Conference on HIV/AIDS and*

Sexual Health. Sydney: AFAO, 2011.
http://ana.org.au/publication

B., Shirley. 'An Indigenous Baby Boomer in a Novocastrian Background.' In *Out in the Valley: Hunter Gay and Lesbian Histories*, edited by Jim Wafer, Erica Southgate and Lyndall Coan. 89–98. Newcastle, NSW: Newcastle Region Library (Local History Monograph no. 15), 2000.

Baylis, Troy-Anthony. 'My Body the Hand Grenade: Kaboobie's Making Camp.' *Social Alternatives* 30, no. 2 (2011), 5–8.

___. 'Queerly Speaking.' *Artlink* 32, no. 2 (2012), 98–99.

Brady, Wendy. 'Colour Bars.' In *Queer City: Gay and Lesbian Politics in Sydney*, edited by Craig Johnston and Paul van Reyk. 17–27. Annandale, NSW: Pluto Press, 2001.

Brady, Wendy and Gary Lee. 'Alternative Sexualities.' In *The Oxford Companion to Aboriginal Art and Culture*, edited by Syliva Kleinert, Margo Neale, and Robyne Bancroft. 294–95. Melbourne: Oxford University Press, 2000.

Brown, K. 'Sistergirls: Stories from Indigenous Australian Transgender People.' *Aboriginal and Islander Health Worker Journal* 28, no. 6 (2004): 25–26.

Browning, Daniel. 'Hand in Hand: Sexy and Dangerous.' *Art Monthly Australia* 212 (August 2008): 17–21.

Chapple, Murray. '"White Man's Disease": Discourses around Aboriginal Gay Subjectivity in the Era of AIDS.' BA Honours thesis, Macquarie University, 1995.

Clark, Maddee. 'Against Authenticity.' *Overland* 215 (Winter 2014). https://overland.org.au/previous-issues/issue-215/feature-maddee-clark

Davey, Martin. *Essays on the Western District Frontier 1835–45: Eye-opening Studies on Secrets Kept since Victoria's Frontier Days: About Our Aborigines, Our Pioneers and Our Unknown Convicts.* Blackburn, Vic.: PenFolk Publishing, 2011.

D'Cruz, Carolyn. 'Black Power and Gay Liberation: An Interview with Gary Foley', in *After Homosexual: The Legacies of Gay Liberation*, edited by Carolyn D'Cruz and Mark Pendleton. 65–74. Perth: UWA Publishing, 2013.

D'Cruz, Carolyn, and Mark Pendleton, eds. *After Homosexual: The Legacies of Gay Liberation*. Perth: UWA Publishing, 2013.

Driskill, Qwo-Li. 'Mothertongue: Incorporating Theatre of the Oppressed into Language Restoration Movements.' In *Nurturing Native Languages*, edited by Jon Reyhner, Octaviana V. Trujillo, Roberto Luis Carrasco and Louise Lockard. 155–63. Flagstaff, Arizona: Northern Arizona University, 2003. http://dragonflyrising.wearetheones.info/mothertongue.pdf

_____. 'Stolen from Our Bodies: First Nations Two-spirits/Queers and the Journey to a Sovereign Erotic.' *Studies in American Indian Literatures* 16, no. 2 (2004): 50–64. http://dragonflyrising. wearetheones.info/stolen.pdf

Driskill, Qwo-Li, Chris Finley, Brian Joseph Gilley and Scott Lauria Morgensen, eds. *Queer Indigenous Studies: Critical Interventions in Theory, Politics, and Literature*. Tucson: University of Arizona Press, 2011.

Drinnan, Neal. 'Bending Over Backwards: Wayne King's Autobiography *Black Hours*.' *OutRage* 165 (February 1997): 39.

Dudgeon, Pat, Darren Garvey and Harry Pickett, eds. *Working with Indigenous Australians: A Handbook for Psychologists*. Perth: Gunada Press, 2000.

Dunn/Holland, Wendy, Maureen Fletcher, Dino Hodge, Gary Lee, E.J. Milera (John Cross), Rea Saunders and Jim Wafer (The Gays and Lesbians Aboriginal Alliance). 'Peopling the Empty Mirror: The Prospects for Lesbian and Gay Aboriginal History', in *Gay Perspectives II: More Essays in Australian Gay Culture*, edited by Robert Aldrich. 1–62. Sydney: University of Sydney, 1994. http://alga.org.au/files/Peopling-the-Empty-Mirror.pdf

Gilchrist, Stephen. 'From Tiwi with Love: Bindi Cole.' *Artlink* 30, no. 1 (2010), 74–77.

Green, Sue. 'Racism within Lesbian and Gay Communities and the Impact upon Indigenous Australian's Health', *Proceedings of the First National Lesbian, Gay, Transgender and Bisexual Health Conference, Sydney, 3–5 October 1996*. Edited by Juliet Richters, Ross Duffin, Janet Gilmour, Jude Irwin, Richard Roberts and Anthony Smith. 83. Sydney: Australian Centre for Lesbian and Gay Research, University of Sydney, 1997.

Hardy, David. *Coming Out: Wagga to Warsaw to Wiradjuri – Journeys of Indigenous Identity and Queer Identity*. PhD thesis, Batchelor Institute of Indigenous Tertiary Education, Batchelor NT, 2014.

Hawkes, Gail, and John Scott, eds. *Perspectives in Human Sexuality*. South Melbourne: Oxford University Press, 2005.

Hurley, Michael. *A Guide to Gay and Lesbian Writing in Australia*. St Leonards, NSW: Allen and Unwin, 1996. See esp. 1–2 'Aboriginal gay and lesbian writing'.

Hutchings, Jessica and Clive Aspin, eds. *Sexuality and the Stories of Indigenous People*. Wellington, Aotearoa New Zealand: Huia Publishers, 2007.

Johnston, Craig, and Paul van Reyk, eds. *Queer City: Gay and Lesbian Politics in Sydney*. Annandale, NSW: Pluto Press, 2001.

Junga-Williams, Rodney. 'For All Australians?' *National AIDS Bulletin* 12, no. 3 (1998): 10–13. http://reconciliation.tripod.com/nab_australians.htm

Justice, Daniel Heath, Mark Rifkin, and Bethany Schneider, eds. 'Sexuality, Nationality, Indigeneity.' *GLQ: A Journal of Lesbian and Gay Studies* 16, nos. 1–2, special issue (2010).

King, Wayne. *Black Hours*. Sydney: Angus and Robertson, 1996.

Kleinert, Syliva, Margo Neale, and Robyne Bancroft, eds. *The Oxford Companion to Aboriginal Art and Culture*. Melbourne: Oxford University Press, 2000.

Lawrence, Chris. 'Sexual Identity and Indigenous People.' In *Working with Indigenous Australians: A Handbook for Psychologists*, edited by Pat Dudgeon with Darren Garvey and Harry Pickett. 53–57. Perth: Gunada Press, 2000.

Lawrence, Chris, Garrett Prestage, Brendan Leishman, Colin Ross, Wilo Muwadda, Michael Costello, Patrick Rawstorne, and Andrew Grulich, eds. *Queensland Survey of Aboriginal and Torres Strait Islander Men who have Sex with Men: 2004*. Sydney: National Centre in HIV Epidemiology and Clinical Research, University of NSW, 2006. http://kirby.unsw.edu.au/publications/queensland-survey-aboriginal-and-torres-strait-islander-men-who-have-sex-men

Lee, Gary. *Malaga to Malaga: Man to Man*. 2nd ed. Darwin: Danila Dilba Biluru Butji Binnilutlum Medical Service Aboriginal Corporation and Northern Territory AIDS Council, 1996.

___. 'Love doesn't have a Colour', in *Lovers and Others*. 54–55. Sydney: Australian Federation of AIDS Organisations, 1996.

___. 'Towards an Aboriginal and Torres Strait Islander HIV/ AIDS Epidemic in Australia', unpublished paper presented at the 4th International Congress on AIDS in Asia and the Pacific, Manila, Philippines, 25–29 October 1997.

___. 'Boys to Men', *National AIDS Bulletin* 12, no. 3 (1998): 18–19.

___. 'Us Mob: Anwernekenhe II – The Second National Conference for Indigenous Australian Gay Men and Sista Girls.' *National AIDS Bulletin* 12, no. 3, (1998): 6–8.

___. 'Vast Distances ... Vast Differences.' *National AIDS Bulletin* 12, no. 3 (1998): 24–25, 35.

___. 'Picturing: Aboriginal Social and Political Photography.' *Artlink* 20, no. 1 (2000): 45–49.

___. 'Black Glory: Aboriginal Erotica.' *Artlink* 20, no. 1 (2000): 62–64.

___. 'Breaking the Silence: Indigenous Gay, Transgender, Sistergirl Sexual Abuse Workshop Report', Anwernekenhe III Report, Australian Federation of AIDS Organisations, 2002.

___. 'Proposal to Undertake a Needs Assessment of Indigenous Gay Men and Sistergirl (Transgender) Sexual Abuse in the Darwin-Palmerston Region', July 2002 unpublished paper.

___. 2006, 'Oh, boy! The portraits of Gary Lee.' *Art Monthly* 190, 15–17.

Lee, Gary and Timothy Moore. *The National Indigenous Gay and Transgender Project: Consultation Report and Sexual Health Strategy.* (The combined consultation report [Lee is sole author] and strategy [Lee and Moore joint authors in association with the AFAO Indigenous Gay and Transgender Steering Committee] is known as the 'Green Document'.) Sydney: Australian Federation of AIDS Organisations, 1998. http://www.afao.org.au/__data/assets/pdf_file/0016/4660/ Indig_report.pdf

Lyster, Britta. 'Anwernekenhe – The Black Survivors: Matthew Cook.' *Talkabout* (May 1995): 12–14.

Macfarlane, Ingereth, and Mark Hannah, eds. *Transgressions: Critical Australian Indigenous Histories.* Canberra: ANU E Press, (Aboriginal History Monograph 16), 2007.

Martino, Wayne John, and Maria Pallotta-Chiarolli. ' "Men are Tougher, Bigger, and They Don't Act Real Girlie": Indigenous

Boys Defining and Interrogating Masculinities.' *Balayi* 6 (2004): 143–60.

Meeks, Arone. 'True Words, True Story: My Journey through the Visual Arts and Working with Communities.' *HIV Australia* 12, no. 3 (December 2014). http://www.afao.org.au/library/hiv-australia/volume-12/vol.-12-number-3/true-words-true-story#.VJje2iMIDg

Moore, Clive. *Sunshine and Rainbows: The Development of Gay and Lesbian Culture in Queensland.* St Lucia, Qld.: University of Queensland Press, 2001. See esp. 51–53.

Murphy, Dean. 'In Translation: Implementing the Indigenous Strategy.' *National AIDS Bulletin* 12, no. 3 (1998): 8–9.

Murray, Stephen O. *Homosexualities.* Chicago: University of Chicago Press, 2000. See esp. 25–28.

____. *Pacific Homosexualities.* Bloomington: iUniverse, 2002. See esp. 23–32.

O'Riordan, Maurice. 'Walking through Time: Indigenous Lesbian and Gay Art.' *National AIDS Bulletin* 11, no. 3 (1997): 26–29.

____. 'Everyone's Business: Love, Magic, and the Art of Resistance.' *National AIDS Bulletin* 12, no. 3 (1998): 20–23.

____. 'Review: Campsites', *RealTime* 57, Oct-Nov 2003, 4. 'Campsites' was an exhibition curated by Malcolm Smith in association with Darwin Pride Festival, 2003, and shown at Darwin Visual Arts Association, Darwin. The exhibition included the work of three gay male artists, including two Indigenous men: Gary Lee and Bradley Alderson. http://www.realtimearts.net/article/issue57/7175

____. 'Change, Ambiguity and Art.' In *Courting Blakness: Recalibrating Knowledge in the Sandstone University*, Fiona Foley, Louise Martin-Chew and Fiona Nicoll. Brisbane: University of Queensland Press, 2015.

O'Sullivan, S. *The Multifarious Identity: Intersections of Gender, Sexuality and Indigeneity*, PhD exegesis and artefact, Batchelor Institute of Indigenous Tertiary Education, Batchelor N.T., 2006, http://eprints.batchelor.edu.au/108

Palmer, Kevin. *Boys' Home to Broadway*, Broome: Magabala, 2010.

Pollard, Ruth, ed. *However You Wanna See Me, I'm Just Me: Stories from Aboriginal and Torres Strait Islander Gay Men, Lesbians and Sistergirls.* Sydney: AIDS Council of New South Wales, 2009.

Povinelli, Elizabeth A. *The Empire of Love: Toward a Theory of Intimacy, Genealogy, and Carnality.* Durham, N.C.: Duke University Press, 2006.

Rea. 'When Will I See You Again.' In *Lesbian Art: An Encounter with Power,* Elizabeth Ashburn. Cover, 57, 114–5. Roseville East, NSW: Craftman House, 1996.

Reyhner, Jon, Octaviana V. Trujillo, Roberto Luis Carrasco and Louise Lockard, eds. *Nurturing Native Languages.* Flagstaff, Arizona: Northern Arizona University, 2003.

Riggs, Damien W. 'Possessive Investments at the Intersections of Race, Gender and Sexuality: Lesbian and Gay Rights in a "Post-Colonising" Context', http://www.damienriggs.com/blog/wp-content/uploads/2013/09/Possessive-investments.pdf

Rosenstreich, Gabi and Sally Goldner. 'Inclusion and Exclusion: Aboriginal, Torres Strait Islander, Trans and Intersex Voices at the *Health in Difference Conference 2010.' Gay and Lesbian Issues and Psychology Review* 6, no. 3 (2010): 139–49.

Teves, Stephanie Nohelani (Kanaka Maoli). 'A Critical Reading of Aloha and Visual Sovereignty in Ke Kulana He Māhū.' *International Journal of Critical Indigenous Studies* 7, no. 1 (2014): 1–17. http://www.isrn.qut.edu.au/publications/internationaljournal/allissues.jsp

Tovey, Noel. *Little Black Bastard: A Story of Survival.* Sydney: Hodder Headline Australia, 2004.

___. *And Then I Found Me.* (forthcoming, Magabala Books, 2017)

Trevillian, Jinki Kalinda. 'On the Romances of Marriage, Love and Solitude: Freedom and Transgression in Cape York Peninsula in the Early to Mid-twentieth Century.' In *Transgressions: Critical Australian Indigenous Histories,* edited by Ingereth Macfarlane and Mark Hannah. 135–52. Canberra: ANU E Press, (Aboriginal History Monograph 16), 2007.

Triffitt, Kathy. 'A Story to Tell: Rodney Junga Williams, 18 February 1962–24 November 2011.' *Talkabout* 176 (March–April 2012): 11–14. http://issuu.com/positivelifensw/docs/176medium

van Toorn, Penny. 'Re-historicising "Racism": Language, History and Healing in Wayne King's "Black Hours".' *Altitude* 5, no. 4 (2005). https://thealtitudejournal.files.wordpress.com/2011/05/vantoorn.pdf

Wafer, Jim, Erica Southgate, and Lyndall Coan, eds. *Out in the Valley: Hunter Gay and Lesbian Histories*. Newcastle, NSW: Newcastle Region Library (Local History Monograph no. 15), 2000. See esp. 89–98.

Willis, Jon. 'Sexual Cultures: Some Notes on Indigenous Australian Sexualities.' In *Perspectives in Human Sexuality*, edited by Gail Hawkes and John Scott. 119–41. South Melbourne: Oxford University Press, 2005.

___. 'Heteronormativity and the Deflection of Male Same-sex Attraction among the Pitjantjatjara People of Australia's Western Desert.' *Culture, Health and Sexuality: An International Journal for Research, Intervention and Care* 5, no. 2 (8 Nov 2010): 137–51. http://dx.doi.org/10.1080/136910501181921

Newspapers, Newsletters and Ephemera

Alexander, David. 'An Australian Story.' *Star Observer* (July 2014): 22–25.

Anonymous. 'Spunk: Exploring Masculinities and Male Genders.' *Spunk Magazine*, 1 (summer 2009).

Baylis, Troy-Anthony. 'Black Queens Talking: It's a Drag Thing.' *RealTime* 111 (Oct–Nov 2012): 13. www.realtimearts.net/article/issue111/10806

___. 'The Art of Seeing Aboriginal Australia's Queer Potential.' In *Blak Wave*, edited by Tahjee Moar, Melbourne: Next Wave Collective, 2014. http://theconversation.com/the-art-of-seeing-aboriginal-australias-queer-potential-25588

Bonson, Dameyon. 'Reconciliation and Decolonisation in Suicide Prevention.' *Star Observer* (August 2014): 35.

Cook, Rachel. 'Out and Proud.' *Melbourne Community Voice* 675 (December 2013): 12.

Johnson, Crystal. 'Indigenous Report'. *Gay NT* 1, no. 3 (2000): 22.

Johnson, Cyril. 'Indigenous Report'. *Gay NT* 1, no. 1 (2000): 14.

Lee, Gary and Maurice O'Riordan. *Love Magic: Erotics and Politics in Indigenous Art*. Catalogue for exhibition held 20 August–3 October 1999: National Trust, S.H. Ervin Gallery, Sydney.

Riley, Benjamin. 'The National Anthem.' *Star Observer* (November 2014): 10–12.

Ross, Steven Lindsay. 'A Lore unto Themselves.' *Archer* 2 (winter 2014): 77–81.

Audio-visual Material

Cole, Bindi, Andy Canny, and Donna McCrum. 'Sistagirl.' 2011. http://www.abc.net.au/tv/guide/abc1/201102/programs/AC0928V001D2011-02-01T220056.htm?program=Artscape:%20Anatomy:%20Eye

Courtin-Wilson, Amiel. 'Bastardy: Addict, Homosexual, Cat Burglar, Aboriginal, Jack Charles.' 2009. Available commercial DVD outlets.

Northern Territory AIDS Council. 'Tayikwapi: Documentary on the Sista Girls.' 1998. VHS video; digital copy held by ALGA, disk no. 403 (26 mins).

Santana, Hédimo. 'Anwernekenhe: First National Aboriginal and Torres Strait Islander Gay Men and Transgender Sexual Health Conference.' 1995. Produced, directed and edited by Hédimo Santana, under the auspices of the National Committee for Indigenous Australian Gay Men and Transgenders and the Department of Sociology and Anthropology, University of Newcastle. (DVD transferred from VHS tape, copy lodged with ALGA.)

Selected Internet Sites

Australian Aboriginal and Torres Strait Islander GLBT Community https://www.facebook.com/pages/Australian-Aboriginal-and-Torres-Strait-Islander-GLBT-Community-0-/178966704435

Aboriginal project e-news 2006 (formerly *Aboriginal and Torres Strait Islander project newsletter* and *A quarterly newsletter from the Aboriginal Project*), AIDS Council of NSW, Sydney (ceased hard copy newsletter and began publishing an e-newsletter in 2012 for email distribution, now published on *ISSUU*. http://www.acon.org.au/communities/aboriginal/newsletter-print

http://issuu.com/aconhealth/docs/
aboriginal_project_newsletter_may?e=2140261/2921899

Anwernekenhe National HIV Alliance ('ANA'), 'Our history.'
http://ana.org.au/home/our-history

Archiving the Aboriginal Rainbow
https://indigblackgold.wordpress.com

Australia and New Zealand Professional Association for
Transgender Health
http://www.anzpath.org

Australian Lesbian and Gay Archives
http://www.alga.org.au

Beyond Blue awareness for mental health campaign
https://www.youtube.com/watch?v=O1P9gmiXOss

Brotherboys Yarnin' Up – Kai and Dean
https://www.youtube.com/watch?v=fTtiYD8GmXQ

LGBTI National Mental Health Awareness Conference.
http://mindoutconference.net

Queensland AIDS Council 2 Spirit program
www.qahc.org.au/2-spirits-promoting-healthy-aboriginal-and-
torres-strait-islander-communities

Queers of the Desert
http://www.indigoz.org.au/qotd

Sisters and Brothers NT
http://sistersandbrothersnt.com

Index

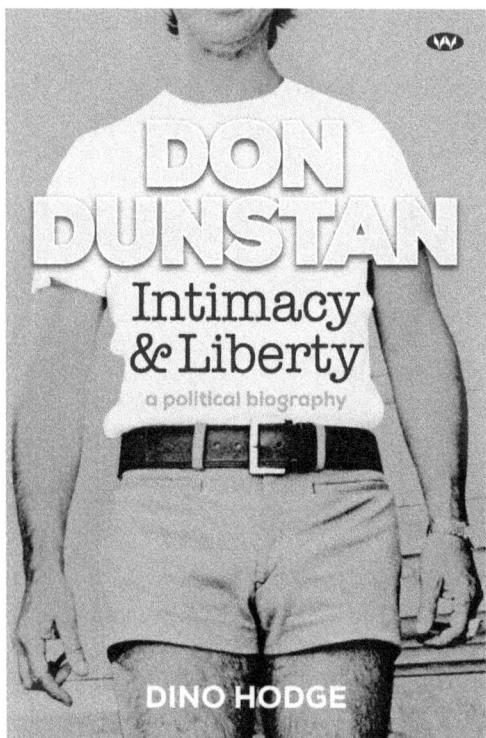

DON
DUNSTAN
Intimacy
& Liberty
a political biography

DINO HODGE

DON DUNSTAN, INTIMACY AND LIBERTY
A Political Biography

DINO HODGE

Don Dunstan, Premier of South Australia in the late 1960s and throughout the 1970s, is acknowledged as one of Australia's foremost civil rights advocates of the twentieth century. He actively promoted the rights of Indigenous Australians and women, and he passionately pursued multiculturalism. More than any other political leader, Dunstan championed the rights of homosexual citizens at a time when they were treated as criminals, classified as insane, and regarded as outcasts. He was also bisexual.

This book records the change in public discourse over issues of homosexuality – from morality to state security and then civil liberties. Dunstan worked as a member of parliament, and then throughout the remainder of his life, to realise his vision of full equality for same-sex attracted citizens. He focused on both legislative and cultural reforms, and introduced changes to the Police Force that were unprecedented and strongly resisted. His efforts and the backlash he suffered are fully documented here for the first time, finally giving due recognition to one of the country's most remarkable champions of human rights.

Praise for *Don Dunstan, Intimacy and Liberty:*

'This book will inform teaching and research across a broad canvas of Australian history. I commend it as both intellectually compelling and thoroughly enjoyable.' – Barbara Baird, *Australian Historical Studies*

'The biography has been much needed to reveal more clearly the outstanding achievements of the Dunstan era and the special humanity of the man himself.' – Maggie Tate, *Global Media Post*

ISBN 978 1 74305 393 5

For more information visit www.wakefieldpress.com.au

Wakefield Press is an independent publishing and
distribution company based in Adelaide, South Australia.
We love good stories and publish beautiful books.
To see our full range of books, please visit our website at
www.wakefieldpress.com.au
where all titles are available for purchase.

Find us!

Twitter: www.twitter.com/wakefieldpress
Facebook: www.facebook.com/wakefield.press
Instagram: instagram.com/wakefieldpress

www.ingramcontent.com/pod-product-compliance
Lightning Source LLC
Chambersburg PA
CBHW021124270326
41929CB00009B/1027